The Angled R
Collected Poen
1970-2020

8/28/22

The Angled Road
Collected Poems
1970-2020

Jonas Zdanys

LITERARY PRESS
LAMAR UNIVERSITY

ISBN: 978-1-942956-76-1
Library of Congress Control Number: 2020935305
Manufactured in the United States of America

Lamar University Literary Press
Beaumont, Texas

Acknowledgments

I am grateful to the editors and publishers of my previous books as well as editors of journals and anthologies for publishing poems now gathered in this collection. Those journals and anthologies include *American Poetry Review, A Baltic Anthology* (University of New Orleans Press), *Connecticut Review, Crosscurrents, The Galway Review, Haunted Voices* (White Hawk Press), *Ironwood, Lithuanian Writers in the West* (Loyola University Press), *Poem, Maine Times, Mirrors: An Introduction to Literature* (Harper & Row), *The Poetry of Men's Lives: An International Anthology* (University of Georgia Press), *Rage of Silence* (PEN), *Sewanee Review, Visions International, The Yale Review*, and many others, large and small, which have kindly published my work over the years.

During those years I have been deeply fortunate to have had the encouragement and support of many people, teachers and colleagues and friends, many of them now sadly gone, whose good word and apt suggestion made my writing better than it would have been without their care. I am grateful to Michael Benedikt, Thomas G. Bergin, Marie Borroff, Constance Carrier, Robert Creeley, Michael Cuddihy, Steven Florie, Ken Hada, Mac Hammond, Michael Higgins, Ivar Ivask, Kerry Shawn Keys, John Logan, J.D. "Sandy" McClatchy, Czeslaw Milosz, Kornelijus Platelis, Aleksis Rannit, Steven Schroeder, Hugh Seidman, Wally Swist, and Robert Penn Warren. There have been many others, with whom I have talked about poetry in writing workshops and in other settings, including my Yale classmates William Logan, Timothy Murphy, Cal Nordt, and Jamie Stern. I hope that they, and so many others, know how grateful I am for the opportunity to have learned from them all, and especially in those early years.

The poems in this collection are taken from the following books: *Notebook Sketches* (Chicago: Virtual Artists Collective/ Strawberry Hedgehog 2019); *Three White Horses: Still Lifes* (Beaumont: Lamar University Literary Press 2017, with ink brush paintings by Sou Vai Keng); *St. Brigid's Well* (Chicago: Purple Flag Press 2017); *Red Stones* (Beaumont: Lamar University Press 2016, with paintings by Steven Schroeder); *The Kingfisher's Reign* (Chicago: Virtual Artists Collective 2012); *The Thin Light of Winter: New and Selected Poems* (Chicago: Virtual Artists Collective 2009); *Salt* (Chicago: Virtual Artists Collective 2007); *White* (New Haven: The White Birch Press 2004); *Lithuanian Crossing* (New Haven: The White Birch Press 1999); *Water Light* (Vilnius: Vaga Publishers Ltd. 1997, with drawings by Romas Orantas); and *Voice on an Anthill* (New York: Manyland Books 1982). *Voice on an Anthill* includes poems that date back to 1970.

Experience is the Angled Road
Preferred against the Mind
By—Paradox—the Mind itself—
Presuming it to lead

—Emily Dickinson

For my Grandchildren

To the Reader

When I started writing poems, more than fifty years ago, I could hardly imagine a time when I would be looking back on a body of work instead of looking forward to the publication of my first book. Such a thought never crossed my mind in those early years, but that first book came and then others came and the years passed. I was thinking about writing and its results while sitting on a beach in Maine some months ago and was struck by the fact that I now do have a body of work, collections of poems and translations, and that I have been shaping it for more than half a century. It was a reassuring thought and an unsettling one. Half a century. Notebooks filled with drafts, a shelf in my living room lined with books that had my name on them. That thought came with the wistful sense that I have written more than I will write, that looking back occupies far more space than looking ahead.

This year, 2020, connects some important milestones in my life. It is the year I turn seventy and it is the year that marks the fiftieth anniversary of the first serious publication of my poems, in the *Yale Literary Magazine*, when I was a twenty-year-old undergraduate. I thought about the significances of twenty and fifty and seventy, considered it a very fine confluence, and decided that I should celebrate those connections somehow.

Preparing a collected poems seemed appropriate to acknowledge that full half century of writing and publishing. I also realized, with a brush of serendipity, that such a volume would connect to that lovely flow of twenty-fifty-seventy: the book would be my fiftieth published book. I could not pass by such an opportunity, so this collection is the result of that process of linking all those numbers and decades and volumes together. The poems in these pages, even after all these years, continue to speak for me. I hope that some are able to speak to you.

JZ

New Britain, New Haven, Newington, Buffalo, Vineyard Haven, North Haven, Vilnius, Kaunas, Druskininkai, Kennebunkport, Fairfield, Dingle, Anchorage, Brooklyn, Wallingford
1970 2020

CONTENTS

Notebook Sketches

Three White Horses

Red Stones

The Kingfisher's Reign

The Thin Light of Winter

Salt

White

Lithuanian Crossing

Water Light

Voice on an Anthill

Notebook Sketches

I invented myself just as I invented you.
It was reason enough to be resentful,
a sensible response to a series of snapshots
that weigh everything down with a sad ring
and the lights cut a frail path that rouses
the lucid air. I chose the wind to fall with me,
the close of day half-buried in the back
of death's particular stop, coaxing the pale
tones of consolation from the terrible stars.
It was a dead giveaway, a measured pattern
that traces truth on sibilant water, the flame
that roots in its buried keel and consumes
itself. I bleed my name. I am open and fragile.
The day has fled and the pendulum marks
its desolate hour. The mirror that held your thin
reflection breaks as it gives mine back to me.

*

The dark-skinned boy in the window
of the tenement building just past
the tracks on the way into the city
rummages through the sounds he hears
on the stairway, his clothes damp
with the burden he carries with him
through the world. When the day
of judgment comes he will feel no
mercy for the world of unrelieved
night, the birds frozen in the air in
mid-flight in a posture he remembers,
the corner of the moon broken
against the water tower's spiral drift.
The postcard I bought at the station
when the train arrived showed a boy
running through a small park between
high walls, his face averted, an imaginary
scene devoid of expression in some
distant country grown old and gray.
I'm not sure if it's the same boy
I saw from the train, some settled
story told in one brief moment
when the day grows dim and the
invisible things of the world burst
enigmatic to the truth that overwhelms
us. I believe yet don't believe what I am
saying: he falls vertically from the window,
runs through the rush of cold air, hides
his face with his back to the street
and quells premonitions of his own panic
as he gropes his way to the last flight
of stairs. Truth comes in winding ways.
It is like memory, a wisp of smoke

in the corner of a postcard found in
a scattered pile outside the station.
There is something else looming in
that picture. Some shapes of it can
only be seen through darkened glass.

*

I was once somebody else,
an old woman with curvature
of the spine playing the piano
in late afternoon in a weathered
· house on a farm in Nebraska.
My children reorganized
the cupboards when I was
sleeping, smiling in every mirror
they walked by pleased with
their wonders and tricks.
I did not think about happiness,
finding no truth in such ideas,
dyeing my hair black each year
and watching it grow out white
with the changing seasons.
No one took my word for it,
there was nothing else I could do,
these things don't mean that much,
these ritual labors and small rewards
of a world that seemed to be
the most casual imitation of events
on a far landscape, out in the country.
One spring, like blood from a stone,
water flooded the house, loosened
the tiles and warped the legs
of the piano. Someone painted
a sign on the door, a dark circle
with a line drawn through it,
like a spell to keep the light
intact, a defiance of circumstance
and death borrowed from some
random circle in the ground.
It was a reassuring, peaceful thing,
as if the present stretched on forever.
My expectations for myself ran along
the same lines, the same dark circles
covered my dress, and it all seemed
reasonable enough, it all boxed up
the world of which I was a part, though
I also admired bright colors and forms,
though I walked sometimes in too much light.

*

She took the train across
the floating bridge, the houses
just beyond the tracks, in the

heat of those days, ruins left
by the swarms of bombers
that came all night, that
juggled the landscapes
to forgotten destinations.
She traveled alone, bed on board,
on the way to see her sister,
the corruption of that war held still
where time was no longer content.
The night settled to three,
the shadows at each passing station
no solace for the hand or eye.
In the strange city, the lights
were out, a terrible darkness
on each face she saw. A horse-drawn
cart stood crippled near the tower.
The unrecoverable waste of history
loosed upon the changing images
of time suffered and moved, hung
like a yellow moon from a darkening
cloud and rushing the crescent
pressures of every life it wrecked.
Her sister, stripped naked, lay
salvaged to ruin by its intolerable stare.
She turned away when the train began
to move again, the night forever on the hills.

*

It's hard to know how to fill up
your days and keep them near
at hand when you know that something
is going to crack open, an unexpected
noise from the deeper silence of a broken
radio that startles you awake to some
riddled end when the rest of the house
is bare and sleeping and undone.
The hours swell without remorse then
shrink down while a coldness grows
and your face lapses like a darkened star.
The year is a patch of dry land cut by
empty ravines. Dark moths ring
the far edges of the world. Time crouches
in a bag dropped in a ditch by the side
of the road, longs to run in the straits
where the expected noises bloom.
I'm at a loss. The sound takes down
its own debris and the great work
is done in other places, in other days.
I would lie to you if I could.

*

I was lifted up by a great black bird,
beyond the tracks, beyond the fall
of water, in a dark alley shrouded in fog

when the flame sawed and the day
lashed and the ghosts on the rooftops
stirred. All of them are gone except
for me, the iron ascending when black
birds flicker in the scales of their long
descent. It was where the street turned
left off the main road, near the edge
of town where the roofs were flat
and the windows long and the houses
narrow and bare. The floor creaked when
I went outside to listen to the voices
that gathered in that other night,
my cold hand inching across the barren
circle, the dust on the stairs pushing
words into my mouth in response.
There was something past the statue
in the square, a shadow floating
in the moonlight, the night holding
its breath, that led me to an empty
space pinned against the light.
A single word floated up from the past.
An unpredictable scrawl numbed the moon.
I stood to let the darkness rise.
And I was falling, falling, like a meager wall,
falling bleak when the street rebelled, and
when I turned, transfixed, dark wings took hold.

*

You can stand at the edge of the ocean
in late October as the sun sets and hold
the whole world in your hand. In the middle
of the night you can hear the thin sweet
voice of the river emptying into the sea,
rocks slipping into water and the wind
coming up like some miraculous thing
finding constant shape. The sky is clear,
an oblique harmony of currents and pulses
in great migration west. I hear birds
vanishing, something unknown rising
and falling in the offshore surges.
There is a point of rest for us all, the balance
between the many and the one, the unity
of substance and abstraction in the white
curve of the tide. Everything here breaks
to possibility, the soft white in heaven's eye.
An immaculate morning will rise.

*

All night I rolled rocks up
and down the slope of the hill,
the grass below transparent,
the dark gray sky at dead rest.
The girl with the skirt over her
head sat on a bench watching,

half-trapped and muffled
in green cloth. Her legs were bent
as she unbuttoned her blouse,
bold and white, and then stiffened
her arm. She felt cold and tired,
a strip of blackness just beyond
her hands, a great silence angling
the bottom of the air like the bitter
aftertaste of love. The sum of these
events is undrawn, the point of the
periphery of a world made and
unmade by the changing stones.
The moment is over.
I performed all the rites.
What is mine on this hill
belongs to no one, what is hers
on the bench belongs to me.

*

Nobody comes here to stay:
footprints disappear at the turn
of the walk, at the edge of the yard,
in the changing sand, the melting snow.
Ideas of permanence flutter by,
fuse in the weeds and gravel
anticipating every random event.
The moon moves only when I move,
rising from the ground and flowing
down the dark river. Bricks flake
above my head, the window glass
rattles. The dead sing in my sleep.
This is how memory is made,
groping like a hand on a cold wall.
Light illuminates both, the end of
each passage blocked by an iron door.
How still she keeps herself, the heavy
posture, unlightened by motion,
generating its own uncertainties,
various truths that cannot be reconciled
at the center of any possibility.
Something summons itself, wanting
to be healed. Something remembers,
something knocks again on the door.

*

The doors were all open around the corner,
windows draped with yellowed lace below
high ceilings and scattered at random in walls
painted pink or white. A row of willow trees
lined the hard street, planted too close
together and tangling to black. People walked
both ways, coming and going, through
the branches, their footsteps weightless traces
on the sidewalk, as if they had touched death

for the first time, its consequences darkening
the shadows of fire escapes and loose railings
on the faded porticos and stoops. Time,
a cold turbulence that opens like a body made
of glass, forsakes the small moment, its
head tilted to one side. The continuum of all
that was born becoming all that will die
spreads its claws across the pure meaning,
the slow retreat of day into night that rises
and falls like an erratic wind caught in paradox
and contradiction. My eye wakens
and stretches, fixed on a stray point of light.
The doors around the corner slam shut.
Let me stand outside myself as this world shifts.
Take this heaviness away, divide the air.
May the dark be forgotten, may the impenetrable
silence at the heart of every form dare itself
to bleed and dance at last in the whole of light.

*

There is nothing he can do
to hold it back, nothing to make
the stillness last forever, nothing
to keep the moment from coming
to an end. Upstairs there is the smell
of cooking, the dark passageway
leading to a half-closed attic door,
the waft of cigarette smoke folding
again in the bed sheets. Her foot
touches his, a deliberate move
that turns inert and cold when
the clock strikes. The candle on
the table droops to a pool of wax.
Shoulders, hips, knees: he is drawn
to desire, tears at the edge of the blue
dress. He wipes his mouth with his
cuff, his skin like paper, and waits.
His finger follows the loop of the chain
around her neck, moves to the cross
between her breasts. There is no sound
but the dripping of rain in the gutter.
Two inscriptions are scratched on
the wall. He makes a separate peace.
He dies for truth. He looks away.

*

The answer is the deflected form
of another question, a dog among
many dogs that howl in the night.
Things are not entirely as they appear,
a sad business that the man at the desk
shakes his head over, nothing to do
but fall, call to God to save him
as he wanders on poor black wings

across a dark horizon. His hands
are dull, the air above the chimneys
smells of ash and gray snow, and
the image of a face he did not
want to see disappears for the
second time at the bottom of the
stones in the street. There is a
desperate smell of red earth, a
portion of a split eternity, nourished
in the yellow lights below. A moment
of silence opens a moment of silence.
Time reverses the vision of time.

*

The light in the kitchen of the house
next door goes out. They are suddenly
blind, trembling to undress, caught
in the sounds of things before the storm.
They stumble in the dark in small circles
hoping to find each other again,
one foot her right, his left   nailed
loosely to the wide planks of the wooden
floor, each arm waving the thick darkness
of winter away. It was a moment neither
wished to keep, the measure of all things,
of anguish, of lack, knocking on the window,
falling to gray dust that coats the walls.
The moon is obscured but I can see
the shadows of their odd dance.
I am looking for a way out for them,
my hand half-raised, time standing
still, my heart beating. She flaps her
arms like a painted bird in response,
fluttering toward the ceiling, pulled back
by the nail in the floor. He strikes a match.
There is a sudden rush of air.

*

She asked how long it would take
until God relented, her youngest
son holding the dog by its tail
and asking for the world to be forgiven.
Or at least come to its beginning again
on some long and solemn afternoon
when children kneel in their corners
waiting for the touch of a phantom
hand and reciting the sufferings
of people asleep in other rooms.
Death is not the measure of all things,
they say, imagining the wild waters.
The cup will fill in time, they say,
in the passion of surrender.
At midnight the dog whines softly,
the boy's grip tightening, and she

wakes once more, hears the high and
silent slide of night, the tremor of
derision at last in God's exhausted voice.

*

It was an odd gesture,
an uncalculated act.
He lies down fully clothed,
rocks himself to sleep.
The day is cut from stone.
The confusion of the world
is like the wagging of a burned
finger on the other side
of the room: he is his own
father now, a new double
under a dust-gray light.
He closes his eyes, his mind
on other things, his father's
letter on the table written
in his own resilient hand,
addressed to himself.
A noise wakes him.
He crosses the threshold.
History comes to an end.
All things are permitted,
he knows, and falls silent
and fevered onto his bed.
It's better, he thinks, to sleep.

*

He had been drinking and came home
in the middle of the night, his mind
wandering like a seizure across no world
he knows. He travels through a wide plain.
Lightning flashes like something reinvented
in the hands of sober men. On the banks
of the river, just past his block, stands
a woman with a dead child in her arms,
no look of surprise or alarm on her face,
just the image of a faint smile, cold and
brittle as drifting smoke, framed by her
falling hair. His voice rises, he rubs his eyes
unsure of what is swallowed in the dark.
He is not sure if he should plead for himself or
call out to the dumb weight at the end of the
world and then turns because it doesn't matter.
He is here today gone tomorrow, like wind
drifting around corners late at night, the
isolation of the heart carried down to the banks
of an unnamed river in an anonymous town.
The glass in the windows above his head is black.
He can feel the child's soft bones fold.
He can hear time break against the solemn wall,
barely containing its circles and dust.
These visions come and go, full of remorse,
fixed on the night and water.

24

*

The black birds leave the hills
and settle in the rushes and reeds
that fill the brown islands
just past the channel marshes.
Darkness comes early, brushes
the tall dead seagrasses to a dry
rattle at the junction of the north
shore and the tides, the air cold
and ribboned with gray, and the
blind valves stiffen with the ragged
suddenness of a day gone dim.
The cycles grow shorter and shorter.
The year died and was buried,
from beginning to end, with no hope
of resurrection, no contritions made.
The birds have a power they do not want,
blending in the illusions of the outer eye,
a bodiless pulse, a vibration, that passes
and repasses with the changing light.
They tell me nothing, and I do not need
to know how they move into a world
beyond the world, the luminous vision
of things unnamed as the channel fills.
The dark reveals the light that it conceals.
I am moved by shapes diving through
the air, by the endless arrival of the sea.

*

She asked that I believe in goodness
and I replied that all beliefs are tentative.
It was an unpretentious life, no majestic
meanings swept up from under the rug,
no grand design that others watched.
Only the joy of subversive acts in the small
middle of things, the integers lost as I
drew my face on the cold glass with a puff
of warm air. It was not all just idle chatter.
It was not all just obscure philosophies that tug
themselves loose from the curtains and shawls.
I'm aware that the struggle has never ceased.
The man with the lamp in his hand
on the street shudders without reason
or cause. He murmurs a word or two
about goodness, counts out his steps
backwards along the inner wall.
The question she asked did not disconcert
him, did not keep the next sentence from
passing his lips. He gathers his wits all
about him, fixes his gaze on her breast.

*

Black water breaks through the ceiling
and the rafters creak with their own truth,

rain somber and drumming the roof.
There was a point at which I awoke, sure
that I had the power to predict the future,
the drops of rain not twelve inches apart.
I started with the past, decided to bring
it down to zero, half a year at a time at first
and then faster and faster until I reached
the perfection of nothing. From there
I could shape whatever next moment I wanted,
skipping the words I did not know, ignoring
centuries like unwelcome guests or strangers
huddled and dangerous. I feel the fingers of time
groping me, searching for memories that
have not existed, for the source of any image
that has not yet afflicted the world.
I won't allow it, won't spend the night
flapping the bed sheets to shake out
the truths and lies that will once again be
new on the face of the earth, won't fret
for any incomprehensible penance that
shapes the shadows of love. And in this
version of my new beginning, when courage
and resolution are put to the test, God will
be a one-legged old woman having a seizure
on a dark street corner, with a cardboard sign
that she will work for shelter or food,
a pint of muscatel, cheap wine in a jug.
History moves quickly once it gets moving,
frames the meaning I cannot bring myself to tell.
I wait for the rain to be falling again,
I start the clock backwards to zero.

*

They took down the tree at the front door
and quite unexpectedly the house was colder
and darker than it was before. It may have
been a hundred years old, its biggest branches
surviving discovery and disaster scribbled
on the winter sky, bewildering the children
in the yard and tempting the migrating birds.
But it was as if nothing whatever happened,
no link in its falling between the living and
the dead, though an order of existence came to
an end and destiny now hung naked in the air
where the thick axle of the world once stood.
The nature of loss is a holy thing. Hope
unravels when all comparisons are broken,
an analogy of a minor kind becoming the
substitute for the deepest truth. But this
is not about that, it's about the loss of a tree
lifted and dropped to earth under a wide sky.
Up in the attic I cry myself to sleep and dream
about stars on a low horizon. The tree
outlived half my family in a grand confusion

of gravity and death, the beauty of the world
waning in the pleasures of its end. This is how
things happen, how everything we call back
travels off again, its price exacted, or at
least this is how we create our lost tomorrows.

*

The ship struck the rocks on the far coast,
gray as a mirror polished with slow care,
tired of the landscape of the sea and soundless
as a dream from which no one wakes.
The war blackened the windows, curved roads
leading nowhere and time beginning to drift
like the slow last breaths of soldiers in the field.
The days contract, blind with their own hard
light, and the nights grow colder. Stars litter
the sea. Clouds are a stiff brush on the horizon.
Something with three wings hovers above the
sand, shivers in slow strokes over dark flowers.
The searchlights fall, the wind wears north,
the air hollows to an inexorable warning.
A hand thrusts upwards from among the reeds.
The iron rod of time bends like a candle in heat.

*

The letter sent never reached the hand,
as if a storyteller lost the thread of his story
in the middle of telling it: a space, a blankness
huddled in a dream that has lost its root.
I sleep on the door sill, wrapped in a gray
blanket, waiting each morning for the mail
to arrive. It's the only chance I have to explain
myself to anyone who comes up the walk.
I drag down the stairs when no one comes,
rubbing against the walls in hope for the cold
comforts of an empty house. Though I haven't
read them, and am not sure I could, I know
that the words in the letter have great significance,
the outlines of civilization perhaps or credible
principles to live by. I stand in the hallway
and scratch the door. I've been through this
all before, know that whoever is writing to me
will fully understand the moral dimensions
of my plight. I believe it will all be revealed
and all will be heartened, if only I can wait
long enough. I want to be an original soul,
leaving light footprints on the floor, be
the only one here who can hear the language
that lovers speak. That all will be explained
in the letter, I'm sure. For now, my fingers
shine with blood, windows whistle like old birds
on the flats, there is a ringing in my ears.

*

The late afternoon sun was low,
trapped in the shop window,
and it was hard, against the light,
to make out her features when
she turned as I drew near. I lit
her cigarette, opening my hand
to catch the ring of smoke and
learning the shapes of the stones
of the brown wall behind her.
She said something quietly,
her words stuttering in the air,
asked if I would spend the night,
said it was late for her to have a child,
added something about visiting friends,
felt she should apologize and call.
These are the habits of a lonely life,
the glimpsed shadows of misgiving
that crease her face. I have lived
long enough to know it doesn't matter,
the needle of the future quickening,
faces dark with the imbalance
of the things that shape the flesh,
that fold the earth. The lights come on.
Children press their noses to the glass.
I touch the scar on her cheek, barely
just barely, hear the traffic on
the corner cut and slow. Her hand
folds under her head. The blur
of a nervous river broods in her eye.

*

The snow was cold and the morning still
and barely dark. Autumn had lived out
the span of its days and there are patches
of white on the sidewalks and roads, flurries
smoking on the lower edge of a horizon
just visible where the town cups the blue
coldness of the air. I woke last night at four,
the window a heavy gray, waiting for the world
to become the world, to come back to where
I left it, whispering the words my mother
taught me to seduce the dawn, to spill the
things the body hides in its own ten fingers.
It is a sad decline and I know I will not save
the weary ghosts as they make their way
to heaven, good for good dying in a vacant
lot and fading blindly on indifferent ground.
I lift the double weight   anonymity and time
from the floor, push it, immense and relentless,
through the unopened door. There is not
much else to bear the quick necessities, not
much else: I woke and fell asleep and woke.

There is no mystery about me. The room is
heavy with the past. Silence gathers like snow.

*

Each morning he counts out
the fifteen white tiles, beginning
randomly every day from one
of the corners and rows.
Each afternoon he counts out
the fifteen red tiles, beginning
randomly every day from one
of the corners and rows.
Each night he counts out
the fifteen black tiles, beginning
randomly every day from one
of the corners and rows.
It is a habit of impatience,
the fall of light and dark in the stark
iterations of the world, the bottom
of the world lined in random tiles
that tap the marble of the blind man's
stick. It is a practical arrangement,
how each wanted life to be: patterns
of sound and sight ever evolving
into satisfactory expansions of
possibility, chance connections of colors
that tap to colorful echoes no matter
the time of year. All things become
themselves when given the right design.
It doesn't matter if anyone can see
or hear them. The everlasting gesture
of arranging the tiles and tapping
the stick calms its own image, both
sides of the sky blossoming under the
horizon of the tiles. White shadows fill
the hollow spaces of the day, morning
steadies the white hand of winter.

*

It was still dark, just after six,
and the back room where I slept
was cold. I did not turn on the lights.
The old furnace made its usual noise,
stoking its fire, and the pipes in the walls
rattled with a dull smell of smoke and oil.
The wooden chair with a broken back
leaned flat in the corner. It was draped
with the coarse gray blanket from my
small bed and a red plaid shirt that was
a bit short in the sleeves and threadbare
at the elbows and collar. There were
a few framed pictures on the far wall,
on either side of the window, and a
dresser the color of dry garden stone

stood next to the open door of the
closet. Something that looked like a
vase held a bouquet of what once had
been fresh flowers. The mirror, which
never delivered what it promised,
reflected the five fins of the ceiling fan.
I got up, pulled on my slippers, ran
my fingers through my hair, began
to think about separating what was
real and what was not, my senses
centered in my closed eyes. I am
only half real; the other half is a phase
of emptiness that circles the earth.
One protects the other from the sorrows
of the world. I hear the cry of the
single giant sky as the sun rises.
The hour strikes its end.

*

The wall in the center of the square,
just past the gray Civil War monument,
is chalked with the names of anonymous
boys who leave the quick pulses of their
lives behind in widening arcs. It was a
sense of triumph, a moment of power
off the main road, that rumpled their
lonely wisdom and gave shape to their
belief that their lives were the only lives
to live. There was no other way to go in.
But the old bones buried there longer
than anyone remembers feel a different
longing, not the eternal now scratched
insolently on a rock but the notch
of the past etched on the barrel by a soldier
who fights for his life as his years contract
and his name is smothered in dirt and blood.
Not a footprint remains in the empty grass
in whatever field this marble tried to save.
Only the name in red of some local boy
sprayed on the pigeoned pedestal. The
clouds of summer hang above the square.
The world steadies like an unmourned
grave. The angel at the top of the statue
whispers light on a passing girl's face.

*

She sat in the car with her head back
against the rest and her eyes closed.
The air was cold and blue and the water
down below so still. Her arm knocked
against the door, the belt drawn tight,
her pleated brown skirt pulled up above
her knees and turned a little bit off
center around her waist. She whispered

30

the name she called him in a low and
intimate voice as leaves blown by a
sudden wind scratched across the
window. Her legs were shaking.
It came on her gradually, like a possibility,
like a blurring of satisfaction. She tried
to think of other things, the unreliable
affections and calculations she came
to expect, but he slowly touched her wrist.

*

I would return to summer light,
would let the long rows of open doors
not fade again, the yards rocking
gently with wind, birds flying past
in endless flocks and the willows
moving. I would return to summer
light, would let gold and vermilion
and shades of green pour down
across the wide horizon to a glory
overhead. I would return to summer
light, would let the grace of water
rise, the air become the morning,
coveting the earth, a blue burning
splendor of spirits and wings.
I would return, would rest in solitary
places, beyond the break in the trees,
beyond the easy breath of air, where
words are unfinished and the echoes
of my voice are a cry of love. I would
live all this again, and again, would
become eternal and whole in a silver
light, would turn it all once again,
as I wait to be reborn, into something
reckless and endless and beautiful.

*

The wind grows old.
I remember walking down
a path at the far end
of the garden, light
twittering like a sparrow
in soft wood,
the air leaning on
vanishing roots, mist
whirling slowly away
through clumps of dried grass
and touching red blossoms.
I have learned to stand quietly
as the light cries out
and stood there for a moment,
for two, as the crest broke
and farther down, quiet
and clear, the green sweep

31

of bushes and birds
tilted back into sunlight.
This is the slow change.
This is the soul's perpetual
beginning and end,
the reality of walking
in the woods alone,
in the curve and density
of unimaginable meaning
beneath my feet, above
my head. Today,
as the wind grows old,
I close my eyes and see
the thing we feel at evening
nesting at its source.
White birds fly by.
The world releases its forms.
Time tips slowly away
on the other side
of the sun.

*

The day is clean and warm,
the town no more than a place
to pass through on a tattered map,
old men sitting on a wooden bench
in the middle of the square feeding
pigeons and talking about the war,
though none had fought in it
and none knew anyone who had,
unless some neighbor's cousin
who had joined, who hadn't returned.
It was the despair of being at the end
of the track that prompted such
conversations, each content
with such clich,s and each shopworn
with old age and its disguises.
Lies, like so much else in their lives,
at least exaggerations, that allowed
them to forget the ordinary clutter.
I thought of them today, of myself,
all of us sitting on those benches,
while the hands of the clock on the wall
moved and the hours grew and the dogs
in the street barked whenever
another man died and the world died
and time seeped away like the blood
of war into water and sand.

*

I used to sleep on her front porch
listening to voices drifting up
from the rooms below when the windows
and doors were open and one of them

leaned, half-turning, out of her lonely life
wondering about her name, her life being
what it was, and grieving about the end
of summer. It was the middle of my life,
some nervous splinter of what remained
under my skin, a shrug of forgiveness
ready for everyone who passed by
on the street without looking up.
Some argued that I should move out
of there then, but I didn't like the bother
of moving, and there was more to it
than that: each night I heard the telephone
ring three times and then stop as the
earth went on spinning and the first
light in the hallway came on. I don't know
how it all came to be but it was enough.
And once a red bird paused on the porch
railing to look me over just as twilight
fell and I sat in my corner like a flaw
in the painted wood, rising lightly to
a small scatter. That hid me from the gray.
All I asked was to stay alive. All I asked.
It was something I was meaning to tell her
when her fingers tossed my life away.
I dissolved like a stone in the basement.
Disappeared in the rain that blew
in from the mountains and folded my voice
with hers in the cracks of the walls.
At sunset, she whispers her name
through the open window,
the shadows on the porch steal west.

*

I woke listening to the ghosts
of wild horses running down
the long road toward dawn,
drifting through old doors
that opened on the other side
of the earth, their dappled wings
singing nothing, singing nothing
to a random wind. I don't know
why the old woman at the window
is weeping, why her hands still cling
to the first beam of light. The ashes
on my pillow vanish in the four corners
of the road. My body, undefeated,
slips away underground.
I pray for the dark bells, for
the lights in the sky, for a way home.

*

He pauses by the dead sycamore.
The light's out on the bridge.
White shadows wheel the old moon.

The city breaks on the marrow.
Time drowns in its own past.
It is the rifting of things.
The steady muster of pale clouds.
The nameless prowl of hollow dust.
The dying shudder of black mud.
He curls the pinnacle of heaven.
He rusts the sludge black stones.
The weather changes, the morning's cold.

*

I keep a kerosene lamp burning
by the window all night, its flames
a signal to keep away the desolation
and the cold that leaks through the shutters
on the landward side and worries
the clapboards when heavy rain falls.
The light seeps into dark crevices,
dusts the doorway, climbs up
the painted walls of the room where
you lay on the unmade bed, a sketch
of pale colors opening, breathing.
Outside, the wind squats in the eaves,
staggers in a tangle of roots. I dream
of the hour when the last lie grinds
through less than half the night,
when I shift in bed and our eyes
meet for a moment suddenly
in the mirror and then turn away,
each of us staring, with a snatch
of breath, past the dimming lamp,
across the empty sky.

*

The boat plunges across the East River
dragging a gray rain to the far bank,
a blue haze locked in a chill spring as
the city sags weightless against the horizon.
The train is finally gone, morning taking
its own time, slouched on a stone bench.
The lives of old men slow to mourn
dull to a cold simplicity and the dock
slides away to the dust of rutted streets.
Life is familiar as a scar. Below the limestone
and granite of the bridge a boy's body
spreads out, face down, and out on the rocks
someone stands holding onto a kite string.
Past the pier, out past the landing,
there were many people walking,
small boats on the water red and blue.
Someone could fall here unnoticed.
Someone could slide quietly into the water
and not stir the air, arms pressing no
darkness aside, float for a thousand

years in the silence of the setting moon.
Someone could sleep and die alone.
This is what I saw today east of the island.
This is what I saw today in the white
shadows of the city.

*

The inexactness of light on the stone wall
is a keystone that drives the holiness
of night to a confusion of last great shapes,
gathered up and swept forward before
they vanish all at once in a rhythm of pitched
lines and oblique circles curving through
the empty windows of the province.
A mile down the road, past the stations
and lighthouses, fog moves in a mournful pace,
solitary and cold, across the fence that
outlines the yard, shallows and closes in
on the coast. Unable to see, feeling her way
by memory and echo, she stands waist deep,
feet apart, water flowing back and forth
between her legs. She shivers softly
and moans. Birds spin around her blind.
Warmth leaves the sea.
She lifts her face, turning to stone.
Out ahead, before she closes her eyes,
she can see the defiant outline
of what looks like a house.

*

The illusion is set off
by an extraordinary thing,
one wing tied behind my back.
Neither is afraid of the other,
coal smoke scrubbing the horizon,
determined as stone, and the grass
carved hard as brown marble.
A sign appeared suddenly
on the roadside, urging salvation
and flattening the long complaints.
I began to feel cold,
my first thought of shipwrecks
and saved men.
It was a strange forgiving grace.
It was the saltwhite emblem of redemption.
Dark water breaks the ice.
Life pauses for a moment in mid-flight.

*

The door had been broken off
the basement and the house and yard
were run-down, broken glass blustering
the porch roof in patterns of light.
Time is the weight of cold silver, coil

within coil trapped at the bottom
of the stairs. The filaments of old
bulbs, crooked with hate, crouch over
wires and vines in the hallway.
Dry weeds sink in a black trunk.
Time is thistle and blood, labored
hands that forget the truth of a bitter
embrace. We are wayward things,
elbows at our sides, devoured memories
in back rooms drawn with faded paint,
cracks on the walls, our lives tied
in a cart near the pale trap. We are
wayward things, and the dead are nothing.
Someday I have to die and become nothing.
But not now. Not now.

*

After two days of bitter cold,
the wind changed in the night.
It has a way of coming suddenly
to an end, adjusting itself, then
coming back to its own beginning,
driven in and out by winter rain
as morning drifts to its blind
conclusions and the resistance
of afternoon wears down at last
to night. I'm tired of this today,
tired of the intricacies of chance
that push away human intention
and purposeful cause, of the dream
or the ending of the dream dancing
like a jagged line in the corner of my eye.
I long for some human design
to take root and work across
the low horizon, want to shape
the world to suit my own purposes,
to rust and smoke and strange water.
I close my eyes for a moment and listen.
I lean into my own darkness.
I will go east when
I want and walk along the sea.

*

In the photograph at the top
of the page, the plump woman
with the sad smile and short
gray hair holds her hat in her hand
and looks in the direction of someone
just out of focus, thinking about
something that happened in her old life,
perhaps, or drawing on some private
wisdom or intimate sense about
them both that rested loosely
like an arm on the railing of the porch.

A willow weaved its boughs
just beyond the corner of the house
and a drab small child peeked out
from behind the angular stairs.
The mortal solace of a moment plain
and fixed from this distance in time.
The body taking on life once more,
growing sharper and lighter,
and then swiftly gone as the sky drops
clear and the dark clouds vanish.
I'm alone when I turn the last page.
The window is darkened by night.

*

The air seemed to grow thick
and heavy without explanation
and they held out no hope,
could not tell us the difference
between that time and now.
He could not remember clearly
who had moved on and who
had stayed, could not imagine
finding it all in the state it was in
today, the ground hard, stones
everywhere, the apprehensions
of old words as redeeming as a bad
dream or short and blasting
as a general alert.
He would find himself separated
in the whole arrangement,
sensible as sitting at the table
of an abandoned house, believing
in tricks and magic doors
opening and closing over the cold stars.
The light from outside illuminates
another view, the bare floor
that parries the darkness,
and, just past the screen door,
the shallow mud.

*

He grew flowers in the winter
in the hothouse window at the end
of the kitchen, orchids and hyacinths
interspersed with small shrubs
of rosemary and pots of basil, thin stalks
of cilantro with white blossoms,
long stems of dill going to seed,
coriander and parsley and thyme.
He wasn't interested in the paper
or the news, wore blue latex gloves
to protect the plants from his own
drilled touch, his strokes
of misfortune and errors in judgment,

the raw face of morning as it toggled
his skin. The presence of life
sustains life, he would say,
the rituals of each day the call
to some pale god to linger
in the room among the flowers.
There were times,
on the threshold of spring, when
he tried to open the door.

*

There are stars, and to the west
Antares hangs above a landscape
where every vibration is stilled,
save for the sound of waves breaking
and the faint echo of the moon,
now two days full, spilling across
the sand. A dark crust of burned
moss drops from the rocks
into the water, a thin unity
along the headlands more than
an easy failure or whirl.
The wind is steady and high
and the land falls to clear transitions,
dry wings abandoned and bodiless
as the year comes to a dead rest.
Don't ask me to ask the roots
to tell me how branches fill the empty
places with inexpressible light,
how the dips and rises of the world
are a miraculous increase,
radiance entangling the core,
how reality's cold waters overspill
the black mountains, footprints
disappearing at the edge of the sea.
I don't know what else there is.

*

She was rocking on the edge of her future,
the ceiling of the bedroom white and high,
the windows indistinct as faded letters
in the corners of the walls.
The sweet wind blew soft as her moan
across the corners of her bed.
The door was swinging back and forth
in the front hall, making a sound so small
that she didn't notice when it stopped.
She picked up the suitcase, carried it
upstairs, and laid it open on the floor.
She was tired of all this irrelevance,
promised herself to do whatever she could.
This is what she bargained for.
This is how the tide comes on the square.
This is why the accusation fails again and falls.

Shadows clouded her way across the room.
When she turned, she heard voices.

*

The mingling I speak of may
take place again. I hope this
is the last truth, deeper
than any memory deeper
than any sense of change.
When you left me in the
mirrored room, with a look
infinitely sad, dark hair
outlined by your linen dress,
I saw myself grow suddenly
transparent until there was
nothing of me in any mirror
or dark glass, imperfection
hidden in the dulls and echoes
of a more permanent night.
Let those shadows
sleep and turn to dust.
Let our love
play us across the room.
The hesitant lie persists.
The mirror swings
like a crucible in blue.

*

The road climbed up the long hill,
past the flock of crows on the flats
seizing what they could from the marsh
early in the morning.
Winter brings necessity, somber
wings beating the air above
the breakers, moving like slow smoke
through cuts and valleys in the dunes
in search of things washed up
by the sea. There is a blueness
in the air, a coldness. Black shapes
turn and take to wing.

*

The shaft of light on the path
in the rain-soaked woods brings
the promise of day low on the sky,
the trees' fiery shade, of hickory
and ash, a contemplation of the first
waking of the world, of something
from nothing untethered at last.
Shadows play across your face.
The note sounds from far away.
I can see the endless wild uprush
of white across the edge of the sky,

the infinite austerity of the stars
waning to a pale flare of light.

*

He planned to arrive in late spring,
when children played on sidewalks
according to their own rules
and people sat along the walls
in lawn chairs and on benches,
an unforced heartiness in their voices
as they called to one another
across the street, gathering together
defenseless in the sun. A silent woman
will walk beside him, thinking about
her children, knowing how to bear love.
His hand will touch her dark hair,
a light wind will flutter off the rooftops.

*

At the door of my house
I watched the birds pass above
the tree line in fearless intervals,
low just above the tops of the maples
and oaks and dark against clouds
smoking along the lower edge
of the sky. Shadows gathered
in the cuts of the visible horizon
and there was a tang in the air.
Something was happening, perhaps
different than what happened before,
and I could not hear what you said,
your faced pressed against my back,
the earth smelling of old leaves
and dust. The moon dropped a thin
shaft of light on the dried rosebushes.
The birds scattered from the trees
and squatted near the door in a rough
half circle, facing in and out, in and out,
shuffling a dance. You wept and turned
away. The whole day there went dark.

*

They warn you when you start out
to do this, astonished to find yourself
alive, beyond the secrets of the moon
and the white hands of the sea.
No trace or vestige of triumph,
no place and no reproof.
The forgotten scars of the ditch
burn their way to wires,
one of the many shadows
where spiders root and weep.
You roll down the hill,
abandoned and bewildered.

You move so slowly that you do not move.
Your voice bends, makes no sound.

*

I am surrounded by an odd light.
The fires of August change
the landscape, trees burned
to the shapes of grief, smoke rising
to an unbroken floor of clouds
that bring no rain. The uplands
merge to patterns of belief,
the spokes of the world revolving
to the enormous night beyond.
For a moment, then, we have
a glimpse of ourselves, the mystery
of being between horizons,
eternity a thin smoldering in dust
and dark patches on cold sand.
We are a strange beauty.
The world is empty as a shell,
its edges wet and dark.
There was a light at the end
of the long bridge.
The light said nothing.

*

They were preparing for the trip south,
away from the cold hill and the black snow
deep on the hill and across the streets
already dark at four o'clock after an
afternoon of ruin and fading light,
the old bones on the hill poor as crystal.
Two hands gather the world, the long
loneliness of shadows waking in the walls,
the anguish of the window sill blind
and unnamed, life uncalculated,
brooding the emptiness that will soon come.
They were preparing for the trip south,
away from the shed skin of the old house,
away from the underbark of black snow
as it uncouples the rails and the door opens
to clarity, to the slag of useless ghosts paling
across the pitted landscape at last.
They were preparing for the trip south.
Two worlds gathered between their hands,
nothing dying as they walked in black snow,
the wind they lived with with the dead
blind and broken in the window, exploding
into roots of ice, breathless as old bones.

*

The lights in the hallway
had been out a long time,
the season late winter

41

or early spring, and the windows
were open and the doors
were all locked. What she said
was not a plea, though the
uncertainty in her voice
surprised him as he turned,
startled her to breathe again
as the hour finally passed.
Her red dress fluttered
by the kitchen window,
in late afternoon at the edge
of the small town where
the plain sky grows so blue
and a good woman's prayers,
in the anonymity of her room,
might reach for heaven.
There was no loneliness like hers.
With each step she took
to close the curtains
she kicked the ashes of dead stars.

*

The phone stopped ringing
at ten o'clock each morning
after my mother died.
She would call to tell me
she wanted to sit down
on the floor, in the middle
of her room, with the lights
turned off,
to be where
she knew no one
and no one knew her,
where no one wanted
anything from her
and she took nothing in return,
to move at last through
the unopened door
and past the dark stair.
The night she died
was abrupt and warm,
midnight lifting up
and down the hall,
something else, more urgent,
coming from the direction
of the door.

*

My uncle drove a dark red pickup truck
with a bottle of Thunderbird tawny port
under the driver's seat.
His mother was swollen and yellow
when she died, hair fine as feathers,
voice quaking across the dim border

of her room, and he laughed
without needing to apologize,
to her or anyone else for anything,
finished up whatever work he could find,
put ketchup on his bread before
burying her and throwing
an empty bottle of wine into the hole
where they put her.
Snow came like a quick errand.
He didn't bother with a coat.

*

Her mind went blank,
couldn't remember the names
of all the saints in all the
congregations that prayed
for the dying and the dead.
Day was an opaque stone,
fingers stained with red,
her arm bleeding,
the night insatiate.
And so she prays:
Blessed is food,
blessed is sleep,
blessed is death,
blessed is the sand of the world,
blessed is the turret of the grave,
blessed the blazing plain.
She trims the lace
from around her wrist,
sees the hole that widens
in the back of her yard.

*

The Finnish girls tug on loose cloth,
their white hands exhausted.
The one on the right taps her foot
softly out of rhythm, the one on
the left hums under a red scarf.
There is someone else in the room,
standing at the window,
gazing into a starry sky.
There is the sudden sound of a body
hitting the earth.
Ukko stumbles through the reeds,
back and forth, swift, ephemeral,
the rumor of his ghost a rush
of breath, the crack of bone
that cannot be mended.
The girls turn: the brush of hand
against hand at the end of the world.

*

The lower edge of Gooch's beach,
along the curve of shore and stone

breakers that guide the river to the sea,
is frozen solid at the junction
of the night tide, layers of salt ice
darkened with feathers, opening
and closing with the cold stars
as the great clouds breathe and
move with water dull as pewter.
Snow falls motionless across the
horizon, crusting in chalky fragments
on the waves. Thin lines of ice weave
to a blind end. The sand adjusts
itself, bursting yet lingering on,
constancy of form an illusion
as the immensity of the ocean breaks
then foams up then slides back again
in a confusion of land and sky
and water. A solitary figure, more
shadow than substance, shuffles
hunched against the wind as if cast
down into the deep places of a world
that will vanish overnight.
Above my head shadows fall from
the roof of the house, pin my arms
to the emptiness that will soon come.
I listen for the sea to call me.
Birds scatter in from the outskirts of town.

*

The gray sidewalk on the closed side
street runs past a house of rented rooms
where he sits in the dark by the window
on the third floor drinking whiskey and water,
thinking about things everyone else he knew
had long since forgotten. An old newspaper
is blown by a gust of wind across the street,
wraps around the foot of a statue of three horses
nothing but skin and bones, blood long gone
back to the river below. He sits looking out,
not sure how much had changed in the street,
in the empty yards and flat-roofed ware-
houses in the distance, confidence and sorrow
both marking the lines of his face.
He lights a cigarette, blows smoke in thin
gray drifts through the open window.
Something calls to him from the hall,
gathering the strength to walk home, trying
to get back to where he ought to have been.
Anyone might wonder what that was.
I wondered too.

*

The mountain and the root
all rise in me, the rubble and the mud.
In the quick white grass, withered things

line the dark rims of the dunes,
forgotten lives at the edge of the salt
hay fields and marshes disappearing
in the pitch black curves of the coast.
There are old women here, fallen in
irregular circles like wild things among
the stones, runes carved on red rocks
in careful revelation of the infinite
and the certain, the triple rhythm
of land sky and sea sweet in the faces
of angels. The dry-stone church
north of Clifftop Dun Beag leans
its back against the old city and time
staggers away on the wind,
hat fluttering, folding in the leaves,
astonished by the ordinary pain
of loving this place in the semi-
darkness of the shuttered room.
I know as much as one man can know.
Two risings that Easter, two risings,
transfigured the ilex and the rose.

*

He wasn't clear in his last days,
drifting farther from shade to shade
each time I went to see him,
his body hollowing out under
the stiff white sheets.
He knew something was coming
from the direction of the clouds
outside his window, and it came.
I found his testament tucked
and folded between the pages
of the red notebook I gave him.
    It read:
I especially love
StaLy and he children
None of which were
mine/
I loved many vimmens
none of whose were my
wife.
I forgive any she might
after me.
And I will all love
her.
I hope she goes to the
after funeral snack
bar.
Say I loved all my 9
old girl friends
even after they brought me
back. and I died

5 to ten months
Later.

I love my Family
Forever.
and all my daughters
and sons who didn't
uses protections.

His eyes see everything through
different glass now, the dulled hunger
of late autumn unilateral as the wind.

*

The sky was the texture and color
of an old gray dog. The smells of the street,
the noise frightening, the threat deadly,
incapacitating, from heel to skull.
Even the living may not have a chance.
It had been dark for some time, smoke
hollowing the horizon and prowling
the streets, the gray spiders of ice
gathering on all the windows and doors.
The snow bleeds on the bird's wing,
rough to the touch, stains the land red.
It is the truth that interrupts the answer.
The dust in my eye sets the dog loose,
nothing becoming nothing in a loud retort.
Pity the sky, the fallen roots.
Pity yourself and me.

*

The country we were driving through
meant little or nothing to me until I saw it,
linked prophecy and travel together
the way fire burns sometimes on the
surface of a frozen lake. The whistle under
the door and old men solitary in the dark,
in the lashing wind in Portage Pass,
dream at midnight of other ghosts,
Tlingit totems of travelers and birds
tracing the edge of the world's rim
where all the roads in and out
of the Tongass are rimed and lost.
The wolves mourn, walk among men,
women's eyes certain of their station,
and the raven shifts its final shape
from being to confusion. The light here
is where it is, sweet and aching and cold.
Bones white in the sun drift inland
across the changing world.
The sea turns, shelters itself from the tide.
Something kept me to the thinnest edge
of the shore. I lingered a while, caught in the

great spokes of light, listening to the dry noise
of sand in the wind, the mystery of being
in the dust of stars. Up ahead, outlined
in fog, the rooftops of a town, the wind
rising, broken clouds flowing east.

*

It was like trying to breathe under water,
a humbling of reality at some paralleling
center. We break across a boundary
of new lines though we reach no new
conclusions, the burdens of the world
finished along the margins, the past
filling its own space and pushing yesterday
into today, what was into what is.
Things turn. Each thing surrounds
each thing as time comes and goes,
struck progressions and bent essences
in the perfect composure of nothing.
I commit myself to the particular,
to the transitions of a perishable event,
but that alone won't end my grief,
won't fix me against a solid wall.
Morning falls out of the tree in a radiance
of light. The small failures of black birds
console the periphery. There is a hunger
in the air, an indulgence of water.

*

It all ends soon enough.
The first days become the last.
The year is a pile of dry bones
scattered near a low brown fence,
the trailing edge of a broken wing
dragging on the water.
For her the world turned white
once more, her blind eye closing
in the high room.
Her life is a thin line written
on the sidewalk in pale chalk
before rain. The lost patterns
of death wear away the hours,
loosen the pale wonders of the sky:
faded, far away, dissolved,
forgotten.

*

The room was sparsely furnished,
made of light wood and dark tiles,
filled with people keeping their distance
from each other. I walked into a place
on the left where I found a woman's boot
with a high heel, dark leather embroidering.
Someone stuffed a gag into my mouth,

eyes wide, and pushed me out and away.
And then: walking through a city with tiered
buildings that I stopped to photograph,
thin black women leaning against white walls.
Light washes my hands like water.
Slow lives sink as the time comes.
Everywhere a cold step, a withering.

*

Early morning was overcast.
This is what I found:
Flames spread out like feathers.
Black is better than white.
Winter, a half moon setting.
A short run across shallow water.
The domination of hard stones.
The ashtray was filled with sand
when I woke in the middle of the night,
the sky blackened by secrets and wings.
Nothing had pity on me, stuck
in the middle of a long rain,
and the invisible owls splintered
the dark crevices bewildered by rain.
I prayed for a road home,
prayed for this green place,
prayed for the vellum and piper and dream.
All this in the time before,
let out of the shadows,
buried in the back of the yard.

*

I imitate the world,
huddle in a small room
painted red, the door stiff
and white as a starched
collar. Everywhere else
seems strange to me,
ghosts of dust and light
recalled in unsent letters,
etched in the silence
of stones and walls.
Persistent things nest
in a corner of my eye:
a patch of moonlight
on the ceiling crying out
in the night, flesh dissolving
to water that fills a roadside
ditch, God's hands buried
in black snow. The clock
in the room is striking,
the hour unclear. I hear
a soft quick step and somewhere
in the east, a world away,

time spins on its point,
the gray mask rises.

*

The hunger of the air,
the inner light of each visible thing,
the separation of black and white
on the wings of dead wrens.
Dawn returns, configurations
of interests and vows.
I no longer care how far I wander.
I am weightless on the old bridge,
my body rises as it falls,
conceives each distance,
climbs each descent.
The circle drives each circle,
each stone the next stone,
each hour the one before
and then the next.
I brush away the ink of time.
I can see the white sun rising in the west.
I am free.

On the Day of St. Stephen, the first martyr, who was stoned to death, and in celebration of L a an Dreoilin, the day of the wren in Dingle.

*

The woman holds the bell
in her dark hand, the death
of the world rusted as a beggar's cup.
There is a face in the glass in the wall,
a man with a stone in his hand
moving closer to the center of the light.
The earth blurs. The moon drowns
in the furrows of the river.
The crow hobbles the air, alights
on the ruins of the white city.

*

It did not take us long
to get there, suddenly transparent
as we face west.
The time before
unexpectedly became the time after.
The change present too,
unnoticed, and we knew
things must be
hidden somewhere,
in the widening scope of disorder,
the abandonment
of the uncertain bottom,
the rising and falling
of the boards of the bridge.
The late sun sinks

red as fire in the west;
the tide washes across the beach,
its slow movements crimson
on the surface of the sand;
in the distance, out past
the curve of the bay,
a ship emerges from the mist.

*

Reason is not ambiance,
no miraculous increase
that spills across an unknown center,
the provisional point inclined
in no set direction
from some luminous core.
Things, instead, dim,
the precise and the absolute
a precipitation of form
that tilts time away
and overwhelms the natural
and the useful.
There are a thousand
close variables, and tonight
as fire splits the sky
and chaos knocks against
the last closed window of the house,
I renounce the blindness of the world,
I whittle the changing root.

*

Some people are not helped
at all, some people miss
the morning when the bus
has come, nothing close
at hand. He sits
in the same chair in the same spot,
reflecting a further decline
each morning, nothing struggling
to the fore, nothing possible
to seize the day. Sometimes,
when he can, he bends
over his plate, staggers
his words to disbelief
and mumbled disgust.
All this so lightly wrought,
the dark grace
of the vulnerable and dead.
I will sit with him
under the dormant clock
until I grow old, watch
as his life peels away
like old paper pulled from
the wall, weightless, thin,
and torn.

*

About a mile and a half away,
along the banks of the brown river,
faltering on the edge of the future,
a distant barking of dogs
hangs strangled in shadows and clouds.
I don't know if I felt grief or love
then and can't pretend I heard
something else slouching past
the stone bench outside the house
and disappearing into thin air
overnight, banished forever from heaven.
Flesh of my flesh, cry of my cry,
the forgotten scars wake to new leaves,
shine mysterious and low in the window.

*

Magical lives, the mournful pace
of a vanished world no matter
how dry the weather, the night
cold and still, everything distinct
along the side of the road, no middle
ground to save or preserve.
I watched women dressed
in white swim silently in the pools
of the river, floating softly
in a blue haze that weaved among
the spider webs and rocks
caught and brittle on the banks.
I lift my arms like a white something,
skim the waters with unfamiliar birds.
The river gathers all that is left.
The river gathers the women and me.

*

I watched it pass the familiar chair,
mysterious and sweet, as a cold
February day rattled the windows
and gripped the front door.
I am up before the sun starts to warm
the kitchen, rattling weak as a lost love
testing the horizon. The eye breaks
to the textures of gray light, picks
time's bones apart as the harmless gather
in the unlighted rooms at the front
of the house. I make myself small,
radiate with a constant light that
dampens the black spaces on the walls,
moves to perfection in the lines of the chair.
I accept my end and my beginning,
the quick shiver when the wall grows cold,
the unsteady night and the time to come.
And then morning, the indecisive thing.

*

Somebody opens a window
on the first great chill of fall
and in an unexpected moment
of quiet I hear the infinite
languor of the world out past
the gray horizon, wayward birds
roweled above a reddened sea,
dreams of old flowers as
stars rain blind, sleep spreading
across the blank hush of the moon,
wood darkening to the vague
voices of a yellow heart,
intractable edges of stained glass
in arms as they fall, murmurs
of lost cities whipping the dark,
the arc of a needle scratching.
The world rolls on, love for love,
riveting that other shore.
I record the tethered graces
of this lengthening night
time a drop of water suspended
on a spider's web that trembles
forever in a trace of air or dries
in the blink of a spider's eye.

*

Nothing remains beneath the surface,
elemental things unraveling
in an elemental world.
I am willing to go along, to accept
that every living thing is under siege,
bent to the changing light, that
the unmistakable cadences
of every sound in the world
loud, tranquil, vehement, rigid,
grave, solemn, and slow
are a defiance of circumstance
and death, the one truth I know
on this late summer night.
I post no barrier between them.
I am high and low in this flying
world, a single continuum of earth
and air, brooding under water,
over deserted sky. I meet myself
when the great wheel spins, dressed
in white, stretched on the floor.
I open the one door I am not allowed
to enter. I give away the only thing
the world has given me to keep.

*

The notes below were propped in various places in the house on the table in the kitchen, on the mantle of the fireplace, taped to the mirror in the large bathroom, left on the carpeted cellar stairs   written in dark blue ink in handwriting I did not remember. I wasn't sure if they were facts or opinions, if they were shaped by doubt or idleness, some hovering uncertainty or passing obsession. I took them as warnings to always wear black and sit dumb in the corner, after a long silence contemplate the consequences of acknowledging that having the idea is much more valuable than having the thing, to be morally unexceptional while taking revenge on the world. Shame descends on us all in this shameful time, we get the refuge we deserve. I rattle around randomly in random places, make detours into different faces, become completely invisible or take flight again. No one will be particularly upset that I am leaving, but I would be grateful if you could explain these to me, by letter or call, let me know how I should read them: together or separately, from side to side or beginning to end. You can find me paling in whatever small recognizable form gestures from the window overhead tonight. It will be as if I was always there. And so:

The door of the bedroom
at the back of the hall is open.
The switch on the wall is off.
The window is covered in fake ivy.
On the floor, there is a trodden deep
red stain, an iron-red cast caked
with the bodies of angels and saints.

_____

I wonder what drives me
to a remove, to hidden things?
Sturdy and accustomed,
like filigree or the hope
for mass resurrection?

_____

One small point on the horizon
closer to God.
And the whales and fish
know I am here.
This black immensity.

_____

I listen to how metal lurches
and grinds, a bleak season,
the crest of the moment
of masks and burns.

_____

The error brought to perfection,
the radiance of the hand
as it touches the grief of things,
whatever it is that at last
suits my blood, whatever it is.

But I was thinking, too, that the ground inevitably eats up everything that walks on it, grants no accolades or rewards, and doesn't care in the slightest for the beautiful and the good. Is that what we call a rhetorical victory, the extrusion of laments and moans colored red on posters and in photographs stuck at the bottom of wooden boxes? There is a seed of vengeance in my heart, the artful dodge of mortality, the paradox of the zero and the one. I don't yet know where it will be planted. No doubt in some sad place subdued in the middle of some sad night by a ghost longing to return to his own life. I'll let you know. I'll leave a note   on the table in the kitchen, on the mantle of the fireplace, taped to the mirror in the large bathroom, left on the carpeted cellar stairs written in dark blue ink in handwriting you will not remember.

Three White Horses

Three white horses stir trapped in the language
of the dead as light empties like an oracle
across the blue smoke of heaven.
                    St. Brigid's Well

1.
The clock strikes midnight.
Night began like a last letter against
the cold, the flat light the color of shadows
and the shaken wings of cicadas drying
to dust and brown grass under the ice
as the world revolved and time passed
in brisk detachments down the road.
It had snowed all day, the sky fading
to brittle knots and lesser birds folding
to dark echoes on the streetlamps and trees.
When we came back, a haze of blue
smoke blinded the wall, the frail silence
of the street following up the long stairs.
Outside the window, past the red tiles
of the rooftops, in the old square near
the fountain, three white horses rounding
the circle turned and swelled in bronze.
They watched the strangers pass,
the secret given them by the world
an allegory of winter and love,
quick as their eyes could count
the lowest number on the wheel.
And the sky turned dark as a wilted rose,
black and brittle at the root.
And shadows leaked unfocused
at the center and the edge.

2.
Your skin tasted like the air along
the river, bitter and quick, one light
shining in the window of the house
beyond the bend of the road.
The silence of God muddled the trees
as the heavens closed and reconciled
with light, and the twelve winds
survived the dream's last hour.
In the distance, rising and falling,
the echoes of stars scratched effigies
on broken stone, gatherings of lost birds
patched breathless near the outer gate.
Clouds of snow spun clockwise
in the timeless glass of heaven
and earth, and the dry bones rode
on clear wings to history and dust.
Wait. None of this may be right.
Tonight memory twists and turns

in a drunken room, passion ending
in the echoes of birds in locked boxes
as the vestments of glass struggle and dull.
The course of the world slips away and
the year loses its footing in the street.
The speculations of what is true conclude
without conviction or success, the points
of the wind rose rusted in the arches.
Consolations of the past darken
to bottomless reductions in the mirror,
the artificial line with no fixed point
compounded at the margins as they fall.
The synthesis of fire and ice drones
in the hollows, wings the white wall.

3.
I watched you standing in the hallway,
red shoes nervous in your hand,
a gray shape of soot and stone in a
silent corner of the night leaning against
the wall like an impossible dream.
Footsteps shake the floor, the secret out,
and the city slides into its own blue light.
The long burdens and spare parts
of this place as the great wheel spins
its last come and go as they will.
The day will not reconcile with night,
peels the muster of the rounding stair.
Things sleep in the tarnish of ice,
cold in a cold world where time
wears out, and the street that leads
home darkens on its steep ascent.
Its shadows tilt the shadows back
in a long-abandoned room.

4.
Try to remember the way
the dark bridge above the dark river
stands against the white of winter,
the way dust coats the thin edges
of the window blinds in the old room,
the way smoke from the low chimneys
in the narrow alley dissolves slowly
in the air, the way the thin street
turns back to the house, filled
with memory and desire, and the sky
erupts with the sound of lost birds
in a warp of November snow.
Truth springs up, heavy with the
passing years, like a mirror
in an empty house that shatters
against a sudden wall.
Take it all in as the year sets low
on a horizon of cut stone, follow

the shapes and signs that lift
the secrets of another life.
Clip the unexpected.
Catch the one who was the first to fall.
It may be enough.
You may remember the way
the moon wanes across the corners
of the house, bleeding away like
a thousand wings, the way
the barrier of dead roots covets
the new world, locked in the tempo
of shift and change, the way
light sinks into an open door
near the edge of the infinite road
and follows, follows, follows.

5.
Nothing will happen.
The single stem of a cold night
will break like a blue vein,
the windows and doors of gray
towns claiming no further warrants.
A brittle snow will bring November
to a close and the trees along
the river in the center of the city
will thin to slow brick walls, crossed
thresholds, the disorder that sinks
to other shapes in a changing sky.
The old gods, carved in runes and
dry timbers, will cave the darkening
shadows of the streets.
The indifference of time will slide
to its quick, a black angel floating
in dark water under an old stone bridge.
Near the yards, the pulse of rolled
steel will deafen the light and air.
Memory, charred in its own dry visions,
will walk out the door into a silver light.
Nothing will gather into nothing.

6.
The faces in the shop windows
grow old in the same country,
turn gray on the same cross streets,
rise and fall in the same small corners.
It is growing cold a mile down the road,
trains stop, death comes hobbling
like a strange dog suddenly at the door.
The sky beyond opens as if created for the
first time, filled with pale flowers, and a red
bird lifts slowly across the dark steel rails.
An old man's hand works the folds
of the empty wall in the dark, midnight
coiling along the bricks in the walk.

Something light and dry touches his face,
ripples and blurs in dead glass.
The next moment falters, then the next.

7.
I live simply, raise no alarms.
Darkness flows around itself
as eyes stare past the green walls
and light glances off the single vase
in the center of the table
that holds no stems or flowers.
Night deepens without commotion,
tilts its roots into the room,
the world in sleep and second sight.
The table is covered with the heads
of matches, carefully arranged
in circles and lines, a dangerous plain
near the closed attic door.
I endure the shift of things,
watch a small brown spider
make its way among the
phosphorus stones, quicker
than a human hand, my fingers
tapping on the table's edge.
It is centered on its spot,
threading through the rows
of matchheads as if some
needle's eye or frightened wish.
Wind rattles the window glass,
blessing the ground
and surviving the ice.
I stay up half the night
awake in every nerve,
the promise of conflagration
in the dusted air.
The great wheel spins.
A match scratches across
the coarse plate, circles
aimlessly for a minute
in the streak of its pursuit.
The spider dances for
redemption on the table
among the yellow flames.
My fingers tap the edge in time,
nourished on tears and smoke.

8.
Truth tastes like ashes in my mouth
as I sit in the deep gray light.
The rust on the posts of the green
bridge unwinds the clocks, cold-eyed
in the water of the brown river that
floods across a dry arrangement
of stunned voices. I walk from room

to room listening. The hard rattle
of night spins on its own black edge.
The shade on the window thumps
like the white flame of a lost love.
Outside, whistles running in the streets
call the raw dogs. It's no use complaining:
these are all clear sounds. Only time
is a ghost whose lips are perpetually
sealed until the bone of chaos scratches
the word and the circles of heaven break.
Beyond the window, where the flats
brook the ridge, it comes to a dead rest.

9.
When all else whitens on the roofs,
when wayward things come home
to roost to a new red deep in iron
and stone and the day staggers to
a brawl in the dying street, the years
howling through the light at the edge
of a breathless universe
you know there is no way to go
but back, to dream in the dead
of night of insistent voices in the dark,
the forgotten places behind closed
doors, the way all lovers move and
pass, hair smooth and loose, in all
the corners of all the rooms of this city.
And then a deeper sleep, so many endings
out beyond the opening gates, the sound
of running horses as the scroll unwinds.
The soul, tangled in its own patterns,
cannot see tomorrow unfold, cannot
lurch headlong into its passive voice.
The night is forever cold and struck
and everything is under siege.

10.
In late November, the hours
turn brittle and dull
as reason and forgotten truth
drive the agitated form.
The days pass with eyes cast down,
things turning inside out
and the ground settling
to black frost as the wind lifts
to thresholds and ash.
Someone throws the first stone,
weeping for the life he's lived,
and old men search
the backyards for their own graves
as light mires the vulnerable air.
It is growing cold and the sky blows
to winter, humpbacked and long.

Life hangs by a thread
in empty windows.
Behind the red door, my hand
in the soft hollow of your back,
we stand pressed together
fumbling in a dark we know
will not come again.
My heart rises like a shout.
The night is a long excuse.
Love is a dark cut
on a wooden frame.
I close my eyes
and think of morning.
May it not be so.
May it not be so.

11.

Midnight kneels in the park
by the river like a blind child.
No one can hear or see
and the light that comes
unexpectedly around the corner
is black at the core.
It drifts in its own darkness,
scattering to shudders
on the windows and ledges
of slow gray houses, remnants
of voices on a rising wind.
The secrets of the street
whisper across the thin cut
of the moon, clouds brushing
invisible through the dust
of the rooftops and walls.
Ghosts loiter on stone benches.
Cold crouches in the passing bell.
The mute white horse sleeps
with eyes open, swept free and frail
in the refuge of dead branches,
one of the shapes of the world
that cast no shadows in the glass.
Its sad bones land soft
and low on the dark street.

12.

The streetlamp casts black shadows
across the curtains that float
to the middle of the floor
and darken the room.
The earth turns toward dawn,
the wind out of the east.
The grief of the unanswerable
question spreads over the walls
like a hard inscription
and the snow drifts down.

Cold owls gather white ice
as the hour passes, time
the mute timber of a sallow light.
The ghost of her blind father
is home again: the white shadow
rising above the black street
after a long wandering,
the last grain of sand in his eye.
The weight of things falls to its end:
the world is a hollow sphere,
the last circle, filled with illusions
of smoke where spiders in the
corners of lost rooms mumble
and weave and the deep of night
cannot shake itself awake.

13.
The shapes reflected
in the high windows
erode in the snow, lights
moving through the backyards
in bewildered echoes, dying
twice on the stained wood floor.
It is the thing that is important,
seeing with open eyes beyond
the mind's eye, the new day
driven through the gate
even when the dark is too deep.
Tomorrow will die by your
hand, the end not yet written,
and the war will end.
The mirror mocks the sky's
decline, ticking like a clock.

14.
You dream of a long hall, dimly lit,
where breaths flutter against dark walls,
a white moth drumming on a hanging bulb;
of a quiet old room with green carpets,
a barefoot woman anxious with love
stretched on a hard brown chair;
of an empty bed at the end of winter,
a black skirt laced with fine stitches
draped loosely on a faded rail;
of arms and thighs wrapped together
in secret, faces pressing tense on a rug's
frayed edge, reflected in the pane;
of yourself, dry as salt in flutters of air,
floating through the ends of a bitter
earth and watching, watching.
These shadows mock the thin
disorder of the night, the paradox
of the zero and the one.

15.
The slow breath of a lost horse
standing alone in the snow
at midnight in winter wakes
the seed asleep in the cold ground.
He leaves no tracks as the earth
comes up out of darkness and moves
slowly toward a tenuous light.
The shape of the sky is constant,
the wound on his leg dark wood that
palls to yellow and stifles with blood.
Black cinders of houses burning
to dust beyond the fences spread
across a world that will never end
and the patience of desire endures
as it grapples for hours and fades.
That truth is always bitter in its own
defeat, no matter the threshold or the
sad impermanence of white stars.
The snow for now has stopped.
The radiance of things loses its place.
The uncontrollable season prods the year.
The horse suddenly shakes his head,
the sound of his mane and slow breathing
in the shallows of the trees an unexpected
comfort to the living and the dead.

16.
A small vine of light crawls
across the floor and snow freezes
on the window overhead, a needle
of ice forever pointing northward.
The old man leaning against
the wall reaches for the soft edge
of the universe or the mercies of time
that transfix the unmade bed.
He knows both will come when
the sun at last rises, cut loose for
a hundred years in the narrow streets,
the scar of a sad truth troubling
the careless door, but desires neither.
He'd rather hold the moon in his
hand as it sinks into its own light,
live forever in the soft rattle of summer
flowers, in a life that is not his alone.
But he knows, he knows, and turns his head.
The few stars that remain fuse to
stained glass in the upstairs room.
Shadows whisper of a kindness that may
come in the end, implacable and white.

17.
The history of this place concedes
nothing as things turn inside out,

infinite and dim, and the constellations
drift down along the red brick walls
and the moon slowly runs out of air:
the last thing we think about
when dreams of journeys bend
like wet grass in running water
and the field in the end is lost.
Hands call back the sky, a distant
sound steadies the eye that bears
witness on a windless day.
The years like black rock roll away,
stretch across the line of roofs
where everything is now,
where the day peels to its own negative
and is locked in a small black box.
They radiate in lines in every direction,
each a pain I no longer want to know.
I dream of love and lost cities,
turn my face to the icing river,
to the darkness, the silence, the wind.

18.
There is a point where eternity
opens, scrawled against the low
horizon in late fall, and love
is heavy in thin white branches.
The world often brings regret
and remains a semblance of light
drifting through an empty sky,
a threnody of mirrors and birds.
Above the bed the wheel unwinds
taking the hour by surprise, standing
still and moving all at once.
The ceremony of time anoints
its own indifference, the blade
of a knife keeping court in a dark wall.
Morning will bring a dream
of summer houses and sad songs,
wild flowers pressed against a face
in the pleasures of another dawn.
I close my eyes and wait.

19.
Sleep overcomes us both,
the empty gesture of redemption
leaving no mark.
You arch your back,
your skin white as winter,
a dream divided against the moon.
The world has taken us over,
exchanging the promise of form
for the breach of shadow.
I did not want to live like this,
the occasions of night improperly

rendered, a gray person dressed
in gray pressed on a hard gray floor.
I could be God, spreading
my wings, flying wherever I want,
navigating the maze even
with eyes closed, drifting safely
to the south along the brown river.
This was a thought I thought many
years ago but have since forgotten,
the confusions of invisible things
racing across the ceiling
with the flickerings of snow
as the light falls and falls.
I fall into the burden of these images,
close myself away from the world
and meet the universe at its rim:
tonight is a stopped clock, a short
red truth that frets its hour, and I am
on the wrong side of the wall.

20.
The carved lines of ice on the window
mean nothing as they dry to the coarse
powder of infinity. There is no obligation,
no period of the moon that frames
grand dreams and blinds the sky to ruin
and void. I stare on, the slate of the future
in the hieroglyphs in the window
useless as the blade of a dull knife.
How do we snare our lives together,
the city at rope's end, how do we enter
again into a late dim light as the world
no longer grinds its firm edges?
How do you choose yourself as the earth
bows to an empty mission and strains
against the hull's black plates? How?
The silence of the unbroken night
has sunk into its past, time in slow descent,
and nothing is pacified by the promise of light.
Fragments of cloud unmoor the stars.
Above my bed a familiar face pities
the winter sky, watches the winged
images of a lifetime grope and addle
like wandering bones down the line.
I reach up to touch it, the ritual all
that this night demands, nourished by the
unspeakable bleed of chalk and smoke.
Too old for history or dream, the words
on her lips are hot as fire, cold as ice.

21.
He flaps his arms like a white bird
and flies along the ground in the old
square, collar turned up to the wind.

Black birds settle on tired
statues, not moving, barely visible
under the streetlamps, and lean
against the snow as it covers the world.
He floats between the ground and air.
The trails of his breathing coil dazed
and pale as he sings memories
of superstition and mud, ice binding
his thin shoulders and wrists,
chasing the slow nothing of despair.
The statues kneel, persistent
in the crouch of night, the hollow
wind on eternity's coast the sad
remainder of the day, and beat his
burdens mourning to the ground.
They know together who will die,
the sound of judgment
as it kicks the door that shrives
the world in the chill of the year,
the clamor of the committed charge.
There is no other way home tonight,
no other custom to hallow the street.
This is what the black birds knew.
This is what the black birds know.

22.

I watched from the window
in the eaves of the attic as footprints
scraped the angles of the wild streets
and silence grew, defying gravity,
like a truth gone mad.
Things fall up, not down,
and the bones of the snow keep rising.
It is dangerous here to consider
the shame of the world stripped naked
near the gate, the moment uncapped in
the cold and laid out on a brown mattress
streaked in blood, whose scars are
a roadmap on the slow flanks of
undiscovered countries forever at odds.
The unstable repetition of a final word
I cannot hear below is not enough,
the self a mournful gesture as the city
strikes its own precisions and history
folds to a bag of rags under the stairs.
I never asked to see my future,
never looked this darkness in the eye.
Life is the threshold nothing can re-cross.
I watch the straggler from the house next door
shriek like a bird and fall on his sill.
Silence at last recants its long refrain.
I am caught forever in the shadows
of these rafters, waver north and south
like the needle on the wheel.

I conspire hand in hand with some
wandering god, trip blindly on the edge of time.
The window flakes with a darkening grace,
ignites with the florid moon.

23.
Overhead, the antiphon of the bell
sculpts the air and the final divide
of the quarter hour is a barrier
against the fragile glass. A continuum
of gray houses is lost in a spell
of desperate mirrors, blind-windowed
arches given sight in a blind land.
The heart and mind seek true north,
chiseled in the ice, the patchwork
of the earth meager against their will.
The mark on the palm of your hand
is the incrimination of blood, rough
to the touch, the intent deep in a time
that does not want to come again.
The doors are draped in black,
thresholds sharp as knives and open
to the accusations of the fall.
The solid air thins and broods.
Memory blows hard from the east.
The cold wind trips in its own tracks.

24.
There is a secret hidden in the shapes
of things as they press together like
the fibers of the walls.
The clear forms rise up when the
light goes out, white wings unfurling
in the circles of a dark interior,
beginning again in the vertigo
of a miraculous escape.
It's been a long time now, long past
the memory of it, eyes blind with
the darkness and the snow,
opening and closing, the absence
they feared girding the world.
The night lifts its hand and sets it down,
the sky a dark color it could not imagine,
touching the edges of your skin.
The wind bends pale near the frozen river.
The year turns in its sleep.

25.
An old dog walking alone in the snow
rounds and rounds into a circle
by the base of the statue, its footprints
disappearing as the snow falls and then
uncovering to new ravels unbearable as effigies
of the past combed into their own futures.

Think twice before repeating it, its one
substance melancholy and steady as a swollen eye.
It is an unspeakable arrangement loosing
the black form, a dark scaffold along
the walls of rooms where lovers sleep at odds
and destiny collapses into its own fate.
Give me ignorance, the husk of a trapped
star, make me deaf and blind as a lost dog
in a steady snow, the ecstasy of a world
of sermons and hints wrapped in gray cloths.
Give me blurred glass, the fiery white
of the indecipherable word, the culvert
by the side of the road where the universe
tangles itself to roots and cold water.
Give me at long last the ragged edge of a dream
turned and tense in its own moral point.
Two shapes in the window behind the scaffold
conspire as one, dressed in the skins of angels
or birds, the void fused with its own pardon.
The blind will creates tomorrow out of sullen
abstractions, form and thing invisible as ash
and unstable as the rough stones in the square
that wrest the dog in a confluence of ice.
Night nails its own shadow to a tree.
A cold hand unexpectedly touches my shoulder.
The wind blows.

26.
All these worlds between midnight
and dawn hide in plain sight, stripped
in the flats as the north wind blows.
The eccentricities of the two beginnings
are trapped in mirrors that talk back
to the black voices in the room,
radiant in their twin convulsions.
The yellow eye bends the orbit
of the moon, quick in the pit and dust.
The snow drifts slowly down, here
and along the white shore, as the shadow
gains a foothold by the door.
The prophetic ashes on the floor
have no end, the deep red of the stars
weathered gray as the boards,
and a muddy light fails in the reins.
Something throws the latch, the day
in doubt, and wipes the sleep from its eyes.
Something scatters the hacked horizon,
the thing itself we do not name or control.
Something lifts the stones with white candor,
flying in every direction like unrecorded ghosts.
The forgotten messengers line the dark
cupboards with penciled letters, love for love,
breaking the spokes of the rootless wheel.
There is a sudden cry on the wind, a pausing

of the deepest truths that flakes across the
moon in an ancient shape and sulks against
the hollows of this immaculate stage.
I am alone. The snow presides. The hour delays.

27.
All that remains is a thin line that rises
and falls in the courtyard, an old dog
following at a distance across an eternity
of wind, and the low sound of wheels
dragging to oblivion on a dark horizon.
Their nameless dance in this hour
folds them together in patterns blue
with snow, magnitudes of ice and fire
beyond the tidings of the world.
I listen for a long time, my back
against the empty bedroom wall.
Something whispers in the curtains
that those who confess go free,
drained of protest and resolve
in the undertones of steel.
The covenant of mirror and wind
lays claim to hard semblances
as I reach for the outline of the door.
This city is a bitter glass rimmed with
interruption, fracturing as it twists
and turns across the limits of the universe.
The simple chaos of the lights
below steadies my hand and eye.

28.
I remembered white butterflies
in late spring falling across the
meadows like snow, the history
of the world on hold, and the slow
touch of your hand in the doorway
suddenly close and at ease,
and how you turned and walked away
that last time down the stairs,
across the cobbled street.
These memories come and go
more often now and time takes me
in the darkness by surprise.
I do not want the silences of either.
I watch this winter night curl up
in smoke as God's mystery covers
the far corners of the earth
like snow that falls for a hundred
years on every living thing.
I see your face in each falling seed,
breathe with your breath in the frozen glass.
In the white stillness of this room,
in the final minutes of a sudden dream,
I bear the name that I've been given.

29.
It was a moment I wanted to keep,
the folding history of the north sky
running its course and the sidewalks
cleared and empty at this hour.
Through the window blind an icy light
at the city's end, the secret of how
the world began: centuries of dust,
small things sleeping forever in the cut
of the earth, a dry road leading nowhere,
shattered glass dividing the white of a
single day, a stunned spill and a long fall,
dark stones underground coming up
and out the way a soul might rise
in the invisible wind, in the falling snow.
A white moon beads the clouds,
steady as a circle engraved in glass.
Beyond the square, a train begins
to move again, its slow wheels
husking against their own decay.
The world sinks into its seed.

30.
Up ahead, a few more hours
along the empty road.
The night sky abrupt
as heated metal.
A flock of birds in the distance
rakes the landscape.
An unfamiliar hand brushes
across your back
under a white half-moon hanging
in the dark clouds:
a woman in a white dress,
the shake of her voice
as she offers water to the dying,
to you, the dry curtains rustling
as she passes, the smell
of cold air on the line of the horizon
calling her home.
Nothing atones for the coldness
of night, the touch
of her bracelet on your face
the promise of things
you think you know that lifts
the burdens of the ground.
You reach to make the world
your own.
She sits on the bed, resting, waiting,
the sky heavy and close.

31.
And the world is white and white
and white. The city is white with fresh

snow and lightning opens a sky that
presses down on the streets with
the weight of dry bone scrubbed to white
tinder under the ground. The glass
clears as the gates open, wind white
as salt at the beginning of everything
and the end of it all. Bare stones gleam
in a bright light, hundreds of white feathers
covering the strange trees, carrying
the longing that abides and startles
the two shores. Secrets die like a white
candle burning in a dark window, midnight
bending across the horizon like
a blind martyr in a crucible of dreams.
The white flame leaps and dances
across the faces of the brilliant moon.
You turned away from the window, hands
falling, as I stood down below fingers
pressed white against a dangerous ledge.
The red moon hung above the house
like an empty drum, a miniature dimming
sharp-tongued in the square of glass.
The moment ended in self-accusation.
Crows in the narrow yard lifted and shook.

32.
The shadows of hands on the
drawn curtains stretch to pale roses
against the dangerous walls.
Photographs of mothers, daughters,
sisters in black dresses on a table
of dried wood, standing at odds
and misdirection in a cold despair.
The face of a blue child in frozen
water under a bridge that cannot
be kept, remorse for the past
reconciling with the slow crawl of dust
in the corners of the mirror.
The future has no fixed address,
already old when it begins.
The eye of the needle hanging outside
the windows is part of a long epistle,
the last word stitched in old cloth
and unraveling in dark gray light.
The crowded night coughs.
The sky redeems its own abstractions.
In the hallway the secret life of
light and shade scrims a wheel
of breaking glass. The half-moon
in the air cambers the thing affirmed,
the secondary intimations that leave
nothing behind in the newly-fallen
snow, the porcelain that pieces the world
together when night returns.

I pay the ransom in my broad-brimmed
hat, turn my collar up to the angles
and lines that trim the stone bouquet
in the statue's blue hands.
I slip eccentric in an abstract wind,
resolve the last questions of the world.

33.
The opposites in the square lift
to their own corners, breathe in the unison
and repose of the long root.
I think by feeling, each turn a quick splinter
of glass, each flicker of the streetlamp a new
incantation for the dying and the dead.
Secrets endure, naked as a sudden pain
under the ribs, the disorder of a ghostly
voice that wakes in the slow dread
of what it has become, its bitter
conviction incautious at last.
The rest of the night is a dry lift
as God bends down to sweep the stones
in the pavement, appall the summit
of the long dust. It is a world of dreams,
a small place in the trees as I become
branch and wind and the white kingdom
of the river moves into its own vague trace.
That is the last similitude, the last silence
as silence at last subsides, the obscurity
of the self in the darkness of the day.
Nothing comes here to stay, nothing grates
from door to door as the summit swells
to a time that seeps through my veins,
nothing tangles the miraculous escape.
It is more like a downward progression
along the meridians of the world,
the salience of marrow and stone
in a center filled with centers,
each meaning bearing a differing weight.
The great night stands still, the agency
of the flesh rising before the great fall.
The moment gathers. The wind broods.

34.
The slats of the window hide all
that is innocent, all that is lost or forsaken
in the random currents of truth tonight.
The crouch of the walls is a white embrace,
a struggle to lift from this place without
a single beat of a wing under the streetlamps,
pierce the clouds above the crows' cries,
feel the hard slam of iron and steel
as the doors below close.
It is all chaos, I know that now, some
random impaling of the light, not

a predicted effect or certain analogy
of action but a congress of limps
and desires unmet when the thin bones
ride the loosed horses.
I need nothing more, I have no need
to know why, no need to understand
the articulations that divide us:
it is the nothing from
which the same new beginnings come,
equally unsteady in a shifting wind,
that veers too close when the ice
unexpectedly turns to flame, when
I pin my shadow to the wriggling moon.
Light is the infinite ash that covers
the floor, all that remains of the stars
when eternity coughs and bleeds.

35.
A procession of streetlamps circles
the statues and horses below, the lost world
crossing its own numbers and letters out.
Their light filters through falling snow,
summoning the sky as it hollows to silence
in the west, the effigies of history thrust
in my hands like a moment of crisis.
How foolish it is to dream, to cross
the planes between these worlds:
you turn and tell me you are caught
in the chair and cannot move across
the room to me, your blouse lifting
like morning on your back.
This room is heavy with the past,
you transparent in this momentary place.
The curious lie persists.
The world is neither black nor white.
The wind continues on its way, pushing
the strangers on their long walk home.

36.
Chance events and the chaos of birds
in a distant light mark your return
home on the first day after the
shadows of a hard winter's sleep.
Wires on poles along the street
sag with the remains of snow.
Hands scratch and hide
in old pockets, fingers grieving
with the indifference of white faces.
Strangers on corners and steps
are imitations of the double thread,
the harsh quick as morning nears,
destiny a dark harbor and endless maze.
God himself has already come and gone,
a trick of light in the shaking air.

The old woman passing by the lost
angels drags the night into a vacant lot.
The mind is caught in the bonds
of its own making, indelible and restless
as the deep tides swell.
In the half-empty room, as the sky
grows black and red, something
knocks against the cold door.
A white-colored man in white
clothing rides past on a white horse.

37.
They lead the white horse
at midnight between the fence
posts and rails, watching which
of its legs, right foot or left, steps
first in the furrows of each marked row,
its halting movements across
the stones a conjuring or divination.
The earth blackens and splits
like a dry seed as the gate slams shut,
the land infertile on the horizon,
and the snow drifts down
to a burial of cold smoke.
I never wanted to see that place,
branching into hard lines
that beat across the street,
the future a single hour under
a dark November sky squared
to a sunken thing under the stairs.
There, the consolations of truth in
ambiguous circles leave no tracks
and silence deepens by degrees,
brittle variables of a temporal mind.
There, the moment before the storm
falls away invisible and time braids
together mystery and faith. There.
The clock unexpectedly strikes three.
The horse in the distance
in the dark by the fence winces
with snow then bites the air.

38.
The moment stretches and breaks
as shadows from the lone lamp
on the corner fall across the sudden points
of the street, unnamed glass and steel
reflecting the last hope of a dry return.
An erratic life scrapes by in counter-
currents on the other side of the light,
the equilibrium of the world balanced
in the symmetry edged between midnight
and the back alleys of dawn, the doors
that never open shaken by a rising wind.

The house at this hour is a dead echo,
the absolute of night's black space.
The mirror on the deep wall reflects
a face that night has turned to stone,
the arc of the moon tracing the end
of everything, the peripheries and centers,
far past the outlines of the half-dark room.
The pieces of the world sleep for a hundred
years tonight with the ghosts on the corner,
the drift of time churning to thin smoke
and the colloquies of dreams.
The restless stars bristle above the road,
falling with the weight of white feathers, and
the noises below list against the last low wall.
In the patience of this moment, in the
loneliest of all my days, I am the secret name
that brings the house down to a drawn
conclusion, the perilous silence
the air yields to in a dimming light.

39.
One circle of bare ground by the gate catches
the flame and snow angles the face of the moon.
Nothing is neglected as the passageways recede,
existence a consolation of a single truth and a
difficult peace in the imbalance of both hands.
I try to keep my mind on other things: the train
at the edge of the city, a sudden pale shaft of light,
the way the future and past cancel the senses,
a quickened pulse on the changing landscape,
and the pity of iron that cuts the surface
of steel as rail cars seep slowly into the station.
I regret that I can't ride them in this signal hour,
regret the erratic wagging of the road ahead.
I stand instead on one leg, head back and arms
extended, turned against the wall, the outlines
of the earth capped in redemption on my head.
The energy of the world is contained in forms
that open again to fill the dialectical void.
Life darts for cover as winter birds sing with
the knowledge that things are as they are and
always will be, that the loose black boards
of the world will forever hollow in their wake
as stars explode to the shapes of red glass.
Fear answers fear in a long pursuit, and in the
interchange around me I see the gate's ajar.

40.
I trace my finger through the dust on the
floor, death an orphan in these motions.
The patterns my fingers make are a
sanctuary of artificial lines, the clarity
and wholeness of existence held fast
in their own source, nothing distorted,

73

the certainties I draw a self-accusation
whose end or meaning I will not know.
Reconciliation is familiar as a scar.
The hour arrives: the hand of God
traces its fingers across my face,
gropes across the harsh walls of the hall,
and then moves on, deaf and blind,
into a cascade of flame and cold snow.
I sketch my life like a long cloak
on the floor, inundations of the universe
that break the light of the eye,
the marks of those fingers on my face
part of the world I inhabit alone.
And then the hour passes: the splendor
of the flying world gathers in the dust.
The shades of heaven fumble on the floor.

41.

The day must be given a different ending,
white and long on the rooftops, as we hasten on.
The lost birds feed on flowers rooted in ice,
trapped in anonymous gardens where silence
gathers under cupolas of snow and fog settles
in the proportions of its own destination.
The body can come to life again, can remember
an innocent love in another garden, the brief light
of summer calm in the calligraphy of leaf and vine,
constant in the interventions of the rose.
We remain there forever, as forms of light,
even as night falls and falls in this flat land.
There is no limit on desire, no truth that
will unredeem the flesh, no sound
that will unwind the fidelity of our voices.
The end already exists and we sleep so soon.
The one truth I know cuts across the air.
Let me be blind once more in the bright yard,
let my heart cry out in joy, in the street below,
for the kind salvation of a faint blue light.

42.

I did not expect to see him through
the interruptions of the gray window:
the odd little man dressed in green
and black turning around in the street
at every third step to count the footprints
he had left behind in the snow, up again
to the yellow stairs that lead to his door:
one foot the frame of a well-worn boot,
the other the foot of a hobbled bird.
He stops and starts like a cold ember, knows
that the clawed foot drags the plow of time,
scratching the earth as it scuttles the west
and paling in the migrant orbits of stars.
He knows that if the burning eye that hangs

above him in the square falls across the sky,
shadows will hollow the walls he stumbles
against, elide the red ash on the doorsills
he hops across on one leg unaware.
He knows the vellum and the flicker,
the involuntary rule that flutters in the charge,
and the woman he has not yet named who
sleeps undone in the bottle and the sash.
His shadow is itself a shadow of a shadow.
His nervous hand still prods the air.
His feet again are cold.
I turn off the lantern in the window
he so watches, lid the burning eye.

43.
I have begun to live in memory,
lay yellowed photographs out across
the kitchen table, read old love letters
saved in bent brown folders, try to
find familiar stars in lost constellations.
It's hard at the outset to break
the boundary, to reach for shapes
that fill the space made by a moving hand,
to hold what can be held and then
let go and float free in a beam of light.
Truth is harmless in November.
The only epoch is my own.
I am a strange face in the mirror,
the sudden recollection of a forgotten place,
dull with loss and perplexed by the glare.
I am tonight the color of wind in a
headland of rocks that binds the old moon,
the world retrieved through a glass darkly
and piled in stacks on a table of wood.
The ellipse of the past folds a universe
of balance and risk into a savage now.
The present drives the moment
to the wildness of snow, time gone
and to come spinning on its axis.
The landscape's face is ice and stone.

44.
She tells me that she sometimes dreams
of going mad. Her voice is every shade
of red, the synthesis and symbol of an old
place under an old and darkening sky.
The night each night howls and sighs as she
trembles with the echoes of her walk.
Her fingers tap the moon in the mirror
on its dark gray brow, desire awkward
in its slide, and the dull knife cuts the last
shapes of white paper, the masters of time.
The table moves under her, swings back in the
dark, a gateway to the sounds this winter mocks.

Every shadow on the street and walls folds to a
new myth freed from the innocence of the past.
This is the prophecy of hope in the attic,
the muddled ghost of our love, that waits
for us out there like the certainty we seek.
She presses herself against the wall,
her voice constantly changing its hues,
and complains about the cold, the night.

45.
I move. Far from the river,
the night dies well.
She moves. Far from the city,
bleak land rebels.
We move. Far from the statues,
broken glass swells.
They move. Far from the windows,
wind robs the bell.
All this is part of a careful layer
that haunts my memories,
defiant and thin-skinned as a prayer,
sinking the undertones of centuries
of wrought iron and the frozen courage
of that other age.
It was the time of glass
when I was glass,
consuming the light of the world
and never reflecting it back.
The conviction of the spectrum
divides the colors of the world
and the life to come.
All tonight are gray and black.

46.
Night hovers between two moons,
rises and falls between two horizons.
On the wall, the hands of the clock
synchronize to a steady habit,
the hour striking three, and the self
bears its own reassurance against
the arch of the sky. The past peels
like a paper wrapper in my hands.
We knew we could live forever
in the long pursuit of color and form,
would not allow ourselves
to be easily found, the tides of summer
and winter buried in time together and
waking only briefly and against their will
in rituals that shorten or lengthen
the night. Each was the first day
of seeing, the world ours for the taking,
as the sky expanded and receded.
Each a push and pull against a horizon
that lies steady on the horizon and does

not accept whatever we had of grace.
The pattern endures, pained by its own
weight at the stubborn edge of fall.
The root of the future is an insolent
myth as it stumbles down the stairs
and deadbolts the door.

47.
There are no objects in the world,
no things trapped by chance events,
that run across the world dressed
in the hides of white horses.
They stride in an imagined place,
witness to what the darkness
of the latticework on the balcony did.
The cells divide, ice into ice,
everything closing one by one
in the blunting of the night.
Why do we forget so soon,
hide ourselves among the lost bags
on the train and see the motion
of the hand that strikes us down?
It hangs heavy from the ceiling,
rises darkly from the floor,
scrapes and scratches through
the wall smoldering to the west.
You drink the wine as blood
anoints your head, the mercy of
God's face in the ice too terrible to see.
No need to bring it up.
Pretend you never heard.
Strip the gains of that other world that
peel back the invisible shores of a lost
city tethered to the snow as it falls.
The blind man rambles through
the house, still searching for the stairs
he cannot find though he knows
they lead nowhere.

48.
It was a temporary covenant of rooftops
gone astray as the streets drifted
to the underline the river made
just past the corners of the square,
binding fast the thresholds of the hour.
Small and sure, the dark rider sits
outside the window, the endless
whispers of a forgotten saint troubling
the bewilderment of her mistakes.
Her life is not only her own,
not just some metaphysical fable
or parable of snow that misdirects
the iconography of the world.
She is the word that resonates

on the other side of thinking,
the surface and the substance
of the idea and of the thing
that sift the earth as the houses
all around me shake and rise,
atonement and redemption
hidden in the threaded grain.
The past is cold and naked
in the window, time a bag
of bones shaken in the street.
Night drags the four shadows
up the stairs, knocking at the door,
and something invisible burns.
She closes her eyes and pays
no mind, the half-moon chalked
in a mist that dims in the mirror.
We can no longer falter on, casting
pale reflections in the darknesses
we wander, we can no longer harden
the world to perplexity and hide
in a sleep that flickers like death
against the spill of the night.
The river tallies the outlines of
tomorrow, sounds across the
incriminations of ice in the square.
She keeps her eyes on other things,
forgives the truth that can't be told.
A key turns quietly in the lock.

49.
The counterpoint to grace leads to a cave
that roots in a deep distortion.
Fire curls like water at every turn and stains
the snow in the square, the web cast and
ours for the taking as night overwhelms the sky.
The bodies of the world hover on winter air
blowing in a narrow wind like loose banners
or carved patterns shaped by heaven's sterile eye.
If he were living now, words heavy as prose,
he would walk the streets forever and bring
the wrecker's ball down on all the shuttered
houses of our lives. Life would no longer
be a culling of all that will die in all the towns
we may have seen, a harmless dream where
the trees have all fallen and the heart has bled.
We still hope for the world not to withdraw
to the point of faith, to coil like a reformation
of the past growing in a long dark line.
I push against the cold damp walls
of this place, outlined by no rules and
modulating this hard pursuit, and time seeps
away slowly to a desolate mark.

50.
Cold numbs my fingers as I scratch
the frozen light from the edges
of the window, my breath
congealing on the sibilant glass.
The church tower in the shadows
that lap the street is dark as the day
of judgment, dark as the day when
ghosts whose names I tap on the glass
will claim the borders of the world.
We pretend there's time to change sides,
carve new images in the ice
and turn the index over in a flat land
where tomorrow, poised on the
threshold, looks in and out,
a narrow orbit swallowing time whole.
Stillness moves into stillness,
repeats itself with no consolation.
The streets are empty and the hour dead.
I am transparent in the window,
float measureless on a mortal scale,
my face and its reflection
a random synthesis that struggles
in history and granite, not sure
which fragile patterns to choose
as the sky looks coldly down.
I hide under the covered table, the
ranks of black boxes precisely aligned.
The room recedes neglected down
the stairs and I make myself small
in a stirring of musty air.
A blade of light pierces my heel.

51.
The water in the river in the center
of the city moves the way all dark waters
move under the ice, the stitch of the last
cold wall a fierce barrier on the horizon
fixed in the middle of things as snow
compounds the ratios of night.
Dressed in black and kneeling
at the end of the bridge, she raises
a divining eye across the banks and the
course of the world creaks and turns.
The stars begin to shine, the meaning
of the moment bleeding to white.
The burials of a thousand years go up
in smoke, wet wood burning in chimneys
and rising on slow flanks of wind and air.
She counts out the flames, the will of heaven
answering nothing in the reflections
of ice among the pilings and rafters.
She balances the soul's fall in the
monotony of insufficient gods, measures

the depths of the forms of the river
and the shapes of the ideas of time.
She sighs with the syllables of my name,
with the memory that keeps them there,
pushing away the white face of the moon.
The shell separates the water and ice,
charting the defiance of a lost equilibrium.
The clock on the wall strikes three.

52.
In the middle of the world,
on a stone bench, near the row
of seven houses whose doors
are perpetually closed, an old
love letter half-covered with snow
lies left behind by a tired hand,
the landmark of a dark interior
where drawn shades fall
to a broken disguise.
The dim eyes of statues
watch the snow fall, filling
the empty streets beyond the green
shutters of borrowed rooms.
The dead weights of all
the clocks in all the houses
struggle toward the black
façade of time, lights fading
in attics like a split moon.
The hand dreams of a
forgotten name inscribed
on the envelope in red ink,
the awkward intrusion of silence
through a black-draped window
indecorous with ribbons and dust.
The past is a stray draft on
a bare floor, some pages blank.
Darkness scatters to darkness.
A small door stands open, near
the tower, to the restless wild
singing of this winter's night.

53.
I don't know exactly how long it
was suspended like a pillar of salt
in the spun glass of the city, moving
back and forth with the sound a moment
makes as it breaks against a marble wall.
It touches the ground quickly then lifts up
just as fast, indecent in its suppositions
of redemption, light and dark as
a heavier stone rolled forever up a hill.
I remember when the sea began,
when the landscape opened itself
to let the waters in, how the moon lies

down under the bridge, never living long
enough to paint the faces of angels.
Somewhere in the history of the world
an aging man stumbles in the street
and understands all the things
he will never be able to do or say.
Time, as always, ebbs and flows
to a sway of memory and illusion.
He walks alone, tapping his stick
against the walls, emerging like a single
cry along the margins of the square.
Shadows perched on the statues there are
the only living presence in the widening arc.

54.
The hand knows what it wants to touch:
a world of glass, brittle and transparent,
history folded to an effigy hung
on the gray stones of an anonymous square.
The awkward wind below turns on itself,
an intruder of salt and cold that divides its
own meanings in the judgments of the moon.
In the private light of this room I hobble
on wings of wax and feathers, rise invisible
as gray smoke against the arched high ceiling,
burn like tinder in the angel's eye, virtuous
to the last. I reverse the shadows of the reticent
world, contradict the uncommon nature
of the angled street as a sky white with snow
retracts to the antithesis of its own beginning.
I know there has been a serious mistake:
this night is black as this day and this day white
as this night. Time falls to the inverse colloquy
of color, its patterns precise on the frozen floor.
It is the salient movement of the wheel.
So let me be sharp and blind as glass,
reflecting and absorbing a place where
nothing seems to end, the negative of light.
Let me float through the windows, prowl
the dark corners as the night withdraws,
nameless as the faces in the clouds.
I feel suddenly uneasy about myself, know
this room is not a hippodrome or stage,
and make a simple statement of fact:
all this nonsense about the living
and the dead, these opposites that
affirm the world, is a dream
that each dreams of the other.
I am perfectly safe from the snow
and the horses in this room tonight.
If anything exists, let it drop like a hand
against the implacable walls,
let it unchain itself and gallop through
the black streets savage and wild.

The air glistens with slivers of glass.
No news ventures about tomorrow.

55.
The year has its rituals, silent and blind,
and the undercurrents echo from every wall.
We pity ourselves with a gesture we cannot
reach, a circle where light fades and an
unfamiliar god descends, cropping the horses.
The second error flays the mist, the shaken
dust passing like a breath on winter air,
counterpoint and dominant restored.
He is suddenly gone among the gray flames,
disappearing around the corner in a private
pace as the doors close. The force of gravity
is different tonight, time no longer counts.
A hand pushes through the snow,
moving in and out, then snaps the last rein.
Everything hangs upside down on a single word.

56.
The moment that follows each moment
is a snare of no use to anyone,
the nothing that comes after each nothing.
I dreamed last night that I would dream
last night that night fell cold through the closed
window into my room and the wilderness out
beyond the river at the edge of the square made
its way back to another bend of the river outside
the closed window of my room near the square.
These images remain and grow upside
down like dead seeds sprouting on the ledge
of the pantry window waiting for the world
to turn upside down again, a mirror likeness
of itself on a horizon that cannot open, and
blossom into horses' hooves grounded in mid-air.
Tomorrow, in my dream of tomorrow
I will send a letter to myself, the end
not written, no signature composed.
I hope to be surprised to see what it comes to
in the end, whose name will close the closing line.
Or I'll contemplate the movements of stones,
the contradictions that tie nature and art together
into simpler compulsions, as I shift in my bed
contemplating the slow movements
and contradictions of stones in my bed.
The season of decay is kept from decay.
In the bright night the dark is too deep.
We can argue either side from either side.

57.
The pigeons sleep on the storm gutters
along the ragged line of the roof and nothing
assuages the odd shadows in the square.

The metal stairs turn away from the brick walls
and wind catches asterisks of cinders and lights
that twist in the windows to a certain demise.
The stirring of the birds as the air streaks
to gray ends the distractions of mortality.
The only end to be found pauses as the wind
unwinds and shuts its eyes so it will not die alone.
Fire comes out of the horizon, low in the offing,
the hour brief. Blood lingers in the utterances
of birds, and the dead will not unbend
the last white star. Footsteps in the hallway
pace and drop, a white glove crumbling
clods of dirt to the outline of an absent dress.
A solitary crow sits on a telephone wire
and a silent wheel revolves in the sky
like an answered prayer in a reticent night.
Black keys unlock the hanging box.

58.
The troubled pacing of infinity on the edge
of an insubstantial light is a half-whisper
of fire that slowly burns itself out.
Night is slow to pass, both absent and
present, known and unknown, caught
in a time that lurks outside of time.
There is no new storm coming, the small
space between midnight and dawn
in which I have lived is fixed forever
in these colors and forms, the horizon
under the eaves weightless with a flutter of
birds against the white of the universe.
Morning smolders around a long corner.
Ice breaks like a conversion of smoke.
I reach for the touch of glass and stone
as I pass by the fountain.
The white horses mount the stage,
spin illuminated at the center and the edge,
splintering the horizon like a shriveled stick.
The empty mirror of the sky opens like
a tragic stare and the darkness of the world's
undone by a gathering light.

59.
I did not find them again and could not admit
that they were lost, the lamps exhausted
in the dead weight of a moment that would not
intercept the light. The statues outside moved
across the square with a loose familiarity,
the wind bowing on the door sills, heavy-footed
and alone against the involuntary grains
of a sky arching from the dark stems of a thousand
nights and the hard paradigms of drift and snow.
The hours of early morning, when the journey
still leads them around blind corners, muffle

the stars that turn among the thinning clouds
and strum the hard walls of a hundred rooms.
Winter will begin and winter will end,
in this country and in that other, and the heart
will break to clarity in the visions of that light.
The chaos of renewal where the lost are found
runs four-footed through the streets, and the
coming day, as it scrapes the roofs, revises
its blank stare, the lamps on the corner faltering off.

60.

Life will sing its lines in the branches
of old trees and in the deep roots, scratching
breathless down the streets, and the earth
will rise to vapor and air beneath my feet.
A shallow light on a winter's day
will hone the buildings and these walls,
shape the balance of the blowing wind
and the ceremonies of white curtains.
The birds on the wires will dance
their secrets, will stir their wings toward
the dry streak of red on the horizon,
and the horses framed in the solitude
of the square will shake the tangled snow
from their backs, the prefigured possibilities
of time and space the brilliant chord
that will tune the illusions of the world.
The clock in the distance strikes six.
The black and the white release
the shadows in the hallway underfoot.
I push back the flow of the seasons, write
my name on the brightening glass,
carve the dangerous wisdoms that offend
the world on the green wall, and morning,
rising on the long screen of heaven, wanders
and strays to an eternal image in the mist.

61.

The year goes its own way,
witness to the indecisions of the sky,
and moves time out of the dark
cupboards of the world in winter.
The promise is kept in the hulls
of the sky, borne on the wings
of black crows and opening like an
unexpected dream of a woman
I do not have in a room I cannot enter.
Truth is a congregation of faces
reflected in the window leaving
as they enter, trembling hands
holding an unburied stone.
The grace of intention reaches the edge,
papers blown by wind in the streets
honing the likeness of whitening ground.

The three bronze horses in the square
turn toward the denominations of day.
The beginning of everything, fixed in the
fall of these things, lifts in its own end.

62.
It's not enough to want to come
into the light, to separate from darkness,
to reveal that aspiration, hidden deep,
to choose the absolute over the original
revelation and weather a harmless truth
that sits still and silent at an empty core.
The end of the year again like the year
before, and I catch my breath.
I fix my attention on the stitches
in the curtain, take whatever cold that comes.
I remember how I complained about
the stairs, the blown glass hanging dark
above the bannister, the idea
of the permanence of light loose
and half ready in a transient light
that wastes itself like an imagined moon
hanging in a noose of dark clouds and wind.
I like the order of that, the consequences
of the pentads and decahedrons of glass
as the universe inches to renewal,
burned by a distant source and struck
to the small fractures of lost afternoons.
The streets unravel, pluck the taut strings
that bind the edges of the dominion of air:
the narrows of a second sight that limits
the white chaos of the sky, the end unwritten.
The slow cold wind sighs.
The bones in my hand, as I lift them
to the possibility of light in the window,
under pale skin are hard and white.

63.
I weigh the results of the world on scales
of fire and ice, my eye fast on traveling water.
I make my way across the old stones of the
square, an awkward parody of myself, seek
the solace of things that angle in the dark.
A streetlamp illuminates another view,
transfixing the horses. Their vacant eyes
sleep in the mausoleum of the city's heat.
In this blank limit we are all frail creatures, wary
and ill-at-ease under the arches, tenuous in our
petitions to the brief dignities of the world.
We are drawn to our own separations,
unaware of the brilliance to come and the
dispensations of migrating birds.
On hands and knees I mark the middle
of the fall of things, the integer of lost horizons,

85

fingers digging for the hidden faults of stones.
And what is protected here now?
What did you see before darkness covered it all?
What stories did you tell in the exile of this life?
The night stirs toward another year,
the ground swelling to a bronze shape
that no repetition can prolong. The sound
of water under ice is a last resort,
long done, of the covenant and seal.
The steady drone in the windows of fading
voices is the only truth I know. Snow hones
the statues and walls, compounds
the margins as they grow opaque.
The corona of the moon drags along the streets
like a dark stalk, stars hung in effigy overhead,
and the balance in my hands splays the bare poles.
In the language of the silent mirror,
I reach the two conclusions, spin the world
to chaos for the timid and the mad.
The balance rotates on my hand as
the stones in the pavement fall and rise.

64.
The only light is a small cluster
of stars and a thin crescent
of the moon that hangs across
an old red roof thick with the
gestures and truths of night.
The strange thing rings hollow
in the annulments of this season,
the black edge of an ancient reward
tacked empty in the gray glide.
The world unrolls like a ball
of wet string through cold fingers,
the path of death in brief stars,
and the last blue light of the past unveils
itself in the loose boards of the floor.
Seven black crows tangle the ice
of the river, the mysteries of their
sidelong dance with the shadows
in the snow exhausting the void.

65.
The horse reflected on the wall lowers its head,
lifts its left front hoof as snow piles on the sill.
The limits of the world are hard and blank.
Overturned jars on the shelves in the pantry,
illuminated by candles trembling in the wake
of coarse red curtains, have been empty for years,
the periphery and center of the bones of dried
insects and birds. Old papers and used books
fill the corners of the room, the moment passing
above them a small defect of light. The man
kneeling on the linoleum tiles crosses himself,

turns his head to the shadows in the hall.
He hears the sounds of clouds falling into deep
holes, sees the woman standing alone near the high
ceiling hurrying nowhere, feels her white hand
write in chalk and fire on the cold black wall.
The signs she makes call them to the light.
They rise in a circle in the snow-dusted square,
stand without moving under an opening sky.
The horse lifts its leg and lowers its head.

66.
All who pass by lose their way
in the streets, all who climb the stairs
contemplate the burials of friends.
The cold smoke of my breath folds
across the window panes, outlining
the shapes of old words scrawled
on the glass in a language I can't recall.
Perhaps the knife did not go deep
enough, its blue sound an elaborate
confusion that swaddles the walls
and cumbers our necessities.
Free will rebukes this world, the end
clear, and the ungovernable fear hangs
its head in expectation, its flat boxes
stacked in the hallway under the stairs.
Something stares with white eyes from
the corner of my bed, something wheedles
the old woman nodding in the fire.
I sleep and wake at every hour, sidle
in the present and the past, each of my
faces whispering to each other, each
reflected in the clouding glass.

67.
The black shoals of air along the river
narrow under a green bridge gray with rust.
There is no entrance, no exit in the ice,
nothing that muffles the stir of morning.
The left bank is clear, the rocks
of the right covered in algae and snow.
The stems of the winter weeds
are marked with invisible wounds.
The abstraction of form falls to
the vacant stare of brown water.
Nothing slows, no wall holds it back.
Something shifts, a sudden breaking, slopes
the venerations of birds in dark branches.
The air is marginal in its usual grief,
unwinding to another kind of death.
The wind counts its fingers, crows leap and dive.
I'm not there, I'm here. I listen, I talk.
I see myself out to a world without end.

68.
I whistle for the silence of another morning,
dance and chant in ceremonies of ice and stone
as stars fracture like pieces of colored glass
burning back and forth in ancient ceramic.
Cold fills the curtains as I open the window.
The ledge piles up and the wind is loud,
recognitions stale in the fade of night
and defiant as a rising shout.
The watchman passes in the street below
checking the doors, the consent and failure
of the green lights of a world restored, but
never looks up, never watches me watching.
The wall on the other side of the square still
stands, indistinguishable from the snow,
a confluence of forms that rebukes the dark river.
I want to be lifted up and out the window of this
place, float like a mysterious bird on a white
horizon, forever avoiding the hard wisdom of
the grave, hurrying down before the shadow returns.
It will be the only bright thing I ever do,
the sky growing pale and blue, home once more.
Or if I step out of my body, into a separate
silence, I may become whatever it is the snow
becomes as it melts and rises, whatever it is the wind
absorbs on its naked slide across the last square.
I open the window, and myself, to find it.

69.
The writing on the wall, the signs
on the window, the marks on the floor
are still as crystal in a changing light.
After she was gone, I closed up the room,
imagining the dust on the brown rafters
falling like snow in a field of stars.
The emblems of the last post in the dead
street are a call to reason and grief.
Old men husk the seed that splits the world,
brooding in dark corners and trunks,
and think about the eternal silence of the day.
It rides along an ancient road, bumping
like a broom into every door, and rapt
like a final word carved in dark wood.
I do not want to wander any more,
will not surrender as the candelabrum
scales the rust that streaks the bridge and
dark birds fly in awkward patterns upstream
against a cold current we will not bear.
I am spirit and flesh on a hard winter's day.
I move over and under the ice.

70.
A world of white, the perfect
harvest of snow and light that

spreads across the scrawls
of love in the distance,
fears the cold progeny of ice
that mantles the outskirts of town.
Something stands on its own
in the mist, the sleep of the
landscape the exception to the
rule as trees interleave with
vapors and roofs.
It looks for something, the certainty
of time or the views of the end
that the wind blows back
to their own beginnings.
The slow perception that names
the composition of the glass
rounds the screen and leans
against the drying wind.
These small moments keep their
high resolve, the one meaning
balanced on the obstinate bridge.
It will not fall.
It will not pale in the hundred
years of snow that stray
to unanimous consent.
It will not hide in past tense.
And the moment comes,
and we cross the hour,
and we run across the blue
horizon, the sky and earth
a single billow in white curtains.
And my life opens like a seed,
dances in two like the
anonymous saint who winds
the clock in the last tower.
The great room turns on its wing.
I touch the door to the watching hall.

St. Brigid's Well

Osclaigí bhur súile
Agus ligigí isteach Bríd Bheannaithe

The starling on the fence in the rain
stares at me, clacks its beak as I pass by.
The white-veined gray rocks line
the depths and shallows of the harbor.
Blade in hand, night clambers at last
up the walls: closed eyes closed wings
across the rattle of the future.
Darkness dreams on flat leaves.
The red shaft of water shudders in the wake.
Midnight blooms in the west.
I am closed and pale, whiter than stars

whelmed at the stroke, part of the fragile
patterns and urgent movements caught
in the undertows of the town.
Sudden sounds trace the shores
of the undiscovered country.
The messenger on the wall as it rolls
to zero drops to shadows in the mud.

A strong wind sounds from the east,
every moment a drop of water
that breaks the skin.
Hands disappear along the shores
of the abandoned island.
The blood will rise this morning,
a dry jar dug up from the thin earth,
its red contours carved with the
fading letters of her name.
The quick of evening in a surface
of wild light sighs for its own green sorrows.
Memory is a hard life, an old window
facing a far harbor bleak with rain.

The smell of salt on the horizon,
colors and lines of anticipation,
the hollow sound of the broken planks
of sunset buried against the rusted gate.
The bitterness of parting and the small
houses of the dead each trace their ways
by the falling stars. Turn here.
Dream again. Keen invisible in the air.
Constellations ward their spells away,
prowl through the black barns at midnight
with red owls as the wind lifts and cold falls
hard across the infinite bridge.

The ashes in the rhythm of the bricks
in the pavement, the slow movement
of people we have loved, under the tree,
near the troubled water, the cold
that wakens again now that the flame
has at last gone out.
It's dark by Brigid's well.
Time unmasks itself and howls.
Stretch out your hands.
Prod the air. Ask nothing.
The goddess waits up ahead
skimming the confident light.

In the grass, the wild tracks of late spring.
The green surface of rainwater flares
the red soil where footsteps trip to silence,
where the suffering of the rocks breathes
and rises again. The horizon of clouded eyes
turns shoreward as trees hull in dust and salt

and the earth scatters to cinders brittle
as the wings of old gulls.
The voice falls quiet into the heart of day.
A door opens slowly in a country room
with dull windows that brood with light.
The spring wind soughs across the sea.

The round peaks of the hills,
the beginning and end of the world
where clouds hollow to flat ash,
the inexplicable disordered rhythm
of the north wind, the pliant hunger
of the grass, and a final vision
of white cities torn whole from
the cold waters of heaven below.
All this, for the first time.

When we closed our eyes the shudder
of the yellow moon changed shape, roses
along the edges of the cold field
shook to dust. A hand nailed
to the wrinkles of the sky sketched trees
on dawn and dusk, opened and clenched
as the black bend of time crawled wet
across the horizon. The day tethers itself
to the walls, lowers dark shades
on the windows. The air sinks
unexpectedly to a sad cadence,
the seed dead on the invisible road.
The black dog wanders aimlessly
down the boundaries of the landscape
then turns, contented, and shadows me home.

The bodies in the neglected graves
outside St. James' are the low voices
of dried branches coupled to failed ghosts,
the sky and sea in a lost hour of fire oval
as evening falls and the shallow day ends
with slow whistles loosening in the west.
The moon is chalked in mist,
the wind half wild with loss.

Birds knock against the afternoon,
the echo of their wings
the sprung wire of a numb lamp.
Spring tastes of salt in the white roots,
the girl is blue on the far wall.

A heart drawn in charcoal on the side
of a bleak gray house: a quiet voice
in a room with low ceilings.
Thin white petals drying in a green glass jar.
A frayed black cloth wrapped around
an old woman's head   weightless, spinning,

uncertain   unwinds through the redemption
of an ancient sky. The living are far away.
Fear, like a spear in the side, knits
the fates together, naked to the waist.
Old men sidle home at dusk, write
the stolen child's name on the walls
in their torn red coats.

Flocks of sheep dissolve to a silent gaze
in the distance. Night plumbs the low trees
where the blind man sleeps.
Nothing further as the clock strikes:
the noise of air outside the window
moving like a slow carriage, the quick eyes
of the moon mourning as it grows dark,
and columns of rain alongside chimneys
scattering in the wind to frayed nets.
I dug a hole in the wet ground, buried
the bones of the burned sky in old furrows.
Resurrection knocked across the rooftops,
seizing the clouds and air as her pale face
sprouted in the empty garden.
Wooden boxes covered in dust
at the bottom of the hill
rattled with broken wings.

The last wall of the empty stone house,
for those who left and for those shut up
in the slant of light in the broken window,
stands along the road that has no end,
along the margins of the weightless sea.
Keep hold of life. Shudder east
to the salvation of air. Show me
the ravens dancing on their graves.
Those who travel are washed anew
by a darkening rain. Here, mournful women
pluck shadows in the backyards of morning,
sing the one true name you tell.

A quick light takes shape and disappears:
the outline of the weary stems of flowers,
the solemn cries of old birds in gardens
filled with roses: the abbess, clean
and untouched, on her way to heaven,
knits the new dispensations of dawn
that unmask the wide horizon.
Strapped in the flats, the gate swings open,
the sky clears.

The last voices of daylight, the moment trembling
in the distance, eyes closed. The world has lost
its colors, nailed to the sea, and the years pass
as unexpectedly as old men in a thin rain.
Some hear the ghosts of water.

Some touch the gray orphans of love.
Some, they say, talk softly of sleep.

The fragile cloth unfolds across the horizon,
the sky empty and red, and still wings
give birth to petulant stars.
Drops of saltwater stiffen on the flagstones.
Illegible letters tighten the walls.
The signs of holy stones hobble in a paling light.
Crevices of lightning above green waters,
enigmatic reflections in the bare circles
that loon and carve dry ground, jostle
the unfamiliar harp as the time draws near.
The spirits of the world hang low in the yew
trees that line the wells. Morning arrives
like a failed river, a bird whistling nearby.

Nothing remains but the everlasting
weight of memory, bodies uprooted,
deprived of water and light.
The broken strings of famine strummed
by the voices of the dead: the cottage
that waits there while the soul sets sail,
with its dry bones, its slow walls,
its auguries of blood and dust.
An old dog gathers the lost world on its shoulders,
waits forever in this sweet morning among
the sharp stones by the brown back door.
Along the horizon, blind stars cadge the hills
and fall.

The sound of sacrifice taps the branching
walls of the folly above the hills.
The man woven from sticks chants in sheaves
of grass, in the absent solitude of willows and stars.
The uncertain mask in the gaps of parched earth
hovers on wings in the swept port of a lower world.
Paths of shadows bend in the haggard currents of sun,
fingers rough from the touch of red wicker and stone.
In the window, the hands moved, abrupt and cold,
and time fell back like one leg dancing,
its slow bones picked carefully apart.

The stars breathe along the shore at dawn,
water the deep shape of memory and black
sea foam unraveling to old nets on a broad road.
Three white horses stir trapped in the language
of the dead as light empties like an oracle
across the blue smoke of heaven.
The small moon closes, the day at last dies away,
and the desperate cry of a dense rain limps
across the roweled fields like the inching
of a broken wheel. I totter inside
the low room, under the eaves, shivering

on my hands and knees.
I grope the wind as the lights go out.

On moonlit nights, the thousand years
I've lived here flicker in the illusions cast
by a small black lamp in the corner
of the garden, the color of the blood
of all the others in the trees far away.
The soft call of pain drags itself
across the shutters, climbs up all
around me from under the worn stairs.
It winces in the yellow furrows of the past,
seeks the bitter taste of the sea again,
its shadows rising to the sudden noise
of each moment and each moment
a moment of all time.

She sat in the snug under the stairs,
whispering like a dry reed
in the shadows of the night.
The black box opens up
the sobbing of a weary breast
that cannot forget, a body once alive
among the tatters of many-colored lights:
the sightless requiem just outside the walls
where the fairies pulse and stun and preside.

Broken masts on the horizon,
hard whispers behind the walls,
and the voice of an old man
in a beehive of rolled stone
on the grazed hill:
the eyes everywhere and transparent
in the emptiness of the moon,
the past vanishing in the reluctant window,
and the radiance of sudden birds
cresting in the eddies where cold pools
shallow and swale. Tonight the stars
are widowed in the hanging shutters.
The moment is undone.
I seek the harvest of the middle ground,
the dark swarms fraying in the dry stride,
the hiss of old things in empty houses
intractable and fixed.

The slant of the sun on the rocks and waves,
the roofs crimson and black where
the high road vanishes, and an angel dropping
coins in the churchyard, whispering names
that change everything as the river swells.
The night is hollow, the world buried
in blossoms and red shells.
I am alone in the empty house,
cast my shadow across the white sea,

hover without a sound at the great back door.
A dense fog hangs over the harbor.
Waves break. I feel hands searching
for memories in my cold pockets.
Birds lifting toward the nothingness
of the sky ordain the rain and the wind.

Wild myrtle translucent as a seagull's wings.
Fragments of passing rain, clouds skimming
the deep brown edges of barely visible hills
as the day folds.
The voice of God, buried in the sand and clay,
stirs slowly on the old slopes, wakens
in roots and leaves.
Time no longer passes, narrows to a crack
in the mirrored room.
The frail shadow of the moor bird descends
backwards like a gash that will not mend
into the scattered roads of the sea.

A wildness contained, a form encased in glass,
above the dotted town.
The circular round hewn from hawthorn
where the soul spins and the oceans wash
the stack near the cliffs of Moher.
An ancient moment in a narrow cleft
that leads to Brigid's well, the world
cut in two, and on the horizon a forgotten sailor
drifts against a whittled sky,
tomorrow intermittent in the open window.
It is the hour when the secrets of the sea
point the way, spill into rested water
and earth and the blood that beats in our ears
merges with the ruins of the hills.
The old laments of the world pass away
and do not fade, pass away
and do not fade.

Bodies disappear in the sea.
Souls nod in a world of carved lines.
The surface where sails sink,
where stars wind to black silk,
binds to fire and ice.
The stones above the well flutter
to a dead calm, the wounded end
of closed water.
Let your fingers fall, riddle slowly
across the flat country.
The heart stills, galled on its back,
and the hand aches.
The world is cast down into deep places.
Trees empty the past to something heavy
and opaque and the night is cold.
As you turn away, scrub rain hones

the hard peninsula, the wind lifts
like an old white glove.

The bell tower counts out
the hours and rain passing
through the gorse bruises the day.
Whinstones kick to cool embers
against its sudden light.
The air among the weeds is thick
as cold blood and the dense forbs
and dried rosemary call the dead to rise
at the far end of the road.
The women around the fire have gone mad
in a dangerous year and even the best men
fail in the lift of the flood.
We turn our collars to the scorn of the wind,
endure as the angels with four faces dance.
The haggard wings of the world tilt to our side.
The earth moves into the sea.

I can't distinguish anything this morning,
clouds and fog plunging to the water
in the harbor: luminous wings spreading
over black rocks, gathered cold and wild
and forgiving.

The dead along the water line
and in the anchored wake weep
with a cold rain as wind
works ashes to pale masks.
Every moment of this night
reddened as the sun set, endless
and unbroken, and the axle turned
across the surface of the ground.
The plains trembled with voices.
I stood at the door staring,
the room abandoned, barely
given light, and the fierce bending
of the heavens brooded on the hill.
I prepare unsteady for the dawn,
for the chattering of goddesses
and saints that drifts
from the wellspring at Kildare.
I listen as they stagger against the walls.

So many pieces of colored glass
out past the echoes of the sea:
as if through a cracked window,
a separate silence at the threshold
of the world, time present
in every measure and seeping away
like rainwater into sweet twists of sand
on Skellig Michael.
The many-textured walls of monastic

houses along the angled road
will not fall or fade, gray shadows
shuffling just beyond the granite coils.
The somber air canters and complains.
The hawthorn shambles to blooms,
healing the broken heart.
I stand outside the iron gate, the present
and future buried in these untended graves.
A corner of the sky glares down like glass.
A black rain falls.

They were all good men, the sea battering
their boats alongside the exhausted island,
the bitter separations of their faces in the mirror
as the future came in unaware.
It slipped past like a woman, quietly
through the half-closed door, staining
the sand above the waterline lucid and red:
the long rows of old guns washed in from
the flats where hearts have broken and bled.
I hear the sounds of night jumping into the fire
on gray wings and the wild weeping of the stones
in the uplands that ports down the track.

Clumps of dry grass beyond the trees
and hidden ditches reach no conclusions.
The wind from the harbor between old
painted houses is steady and high.
I have drawn no lines against the naked roots,
have not cut a new thread of morning
with a sudden shifting of stars that mirrors
the blue ground. All is one here:
the possibility of order in a moment's events,
the long wounds of birth and death
on the exhausted sea.
The stirring of grief in the distance
when the wind pierces and burns
is quick as a lost star.

After the door shuts, the odd angles
of the roofs break with changelings
in the glimmer of an old room.
The long vigil of the moon embraces
the wet matted grass of the hills, clusters
of birds inexact in the changing light.
We have lost much of what we said here,
the burdens of the world perched among
the crows in the whitethorn trees,
night a recalcitrant dark green.
In the long swell of sea fog and dusk,
in the visions that tap insistent on the walls,
I am diminished to white dust, to red.

Along the edge of the steep dunes
wind blows through the spear thistle,
thorns loosening to pale stems
and deep purple flowers along the stone
boundaries and sands of Brandon Bay.
At the bend of the road, bleached by sun
and the watch fires of hunger and revolution,
they search the headlands, the dry hills
of the south, for the augury of birds
flailing against the heavens, rushing before
the dark creatures of the ocean catch them again.
They flutter into dead hands and flames,
pray to the black shawls of forgotten roads,
turn their backs forever to the sea.

All these shapes of bones.
The anguish of time fractured
to somber rocks, the significance
of the last full moon as it risks
the pulsations of swirling wings,
the disorder of the eternity of mud:
harmless truths in the pale scroll
of morning as it stumbles and falls.

The next day came out of the earth,
its invisible center taking on the colors
of vineyards and small leaves,
vague gray nets of God held
fast by rain, and the endless sounds
of sea waves and deepening light.
Tonight, love gleams empty in the wild range,
the moon in my hands is cold.

Sometimes I dream only of alabaster flesh,
stone with the face of an old woman
and water that rusts a closed hand:
after-images of darkness and light.
The sea below is calm today,
flat as a yellow pulse of rain along
the west slope of the Blaskets.
The starling lifts beside me from
the bluebells, startling me to joy.
I lift my hands in greeting,
spin around the horizon over
and over again, sing and whistle
out loud as the low sky pales,
my heart reaching out like a lover
to touch its flame.

The water is brown and grained as old fruit,
the meek obscenity of fading fire.
I hear each sprawled body below
in its enchanted sleep turn in ecstasy
and cry I am I am I am.

She tore the cloth from the small columns
of the old house bent in the rocks,
spirals of straw drifting unexpectedly
from thatched roofs.
She tamed the wind and hidden water
where the land came to an abrupt end,
luminescent with possibility and form.
There was music in the afternoon:
uilleann pipes rising in a parting of the fog.

Morning comes differently by the ocean,
pushing aside dunes and shrouded waves
to a pattern of silver lights, ceremonies
of glass and invisible moorings
innocent with the songs of women and wild birds.

The shape and loss of form
as the petrels lope along the clouds
and shearwaters puff and bathe.
The ancient tribes flick through the thickets,
safe in this green space among the yews,
and the world is once again contained.
I hear voices whispering under
the closed door, loose boards echoing
the transfigurations of the walls.
I sit for hours, ridding the sky of light.
A sketch of blue paces in the strange room,
strains in the darkness beside the cold stove.
I don't know if we live again, take new form,
or leave only vague traces tangling
in the passages beyond the shoals.
All might yet be well,
trapped in this last conviction.
Up on the cliffs, the wind is rising.
The high dawn flees like a star,
antiphonal and white.

The horseman passed by, saw what he wished to see:
if he looked long enough, staring west, out past
the round tower, the march would at last begin again,
the sorrows of a forgotten dream, lost by a man alone
at sunset in a field trying to see the night,
would trace the wheel marks of an uncertain journey.
Love builds its nest on a narrow ledge.
The ghosts of small trees drain endlessly to green.
In the confusion of the dark, where the dead rise up
on that other shore, in that undiscovered country,
he can hear the armed man speak.

We walk in a transient light, freedom ours.
This moment will pass to memory and myth
and our bodies will float beyond
the resignations of time and death.
We will be shaken to dust, the world

as callow as the new moon climbing
the window sills. The currents and tides
will yaw to a low moan, scarred as a scorned
voice at dusk. But here, everything dies,
everything mourns, everything grays
in the indifference of these changes.
Time does not heal, just layers the world over,
the years a threshold of unsteady glass.
Look: night rolls down the blind river
and lost souls sail into an empty glare.

The whole town is made of hewn stone,
rusted as evening and gathered under
the secrets of cold wings.
Today, well past the middle of my life,
I walked along the side roads
touching the walls, naming each stone,
wanting to leave the brush of my shadow
behind in the irregular crevices and creases
of these houses, to outlive death
in the perfect dance of this brief season.
I stand between the houses breathing
their familiar air. Down below,
I can see the fingers of the world touch
the undone thing, the difficult edges
of the imperfect sea.

The past is startled by the quick turns
of country roads, the colors of vacant
town squares. The mist on this island
comes in like the ghost of something
greatly made, the windows of the church
the shining coffin of a beautiful girl
who died too young. The bell drifts off.
Afternoon sleeps in the incandescence
of the sky. The hands of the woman
out hanging clothes tremble
in the doorway with cold.

The pitch of the rag tree across from the eternal field
is indifferent to the solitary bird hung like a piece
of old cloth on a branch with a thin black wire.
The silence of dry grass ripples down the rows
of ordered fences, darkness lumbering toward
the barn, one lit lamp in its hand. On the pile
of strange rocks, a blue rag flutters toward the hole
in the ground, marred in a helpless sprawl.
The hour passes, lost in the shape of light.

Rain begins as morning rises,
circles and passes on the clear
surface of the bay.
It's summer now.
The holy fire, narrow and formless,

moves among the spider webs
and weeds up across the headlands.
Tiny azure flowers, moulting feathers,
three of us dreaming of small winds
as lights in distant houses go out.
As they gather their nets
from the prophecies of darkening water,
fishermen pray for a way home,
for the taste of dust to settle again
in their cold mouths.

The shop windows obscured
by night mark a desolate hour.
I think of her this early morning,
hear her keening, buried under
the solemn stones of the red earth,
pure as the holy tree in the virgin's
garden in Kildare.
Fire is coming into my veins.
Storm the air. Unlock the gate.
The harrow dances in the holy flowers.
Her face lifts like the rising sun
in the brittle graveyard of the window.

Where does the world
separate darkness from light?
Where does the brook ridge
unilateral as changing air
and the earth unlock,
brown-necked ravens grating
against the uncertain
boundaries of time and space?
Centuries of rain fix
the day on the long wall,
night walks heavy and old
on hallowed ground.
Breaths mingle in a private dark.
The immaculate morning
roots itself out of its
nervous grave and yearns
itself toward the sea.
That is the first mystery of faith.

The old man taps his stick on the cobblestones.
The moon suddenly stands up to a cold bloom.
The top of the roof dies on the wing
as the ghost comes home.
The stars are brilliant in a blue wind,
the uncertain night undivided and whole.
The world ends but cannot end.
Anything can happen. Everything does.
The stick taps out its time on the worn cobblestones.
The branches and roots of the sky swarm after me
and the oceans run ahead untangled and blind.

The hand of God touched the wide roofs
of An Diseart, the long box empty.
The unbraced corners of the sky
lean against the walls, the long afternoon
light scattering to thistle and mud.
The air sounds with a distant horn
scrubbing the fog.
I asked
who prayed for me,
who pitied the dead,
who poured the cold waters
out when the days were done?
Far below, the stars pushed and swept
against the circles of the tide,
forgetting that a god exists, and my easy
grievance was added to the rest.

The consistency of birds in the higher branches
twists to a weaving of black threads
that drift along the dimming hills.
Rain hovers evergreen above the back
and forth of water and the sun breaks,
mixing with time and air.
To be sustained and free in this place
is to conjure a world of unbroken
circles and denser meanings, the open strand
perfectly designed, perfectly contained.
Five miles out past Dunquin, the last parish
folds to the west. The earth rises from
a hard shore and the vastness
of the sky is more tangible than the sea.
I stand, arms extended in every direction,
in a pillar of light, triumphant and immortal.
I know at last the brightness of all my days.

The first words took shape inscribed
on tree and stone, the naming of the dead,
coiled deep into sky and earth, cries from
the ancient narrows and the sudden
unfoldings of truth in the voiceless sea:
the interlaces and plaits that struck us
with the radiance of an eternal light.
We are not yet there. Sing me home.
I am the word, the dust in heaven's eye,
my skin carved in hieroglyphs and runes.
Divinations of light huddle against
the summoned ghosts and wind inherits
time's hollow stump.
A sweet breeze blows on blue wings,
the sun clouds over.
I stand ready in the tide.

I am overwhelmed by birds:
cormorants, egrets, guillemots,

grebes and gannets,
gulls and terns and auks,
skylarks, swallows, blackcaps,
shearwaters, petrels,
pipits, dunnocks and chats,
and the hooded crows
that follow me everywhere,
everywhere, follow me
with their song and their whirl,
shaping their own full spheres.
Here, by the harbor wall,
their world perches on my head.

The reflection of the sun on the ample
passing clouds comes in angles and planes
along the rooted wall and through the kitchen window.
The past is peeled away and the present moment
shelters and flows. I know I can live
forever in this quick coming of light,
in the echo of the world in these words and art.
The sun traces truth on the changing air,
musters the essence of love and night.
Ephemeral and eternal, it awaits the dry
blessing of salvation along the edge
of the distant ridge, grays to nothing
here in the thousand shadows of my hands.

I pressed her down
among the bluebells
and sang to myself
as her eyes opened
and closed and her hair
brushed lightly
against my face.
The blossoms fell
fresh and alone,
sunlight glancing off
her arms and thighs
in the meadow
near the sea,
and I knew then
that God and I
are both still alive,
still magical and rapt,
in the flowers and reveries
of this secret place.

I heard my name called by the trees,
saw my face in the meadows and flowers,
felt my hands wrapped in spider webs and down.
Wings open at the other edge of the sea,
tip to flight above gorse fields and marshes.
I want to be lifted up where evening falls,
move high above the dancing waters,

sing like the pipes across the crowns of birds
letting go letting go letting go
of the constant sorrows of this place.

The sun cut early across farmhouses
and stonewalls half up the blue mountain.
White butterflies, faultless on the horizon,
transformed to rose petals and seeds of wild
dill in the cold of early morning and the dogs
in the barnyards scuttled and coughed.
A strange world lingers here, stubborn as the sea
recedes and the wind blows its own unrest
then the lift of pure sound as the soul ascends,
dark green and gold, and skimmers for hope
in the grasses and ferns.
The turf embers cool in the open hearth
in the corner of the front room and the blue vase
on the wooden table breaks with white flowers.

Whatever I wept for with the loneliness of a child,
whatever I longed for with the cold stare of grief,
whatever I forgot with the intricate shadows of love,
are here today, silent as the feathers that float
in the wind just outside the corner of the back door.
And the lights are going out at the inn, alongside
the hanging branches of the last white oak.
At dawn it will wake to new leaves,
will pity my mistakes, will thank me again
for the gift of the things I longed for and forgot.

The seasons turn and endure,
calm once more.
The heart endures as it turns,
the moment over.
The deep tides at Dunmore Head
crest against the cliffs,
the scars of centuries of seawater hard
as the men whose voices echo
on every hill.
One world at a time,
I hear her thinking,
one world at a time.
And far away, in the well
where she sleeps,
where time haunts and rests,
where love radiates
in ancient patterns and knots
that agitate the world
to fertility and spring,
she breaks the barrier between two.

The margins of the meadows and sands
are diminished by the changing light.
The balance of the day shifts to its close

and time is arbitrary in the bodiless disorder
of becoming and being.
All around me are the opening patterns
of the flights and calls of birds, incantations
that rouse the wind and sea, the divinations
of spoons and waters where the future rests.
On these cliffs, the sun sets to a darker blue,
a sanctuary for the struck and blind.
Their visions heal the hidden women
as they rise from the liberating ground,
dancing white in the ashes of the holy fire.
I ascend and descend, reach through the light
for an easier seeking, prepare myself
for eternity, for rain.

Red Stones

I
The wind stirs under the back stairs,
drifts across a transparent dark
where nothing begins, nothing ends.
The day gives form to scattered dust.
The present is an open door
in the hours of a broken room.
Muted voices hover above
the revelations of old walls.
Stars lift on a bent horizon.
Gaunt birds above the tiled clay roof,
wings angled in a feathered cross,
sharpen the hardened edge of time.

II
The mind is a still distraction.
The white blankets burn in pitch black
and night salts the blood of heaven.
The men at war at the turned gates
of the torn city plant their heels
among the spider webs and dirt,
not terrified of loss or death
or the hinge of mud washed across
the hesitation in their eyes.
Think of nothing. Let the body
become a pale reflection of
ancient wings in the wind's cold glass.

III
The short breath of night runs shallow
and slow across the city's streets
and rain slides, thin as hunger, on
gray diagonals of iron.
Angels made of straw, luminous
as wind in bags of vague paper,

turn their backs to the old red house.
I touch the star above the black
canal, bewildered and endless,
and the world quickens at my feet.
Beyond the square, the lost dogs bark
the secret names of fire and ice.

IV
Darkness sets cold against the wall.
I open the shuttered windows,
lights crowded in the graying panes,
and the brilliance of the year
comes to its full circle, recurs
in the instant that penetrates
the heart as the day moves to its
radiant decline. The air lifts
and the stars drift down as night falls
absolved by the brittle eclipse
of white shadows on black water
and the passing of time to clay.

V
The stars in the sky have been dead
for a thousand years, their slow shades
absorbing the last night until
the present moment, consonant
and urgent, is at last reversed
and our lives are renewed again
in the invisible season.
Every hour has its true color,
every minute its note and breath
our last necessities whispered
on our search for eternity's
blue dream paling in a flat land.

VI
Lone Woman of San Nicolas,
the ashen feathers of your dress,
torn loose from their strings of sinew,
float down across the southern coast
of ancient California.
Flowers in a distant meadow
the artifice of truth and light.
The flat roads of autumn count out
the tallies of a world in gray
that spins across the universe
as birds of Santa Barbara
drift low above your unmarked grave.

VII
There are nights when the moon rises
and the air is comfortable
and slow, and the late stars thicken
high above the far horizon,

and the ache of moving water
circles to things thin as smoke and
tipped with flame across the heavens.
These echoes of the infinite
held in the voices of others,
the language of gods and children.
You gaze far out, and when you wake
and lift your head, the world is you.

VIII
The day is a discarded stick
in the ruins of the garden,
the outline of a worn silence,
wordless and alone, that traces
the edges of the first real night,
ambitious and blind as dried weeds,
to the shape of an ash gray bird
in the branches of an old tree.
Conscience wakes despair: the three notes
they heard were a call to death of
the universe of old knowledge,
the world's history pulsed away.

IX
Snow falls cold and thick in the fields
of asphodel, pale meadows near
the margins of a pallid sea.
Waves break on the dying embers
of afternoon, the blank corners
of the sky waking at twilight
to spare colors and the hollow
pausings of ice among the stones:
an inexorable world where
the lamentations of gray ghosts
gutter above the empty plains
and narrow orbits of our lives.

X
Bent gray figures in the thin grass
scythe the earth near the fragile edge
of land along the water where
dry spaces turn to root and air.
The day flows down the deep river,
the sky whole and undivided,
the world brittle as withered leaves
in a thick stand of white birches.
There is a source of constant light.
I watch them take wing like shadows
on a crest of easy failure,
turn and sing testaments to night.

XI
Evening falls to the cool silence
of silver willows and slow fish,

the cries of fishermen and gulls
that float across the water to
outlines of possibility
and the narrow order of grace
glowing like new fire in the sky.
Small bells ring above the old boats
as light slowly washes away.
The image returns to itself:
the white moon pausing in the wind
as weary as the dead must be.

XII

This is marshland and undercreek,
the place of sleep where birds breathe their
first and last, where darkness and heat
along the edges of water
settle in the long yellow grass
and in the cold curved light of dreams,
where twilight deepens downriver
and autumn crests, pleating to bone.
We watch infinity open
and close the veiled wind in the trees,
and the three day rain crowds away
past this and that other country.

XIII

Winter came as the chestnuts fell
and stars arched up from the bottom
of the world, winking at the cold.
The last bird across the river
made a small sound in the dark, like
a far wind crying in vigil
or woe out past the dry roadside
dotted with hawkweed gone to seed,
deepened beyond recognition.
Deliver me from this fragile
interruption, let my body
rise once more to silence and light.

XIV

Morning was unconcerned as fog.
The long walk in transparent rain,
the climb through violet shadows
shaped like birds above blunt water
far off in a gasping of air.
The momentum of naked grass,
the old lie of earth above earth
and stones that shift in endless chains
to the inarticulate sound
of heaven past the triple wall,
the broken branch that grows again
death's tangent on the horizon.

XV

It was the place where time ended,
the pale drawn shade of history,
as gathered as a sudden dream,
no longer present or past but
open and splendid with quick knives.
The year ends with patches of red
on the water and hands that reach
far beyond the isolation
of the world, fleeting bone that bends
to air and whispers to itself
in the eternal moment that
cusps the last rising of the moon.

XVI

We moved at last toward the flat banks,
our voices thick with mud and haze.
I heard the young woman singing
across the transparent water,
smoke in the distance on the lake,
and the whisperings of others
as the moon rose in filaments
and bars of light that swarmed the clouds.
She made a sound I had never
heard before: a free soul rising
through the white season on the edge
of God's long journey filled with stars.

XVII

The buried day unhinged itself,
flowering into an eye closed
at the center of a circle.
Afterwards, on a strip of land
that dulled against the horizon,
I came whispering with lost leaves
on the white water, came rising
into the sweet air, came gliding
out of the deep bones of the wind
unafraid, both spirit and flesh,
touching the glory overhead.
And I am here, am everywhere.

XVIII

The present fades away slowly,
the last geese crossing the edges
of the lake as the light cries out
in its own slow death and the grass
turns white and bends its own last way.
I touch the shadow of water,
live quiet as a widowed god
or marked bird in a far corner
of a universe of branches
and roots, delight in the silence
of a denser shade. My day slides
with permanence and ease to night.

XIX

I have learned at last what love is
black alders near ice gray water,
the abrupt single truth of air
curling the window, the blind heart
lying in wait for words and years,
the last drop of time unable
to tolerate the emptiness,
the spirit lost in lines of pain,
the bitter vacuum of low land
where a pale girl gathers flowers
with cold hands that ache forever
and I temper myself to steel.

XX

This thing can come to life again.
I watched slowly as shadows dipped
like a summoned vision cut loose
from the dying fire of heaven
and radiant lines of stars traced
the cold melancholy of time.
Old birds whistled among the reeds
and angled undertones of light,
their bodies transfigured to pale
winds by a moon they no longer
remember in that other place,
in that other darker season.

XXI

We must be diligent today.
Waiting until tomorrow comes
will be too late, the arising
of form and the ending of form,
and the moment of our dying
will be unknown, every minute
grasped, the oblivion and change
to emptiness from the senses
of the body penetrated,
realized in the here and now.
Up ahead, the raft abandoned
long after we have crossed the flood.

XXII

We are ghosts when we see what ghosts
see, when we do what ghosts do, when
we hear what only ghosts can hear.
A supple body remembered,
the metal echo of flowers
of mourning near the passing sea
where the silhouettes of birds lift
along both center and edge, hard
as the wind that cries in the dead
salt of water and stone. I hear

the glass break red in the morning,
see the mirror mindless with night.

XXIII

I measure the passage of time
outside the smallest window with
a stick that scratches the outline
of the sickle moon on the dust
of the floor, watch a thousand years
lying gray and naked under
the wounds of the cold horizon,
count out the abrasions of rain
on the old woman's umbrella
and understand how to endure
my longing for eternity
and the impermanence of birds.

XXIV

Green water flows in place of blood.
Eyes of inconsolable birds
in the duckweed and dry sedges
burn with the vermillion heat
of Hesperidian apples.
The white erosion of being
gnaws the bones of heavy flowers
and the absent shadow takes hard
form at the far point of the world.
I sleep in an undiscovered
place, trapped in a pocket of air.
The season drifts, the moon slides west.

XXV

The bridges and streets are patterns
of light fragile as glass, the sky
silent with the disillusions
of the world that seep like water
into the dry sand of the years.
He had studied his life, had seen
the eye of Providence hiding
among yellow blossoms in clouds
and dust, had heard the porcelain
footsteps of angels walking through
bolted doors, had been bird and stone,
and when he turned it was the hour.

XXVI

I have learned to sit silent and alone
as the rain falls and evening lays flat
and coarse against my skin, unbundled
to the mystery of the world. An erratic
wind in the distance abides in small far
corners, in the last dry hold of the sun.
Vulnerable things pared thin by the moon.
The shadows of the sky slant
across the earth, tracing the outlines

of the only truths they know,
and the line cuts deep in the glass:
I see myself there, suddenly transparent.

XXVII
When the dead thrash in the pale east
of morning as clouds strike their end,
after the door shuts and the sky
sinks green in the changing street,
after time tilts away, scraping
the bottom of each consequence,
after the recognition of the wholeness
that blinds the radiant source,
there is a sudden perfect memory
of the contradicting image,
whispers in the shadows, cold and bare,
the lost and unimaginable light.

XXVIII
She held the dry grass in her hand,
the clarity of a long threshold
across the clusters of rain:
she put the last star to her lips,
defiant in her narrow orbit
and coveting that other world:
she pushed away the circle's shaken dust,
the synthesis of fragile patterns
that peels away the ragged form.
This is the hollow of a lost blue,
the abstraction of the moment
where the sky ends, disintegration.

XXIX
The yellow essence of summer
at the end of the street,
ancient voices in the unlit windows,
the talking in sleep as the lights
rise in the square monotony of the sky.
How does a man die?
Quick as a broken net early in the
morning or like salt drying slowly on
red rocks washed by a late white rain?
It isn't much. It is his death.
We will grieve with the waters and sparrows.
The wings of strange birds will break with cold.

XXX
When the music stops, when the wide-winged
shadows pass by, when breaths mingle
in the patience of the red rose and the dance
is motionless at last, when all the edges and hollows
are caught in the moment of change and cold air
fails empty and calm, let your hand take root in
a world in which you play no part, in the wandering
scrawl that remains when the sky is closed.

Rise up like a shout in an empty house.
Stand naked in front of the mirror.
You are revealed in every element and truth,
your face is drawn and marked on every wall.

XXXI

The least motion, the vulnerable descent
at the beginning of winter
and the pale stones behind the barn
wet and bare under a half moon.
The sky smells of rain and dust
and the white oaks outside my window
hold on as the landscapes shift.
Alone that evening, the train gone,
I remembered your fragile hollows,
the stark shadows on the wall when you left,
the sudden light on the other side of the door,
the brittle scent of the air as I fell.

XXXII

I reach no conclusions
in the foreign light, the day's boundaries
abstract and shattering to origins
and eddies in the rigid angles of night.
Rain echoes slowly in a high wind.
The simple attestations of a distant solution
the broken heart begging to be healed
spiraling out from the lost corners of October
until nothing remains, only the drift
of voices bent in the clear sweetness of air,
and a woman's body, deep as the earth,
shaken free at the edge of the sea.

XXXIII

It was an artificial light
reflected on a curtained wall.
The continuum of stones muffled
against the white self ledged
in the requirements of the moment.
The sum of those events released
like scraps of old paper in the street,
the rain beginning changeless and particular
in the distance across the bridge,
and a quickened vision of isolation or love.
The clear line of the roof descends
on the other side of the setting sun.

XXXIV

The well-lit room with two yellow vases
echoes with the sound of something
unexpected mounting the stairs.
Outside, in the hallway, love goes dry.
The street is full of old stars
and the ashes that outlined your face.
The night is endless and the mute sky shudders.

The day will be heavy after rain.
Time is swept away, vanishes among the dead stones.
The moon falls on the windows, works across
surfaces and lines I no longer remember.
Behind me, something whispers lost fire.

XXXV

I woke late in the empty house,
the bare bones of the sky washed
to metal and stone overhead,
and watched dim shapes move across
the clouds as rain thickened to snow
and ice, swinging into unguent light.
The radiance of the day is without intention.
I am overcome with amazement
and fear falls away unclaimed.
Let the others down below run. I'll stay.
It keeps alive in darkness, in dust and air.
The pattern at last intends its own course.

XXXVI

The responsibility of love realized
whispers something beautiful and old,
the perfect edge of a hand as it moves
across your face, constant and white,
and folds away as your body shifts,
a summer bird above the wilting flowers:
the sudden lines around your mouth,
the weightless stones gathered in mourning,
the thin light along the cold back stairs
and the shadow moving down the page:
the stub and halt of every horizon
as it quenches the changes of the moon.

XXVII

It was when the last bird flew by the window
wounded in the leg, its feathers a curse to be lifted
by a still wind and the sun's red crest as it slides
backwards to its fine collapse, that he stood an exile
in the streets, shadows anointing the cobblestones
to the deep gray glow where the dead preside.
It was a drifting across an inaccessible ledge
to a place of familiar wonders wide as a span of wings
and short as the pain of hands that draw away
to the cold fissures of dirt and distant truths.
The god of flowers sustains undone dances
and obscure visions, and the parted waters burn.

XXXVIII

The stolen hours carried him beyond the lands
he surveyed, following the arches of the moon
hanging in the sky like a guarded mirror
that reflects horizons far and wide,
the high bridge of salvation that whispers his name
as the rains pass somewhere in the east

and float up across the garden's trance,
the nearest exit a periphery of space and light.
All this was out of reach: the hawk of redemption
freeing us one by one from the darkness of the world,
bent westward by the spears of miracle and sin.
The trees around us shift their inconsolate roots.

XXXIX

Fish and flocks, the unsummoned image,
matter and form, the earth-brown core
of unbordered lands dreamed like the broken
ghosts of absolution as the branches spread.
The stitch no world can offer, the dream that holds
the last lease on time, the moment that swells
and dies, unwinding a spirit that will never fall.
And when he turned, the sea drew back into the river's
cold waters that cannot be crossed and whose sands never rest.
The two halves of the horseman of God broke the tunneled heart.
The stolen hour widened as infinity staggered the earth.
And the darkness, the darkness stayed alive.

XL

The certain solitudes of the blood moon
drift through obstinate glass, lift the errors
of the blind man's eye. Everything changes
in spite of the light, the black marl of air
waiting to be moved across the bottom rung,
the blind interiors shuttered like blades in the dirt,
fading from dream to dream to attics and vague smoke.
At a time like this nothing suffices.
The horizon falls indifferently on the veranda.
Tomorrow is a warp of earth and myth.
The rapid pulse of orphaned hands
drums a miraculous escape, sibilant and black.

XLI

We stepped across the broken glass
on the icy rocks and the tide stirred
skeletal and thin in the tethers of a colder day.
The weightless stone displaced the air
and time scatters, a thing of hunger,
to an innocent flutter of sand and dry seed
somewhere in the nameless folding of snow.
I make myself small in the dark grace ahead.
The waters recede and the lights
in the distance finally flicker out.
The white hills whisper: late winter.
The marrow cries: dead sea.

XLII

The indifferent night writes an old history
in the corner of the room and dark clothes dry
in the moonlight like a memory of absent flowers.
She floats across the bare floor, arms open
to her own reflection in the window.

The city is frozen. The streetlights fail.
Something fills the passageways and makes
no sound as the season ends, descends
and circles the constellations overhead.
You will never sleep, wrapped in red blankets,
will stammer on all fours with unwelcome ghosts.
Outside, eyes closed, the future taps its stick.

XLIII

Snow falls on old statues in the square,
the rumor of other storms drifting
across the empty spaces of the sky.
You stand in the doorway, a cold inclination,
lost in your own reasons and whirls.
The moon splits above the rooftops.
The curtains in the window fade.
A dry light from the attic falls in the street,
waits to be moved through the shadows
when the last doors close. The pale statues
watch their dreams end, the moment over
as darkness breaks, a sudden quiet in the air.

XLIV

We each close a door to a small room
and the windows slide blindly into dusk.
We are each gone a little more each night,
backs pressed against cold walls,
bones folding upward across the ceilings
and drifting downward to asterisks of light.
There is no true measure, nothing past
the circles of hanging bulbs on bare floors,
the ending banked to a graceless touch.
The narrow orbit of the earth rounds
to a deep dead calm, the sharp profile
of the moon a small mercy that turns and slips.

XLV

Day at last turns into night
and the small brink of the world
shifts directionless and grave
to a damask of lost voices,
a mosaic of fragments and shards
that folds across the immaculate hills,
a play of dense and faint light
weeping like the last embrace of death.
I go backwards in time, wind through
glass and air, return to where I rise and fall.
I lean forward in a world of slow dreams.
In the distance, a black dog howls.

XLVI

Those old things that filled the room
move unexpectedly to a sudden indifference.
Memory keeps them the way they were,
half-hidden in a bodiless light,

as moments come and go without intention.
This is what it means when mirrors burn
like harsh wounds and the windows fill with ash,
when the deep crimson of time falls away
and I hear the cold smolder of broken shadows
faint across the corners of the crescent moon.
I listen hard for a long time.
The walls begin to whisper in the night.

XLVII
Endless clouds of smoke fill the horizon.
Night glows: embers of wood and charred bones.
Sleep: we press against each other and tremble,
morning somewhere far off around the corner.
I long for the one who is not here, I do not have.
I hold her wandering soul in my hand.
It moves like an old dream that hastens
to its quick delay, dark and secret in the dust.
The shadow in the hallway gathers like a gesture
in the small folds of the stairs.
The dreadful joy of the window blanches the floor.
The wall stands still in its own pale light.

XLVIII
A heavy vine of wings covers the stones
scattered in the far left corner of the garden,
twilight gathering and the roads thinning
along the edges of the cleared fields,
a thousand knives cutting through the lost voices
of all the dead who lie in wait there forever.
Time blackens to the core of a great wheel
that turns without stop in the blood red water
and white words reconcile with the blind
lashings of the flat wide stars. Alongside,
a hesitant step. This place alone is my own,
my only measure however brief this light.

XLIX
An abandoned child sleeps alone
in a nest of grass and wire.
I lift her, light as a bird, and coat
her in layers of wax and dust.
She floats between two suns, her hands
seeking what she already knows,
a single continuum, hollow as bone,
lost in its own long slide.
I dreamed of a bridge in a silent world,
saw the sad light of her eyes and low voice
floating like the present and the future
linked far below on the lucid water.

L
The weather changes, separating shadow and light.
Beyond the fence of vines and wild myrtle,
the hesitations of the coddled edge,

the interventions of a universe of lines,
the dead cedars of abstraction and grief.
He was not the last one home again,
birds whistling down the river, the blue haze
widening to deeper sounds, lifted up like the moon
in blind hands pressed against old windows:
I set fire to the deep roots, watched the long grasses
vanish on the hill, coaxed the stars at last awake
the eastern sky full of the dark, of me.

LI

The curve around the bend in the road
speaks in a flat voice, staggers to its feet
on a slant of wind in a sleepless dawn.
When I stand upright as the rains fall
like dropped coins begged in the street
across from the closed doors of old houses,
my bones turn to feathers and wild leaves,
the sympathetic colors of some more distant
source of light taking root in the grim speed
of roses blue as slate as they open and burn.
In three days they will rise again to time and light.
I will stay the quick dust I was made to be.

LII

At the other edge of the field, toward the end of May,
just before the sun rises and the season fully changes,
an unexpected fog roots itself among the poplars,
dangling loose across the empty places in the grass,
caught and held for hours, and then drifting
to the still light that holds the world together.
It is a perfection of motion, a moving brilliance,
a secret beyond the silent corners of the sky,
the old contours of my life forgotten somewhere.
It would not move through the cold bones of my hand,
would not whisper to ghosts when the moon went black.
Forgive me. I dreamed your death, the paling of red stones.

LIII

The rage of summer fires in the distance,
the sky layered with patterns of smoke that paw
the dry shadows overhead, the pointed stick of time
scratching its thin lines across the horizon,
and a woman who cannot speak walking beside me.
The palm of her hand tasted like the sea,
water that rises on the wind from a hard lake.
Pale images in her pale hair darkened as a white streak
of soundless birds creased through the brush,
stirred ashes rising into an afternoon of ripples and weeds.
The day, one wing broken, coils round itself into night.
Look: your name glows white in the burned grass ahead.

LIV

Winter is hanging on, a cold fire.
I rise up out of the snow, following

my own shadow, and burrow sunlight
all evening in my arms, looking for
something simple and familiar under
the roots of the dead sycamore.
Everything is silent here, drifting
face down in the clouds, the light pitiless
and close to the quick of evening.
I hear the owl settling into the furrows
of the dark barn, the spider climbing
along the numb spine of the far wall.

LV
Evening offers no relief. The incandescence
of late afternoon continues to smooth the blood
and the black birds in the tangle of trees
across the way dream of the last white shadows.
The woman who was weeping, who loved me
all this time, belongs to someone else.
When I close my eyes, I see her walking up
the long back stairs, waiting to be touched,
see the hand that floats away on the blind air,
the breath that thrives on longing, the door
that shuts forever under the unpredictable moon.
White shadows huddle together, dreaming of birds.

LVI
The broken boxes the moon fell into last night
were kicked down the center of the street
by the wings of horned owls hunting for the promise
of obscured things, the slow fade of lost words
fumbling in a cauldron of cold air,
the tiny bones spinning secrets in the white ground.
The doors close when an unborn child dies.
Stone walls shift their lenses down through
the bewildered formalities of time and winter.
The sky shatters the isolated bridge.
The rattle of old leaves lifts the world to tears.
The radiance of vacant boundaries says nothing.

LVII
The rituals of time mock the rigid stars.
In the opaque mist, dun-colored birds bind the sky
for hours, sift through the halves of light
shifting in the banded water, the synthesis
of loosened day and endless night.
In the distance, yellow light falls from a window,
lenient and old, and the half-buried moans of dry wind
across the roofline are brittle as burned grass.
My broken soul leans back against its hour,
startling itself in the absence of sound and air.
I am at the center, released from form.
The pall of infinity tilts. Desire broods.

LVIII
The private certainties of time, when the tide

flocks against cold stones and night lengthens,
rootless and ridged, against the hollows
of a safer ground, are caught by chance in circles
of black water and grow opaque as bone,
mute smoke and dust dancing in dead air,
the abrupt landscape insolvent in its ebb and flow.
It will be like this when I die: breaking loose
on a high wind from the vacancies of this place.
Now, the small town past the bridge outwits the day.
Far below, small folds and footprints in empty sand.
The final grace of a brief and running light.

LIX

The last white leaf on the birch tree as the storm passes
recovers in the muted shadows of a secret light.
The wind off the water quickens to a drift of gray,
the sound of darkness moving slow and alone
through the creviced roots, and the long
low waves gather the river to its banks.
At the high window, watching the air scrub
the moving stones along the far lines of the yard,
I thought I saw your face in the glass,
your hands falling empty as the angel wheeled past.
One feather of one wing plumbed the night:
I am afraid of the dark, of the earth as it spins.

LX

The river gathered itself quickly near the fallen trees
and the black ridge narrowed to roots and deaf stones
at the field's closed edge, its somber hands opening
the flat hard landscape where bodies rise from the dead.
The stars have gone to brown water, sad and beautiful,
and a lost skirt lies on the ground near the low ring
of dry weeds by the last still bend in the road.
The day grows old. God's gray hand touches my face.
Through the walls, the last lament, huddled like a mute bell,
echoes in a fold of sad feathers and bones.
Wait for me. I'll come home when the shadows slip below.
We will rise together, soar back into summer light.

The Kingfisher's Reign

Creating the World

I heard something fall in the early hours today
as the wind blew on its journey in the first day
of this season, whistling through the thin branches
that huddle hard against the last trespass of winter.
It was an unexpected sound, the abrupt rattle
of ghosts in the attic kicked to the habits of earth.
The minute would not focus, the aging colors
of whatever drops by the wayside would not heal,
the abandoned measure of a heart that knows
the sky is suddenly too close sidles and bleeds.

Nothing stays. Nothing in its characteristic light.
Nothing in this moment of dispersion.
The dust in the window slowly learns its still craft,
the night points elsewhere, and I hear myself,
wherever I turn, hands over my eyes, falling
in a hail of wax and feathers, far from the sea,
a ball of glory, the blood pounding, all fire and joy,
against the walls and roof of the house. I saw eternity
in the sky's blue light, forgot the old artificer's warning,
sang to myself, helpless and free, until the strings
of the universe stretched and broke.

City Evening

I wrote in response to the gods of the meadows
and trees, drifted across the yellow moon
like the clinging smoke of heaven.
It had all meant something, I know that, poignant
as a glass that breaks when cast against a wall,
reputations made and lost in the sensible marvels
of yellows and browns pricked by a harvest of red.
The hours recede, faceless and hard, and I walk
backwards toward spring as the day holds a
long thin razor against my cheek.
My hands fold the gaps of this sensation.
The blood between my fingers groans
in a burden of fulfillment.
My lover calls out again and flees. See?
The side streets stumble, white-faced and illegible,
and the graves that light the edges of the world
sing I am I am I am.

Icarus in Maine

I keep good company with myself, drink the rain
as the moon climbs across the hard wires
and circuits of New England. The day was like
unopened mail, the truth of this small house
imperfect, the red coal of being alive tossed
with the hollow breath of forgetting and free
as the trail of ashes in the splendid void
I climbed the clouds, found the sun, whispered
across the intricate shadows of the hopeless cause.
I was the evening star, the song half-sung,
the slow fire of stray things left behind as she sighed
and quivered like a lost swarm of birds at dawn.
It was that way each morning, the card and cramp
of markings on the page as daylight uncovered both
our shoulders. The wind lifted, the shallows repeated.
My falling was somewhere else then,
a long time ago, a long time to come.

Dragonfly

I'm still not sure where I should live my two lives.
One, I know, beats like a quickened pulse
outside the window I open each day as the sun dulls

to the color of the old stoplight on the far corner of the road.
The other, whose name I cannot hear, enters the house
and floats freely through the walls, trails after me
like a white flag above the chalk-white towers of the cities
of the plain, the waddling companion of ghost
No, not these, not these. I want a third,
the perfection of an endless summer.
I'll be a dragonfly on a sky filled with water
and light whose fragile wings, when they move
against the wind, dispel the shadows and crush stones.

The Veins of Flowers

I saw her moving slowly through the trees
on the back hill holding a thin green cup
filled with yellow flowers turned delicate
toward the rising sun. She walked without leaving
a single trace or footprint on the maternal ground
or a brush mark against the air of heaven.
I hid naked in the wet hollows as she passed by,
knowing that I could not choose to draw the line
between this world and the next, could not reach
to touch her, could not right the time that whistled
with the hour of my death. I forgave everything,
sprang full grown through the eye of the day
to the place of my exile and madness and dissolved
to dry yellow flowers scattered across the gardens.
In this harmless sharper night, when the body
will not die, my wings furl against the inviolate
salvage of her hands and veins.

Prelude After Rain

I dug a hole in the saturated ground, deeper
than the roots of the bushes I'd planted,
and stood watching how water seeped slowly,
the last needle drops of truth, from its silent
edges oozing across the uncertain discussions
of night and earth in the red mud.
It was the miracle of my beginning, my hands
shaking, as I slid my arms into the opening searching
for her, the prospect of God's last narrative rising
in fits and starts like a scrap of paper blown across
the grass as the soul groans against its invisible back.
There was a sudden scent of roses in the hollow,
the sweetness of her breath. She whistled and
turned in the twilight of my yearning, stretched
in ecstasy as we slept beneath the arch. Blue prodigals
reworked the sky as I staggered to my feet.
Tomorrow the hole will fill itself with whatever finds
its way from box and pail. I will lie awake imagining
the crescendos of this desire. Impossibilities will veer
to shadows that call the crooked sign.

Incarnated

The blue jay on the gray thin branch

of the red maple this morning looked up
and down and then at me as the shadow
of circling wings passed over and again
across the yard, spinning steadily
like the hub of a small world washed awake
by the uncertain light of sudden warning.
He knows the ground will shift unexpectedly
like a thing in hiding, that death will come
like the easy setting of the last bright star.
The rawness of appetite, the half bottle
of memory, the lost nerve of the unredeemed,
and my own heart catacombed by a familiar fear
as the days take root and the universe mumbles
against the bricks and windows of the house.
There is little transcendent to live through
as the shadows rock and tumble on their heels,
as the wild eye of darkness curves the compassions
of the sun and the undefeated weight of gravity
falls back. I watch the bird and circle, stumble
to holy sign and seed, breathe fast and hard in
the consummated shadows. The thin margin
of survival for us both here is a radiant thing,
its name rising and falling to a death it does not want,
the light in the sky the color of time and blood.

Icarus Remembers His Lover Dancing
The look in her eyes each time I enter her,
the sound of her breath against my face,
the weight of her fingers on my back and arms
these moments of rebirth, faint cries framed
by a window dulled by guarded light,
a dance in the sky I have waited for all my life.
The white ring, the shift of things in the wind
she wakes to hear, the mask of desire
pulled out of the air and a thousand flowers
passing to dust as her legs bear down.
I float above the clouds as if to breathe,
imitate the calls of other birds.
Child of light, I spin from world to world
as the grass grows green.
I sprawl the bones of a buried life.
I rise, I rise.

The Late Afternoon Sky
It was a rudimentary sense, an outline
of how to dream. I turn my face away
and try not to notice, sigh hard and flat
unsteadily at the window. I see the future t
hrough the glass, realize deep inside
somewhere that nothing would be the same,
and a kind of contentment came over me.
Tell me your name, I think, and listen
to how lightly she breathes, every day farther
from the place she believed had an impenetrable

pillar at its core, holding up the roof.
Tell me your name, I think, and see the instant
move at random against the steady walls.
Tell me your name, I think.
Her hands stretch tight across their bones
and a cup of tea dark as the afternoon sky
grows ever colder on the table.

Apotheosis

I was walking down a long road toward the hills
and found the dead unaltered and confused:
a hundred then a hundred more, the lost
innocence of lightning crossing the unchanging
sky and the tin of white water lucid as stone.
Then, I was standing on a ladder, my weak eye
seeing the world for all it had become.
Then, I looked out the window and saw the dry grass
burning in the distance, the gray dogs of morning
dragging the shadows of dusk across the blind street,
the empty attic above the cold-water flat
grown desolate and pale.
Then I could see my life blowing in unstable
rain toward evening as the sky pulled back,
the edge of the knife of darkness pressed
hard against the hungry air.
Then I could see.
It was that kind of window.
It was that kind of eye.

After the Fall

Was it later that his innocence was revealed,
the old glory of a fading dream,
the cuts above the hesitant self?
Was it later that he began to talk about the stars,
about an old god buried in the iron earth,
about the tattered dress he saw her wearing
when she walked so easily out the door?
After the trials of winter, did he move exhausted
and afraid across the scattered crusts of clouds
and soil to the coming infirmities of age?
Did he wish for the navigation of voices
and the hard rudeness of late rain as it washed
the salt of moonlight from the back stairs?
Did he long, once again, for the whistles of love
and the expiations of water, the hopeful accidents
of touch as the remains of her closet
became a dominant aching of his heart?
His mind and body tremble with such knowledge
and the long perspectives of his history resound
with the tense snap of brittle metal as the horizons fall.
He remembers the bent circumstances of his soul,
sees the manifestations of a broken advance,
feels the feathered worm of human want
as it crashes through the trees.

He is at peace with an uncertain sky.
He floats beyond the narrow straits.

Resolutions

It was unexpectedly warm today and the air
was filled with the sound of the thin edge of the ocean
moving back and forth across the rocky shore.
It was like a creaking door or the low sound
of your name as you avert your face as night falls.
Out ahead, the water wears the stones
and the north sky is knobbed with paradise.
Time bends forward, solitude its only verdict,
and the slow moon overtakes its own shadow,
the dark colors of the opposite shore
the discontinuity of secret events.
Death roots across the bluing sand.
I keep my distance, explore no depths, climb
across the steep ascent of coarse clouds set awry.
The hour slips and the sky bears down
to the apprehensions of a living name.
There are voices in the surge around me
and the sea is still.
I see what mind and hand had done together
as the constellations turn.
I ride the crescent of the darkened moon
across the blinding hour.

Parable

The sun reflected at an odd angle
on the study window this morning,
the breathing of daylight counting out
the time, the dust of time, in this place
I have learned to live in far ahead of the others.
In the light of midday, I listen for the sun
to fall, lean back against the air, my motions
to and from an imitation of destiny or random chance.
I want to live forever.
I search the sky for portents and signs,
the day too green for comfort or perfection.
I lack for nothing, forgive the unmentionable sin.
I reach for the invisible root, for the inextinguishable fire.
I foreclose the unmeasured retreats.
On days like this I leave the traveled road,
pretend I can escape, forget that I have hands.

Lines on His Birthday

I am old today, a hundred years older than I was yesterday.
I don't know how old I was in my previous lives,
don't remember the color of the coat I wore last week
as a cold rain fell in the distance. I am not sure if I should
move or rest or watch as the float of the world glides
at dead noon across the clouds that fly to your defense
and smooth the blind walls of your heart and eyes.
Love blurs the spiraling gardens, struggles like a loose bridge
in the dissenting air. The bed is cold as a drowned woman,

the apprehension of still water, whispers caught in frozen glass.
The years hoot in the trees to reassure themselves.
The world is flat and rattles against the last candor
of the uncut moon. The white woods face the reddening east,
both hands full. All these turns toward the light,
but who could break them? The intimacy of passing time
keeps its place. I will be a hundred years older tomorrow.

Sunday
Night still hovers somewhere around the corner,
turns in the wind like a sliver of glass in an open wound.
The old man tells me he lives in the dark in a grayed
unfinished house, that his body is as nameless
as the suffocating air, the deep cuts in the cells of his blood
an argument washed by the bitter scent of her excitation.
An arm rises and falls in the empty kitchen by the cold stove.
In the room beneath the roof, a fading note as the white sun sets.
He holds her soul in the palm of his hand, fingers spread
around her like the trellis of a silent cage, her arched back
a heel-print on the long grass of redemption.
I've seen it all before, heard the gathered cry where
the future begins and the rainbow ends. I am given away,
provoke a dark and motionless beauty. The season burns in me.
The sky grows pale above the unmade bed.

Interlude
I am not afraid of the dark and turn off
the lamp under the tree by the back porch.
I count the closing minutes and explore the corners
of the yard, walk through shadows that float
like black swans across the white flowers
of the mock orange on the patio as night falls.
The bush moves each spring from nothing to something
and then back again as the flowers spoil to the color
of hesitant bone and lodge in uneven lines
across the top of the pale stone wall.
The stars on the other side of the hill are vulnerable
and startled as the seeded roses take root.
Something old as a slap across the face
buries itself in the leaves alongside.
Sometimes I wake to hear my own voice calling out
in what the last sound of the universe must be.
The heaviness of memory a seduction of two souls,
this ebbing twilight of wind and eye.
Your blouse was a mayfly as I kissed your mouth
that night, my hand a lost soul on your breast.
I knew then what the center of the world looked like.
I know what it looks like now.
Come again to what I was. Find your way.
I'll leave the back lights on.

Quintessence
I am a thing thrown into the air, one small point
on the pale edge of the horizon, the blood

that simmers in the wind and weather closer to God.
I am a thing cast into the water, a spider or wingless
creature skimming the thin brown tide, the retrospective
of light that lags the comeback of parenthetical waves.
I am a thing preserved in fugitive soil, the dark strip of life
and death in this wilderness at the end of the world,
feathers trapped forever in the permanent freeze of last year's ice.
I am a thing sired in flames, the infinite hanger on the rising
smoke that scorns the widows of my father's words.
I have learned to live in these elements and corners.
I have learned to shape the covenants of my life,
feed the ecstasy that falls from the sky
and drown eternal in the cold black stream.
I have learned to shout my name.

The Wandering Light
We heard something give, the mud of night
broken by the gate, the colony of the blank page
and the lash of being wet and hard across my back.
The future slips between my fingers and converges
in thin columns of smoke in this black immensity,
the land below a sign transfixed and an ambiguous welcome.
I was vigilant. I listened for the wrinkling hole
to unlock, for the final significance of this moment,
the yellow circles on the horizon quiet as the dead
echo of old wreaths on lost doors.
I touch the outlines of the fence and closing gate,
know suddenly that I am sky and earth,
the deepest woods and the rising water.
It is always such an instant, sown with white,
and I have told you all this time and time before.
Wait. It is a terrible struggle this time.
This could be heaven and the trees and birds
may know I'm here.

The Metaphysics of Gardens
I held it lightly in the hollow of my hand,
the night dark early today like stones or wood
evaporating to the fracture of things.
It may have been part of a life I lived long before,
part of a white garden outside a window
behind the corners of a red house.
It was as constant as a wild rose luminous
against the black silhouettes in the distance
as I opened the window. I heard their voices
ebbing from the rocks, burning, revolving in the air.
They say: each day is a cold release and silent
as a star, if only the sky is clear enough and time
is thick enough with salt and dark feathers.
And then it might choose to stay.
I listen for footsteps on the stairs, see the drift
Across the leaden ceilings, open every crack and door.
It passes by faint as a dried leaf, fragile as white glass
that traces the night off to its edge. The shadows sink

and rise. The horizon dwindles to despair.
I snatch and turn again, sleep pressed against the wall.

Epithalamium
My hands reached into pockets full
of blue dust and crushed red stone.
I felt the blood in my fingers, the shifting order
of the world that seized the day, and stood
motionless and inconsequential as a wet match
that's lost its freedom to explode.
The hour came like a feather in a drifting wind,
the fine dust that irritates the eye.
I was in a room with green walls
and dark curtains on the windows.
It was difficult to get up. The woman
dressed in white nodded her head.
The blackout came. I was reborn.
The brief light of apprehension intruded
into the room, against my will, and I saw
the sky sink on the walls and floor.
Or was it later, when the slate of day inevitable
and blank as night became tomorrow and the earth
turned toward summer, pawing the air
like a straw dog from pole to pole?
I heard what I needed to hear,
saw what I needed to see,
the lapse of time in eternal past tense.
I flashed the patches of the present, molded
the future from what I loosened in my pockets,
rose up with a loud noise into the air.

The Kingfisher's Reign
You have come to know what knowing is
and find that place again and your own life
finds its way to you. At the door, standing
as if waiting for someone, you see the year
change and the sky break to deep greens
and blues and warmer winds cross west along
the river, haloed by a sun that shifts to white as it rises.
The horizon is miles away. The echo of time passes
by in the water below, shining and falling to light
and shade on every greening leaf and flower.
Flesh and blood and bone planted on the path,
your eye an old man's knife cutting along
the thin perimeter of the day wherever it opens,
taking in whatever bits of life that come to hand.
The quick stutters of the closer edge, the incidental
passage, all of us rising, and you insist on yourself,
think it will all go on forever, too late to know anything other.
You will never untangle the circumstances
that have brought you to this moment. Listen.
The kingfisher above the river exhorts the water,
angels above each blade of grass sing grow grow.

Canticle

It was the only thing moving then across the hollow
of a thousand flowers: an old face, slipping lightly
through the silver on the horizon, reverent and vulnerable
as a distant whisper skimming the surface of water
or a gesture of renunciation taking me home.
It was a history I had somehow forgotten,
summer full again, and a hole in a window
at dusk a last way out. I had written it on the back
of an envelope I found in my pocket:
There was no perceptible change and we buried him
in the rain that day and the air cried.
The air cried like a treacherous drop and the earth was flat.
The earth was flat and covered in flowers.
A woman stood like an old flower in the distance by
the stone wall, moved back and forth in the meadow
as if she had come by mistake, a voice without shadows
as the metal gave and the road turned west.
I knelt down to touch her, traced my fingers in her flesh.
I could feel the sky pressing down, brilliant as a memory.
I pulsed like blood across the floor.
That day had become a transparent sheet, the night
two cold hands that keep the world from shattering.
I refused to let it end this way, destiny a narrow fraud,
fingers pressed against the darkened sill:
beyond the window, in transparent luster, I heard noises
in the river, saw light and a rustling of forms.

In a White Room in Late August

I watched him walking hard across the dusty field,
breathless, carrying the blue door.
The road curved to the left and the sky lay flat
as a full moon in mid-summer.
He tried not to make a sound, thought of nothing,
moved like a bony finger scratching slowly across
a horizon half full of stars.
He remembered yesterday and the day before,
the woman and small child beside him,
a chair by the window, a table in the middle of the room.
Sunlight fell in a thin gray plume through the shutters,
touched her folded hand before setting beyond
the trees with a soft knock on the roof.
He remembered steps, he said, and saw a solitary figure
moving back and forth looking for a way out, a way back,
heard some unknown thing beside him silhouetted
against the frame. It was then, he said, that he took
down the door, carried it out on his back to the field,
walked barefoot on changing ground into the close
stillness of the warm night: if he keeps to the edge
and finds the right place, he knows, it will open
among clouds of dust to heaven. But for now,
in this eternal absence, let them sleep, let time stop
and the small white room fill once again with light.

Wooden Wheel

A wooden wheel turns across the sand and clay,
a wooden wheel turns homeward like a lost beggar
through the kick and harmony of the light.
The words come slow as the fog that cottons across
the banks of the river early on a mid-summer morning,
just as the shadows of trees tip west and the first blue smell
of water touched by sunlight strums across the far fence.
A wooden wheel turns up the slope of the ridge,
a wooden wheel turns homeward like an old woman
dragged on the ground of a thousand lives.
He watched her talking to herself as light closed off
the doorway and suddenly opened his eyes,
lurching to clouds, so he could see the unlocking of the gate.
A wooden wheel turns above the tall clear grass,
a wooden wheel turns homeward like a red blanket
twisting down the flutter of the last hill.
Up there, on the screened porch, beyond the voices
of the house, I could touch the cruelness of the startling
light that turned itself to air, the postures of a bleak
complexion that no longer cuts the road.
Still later it rained on the horizon.
Grass burst like fire across the eternal wheel of night.

Discovered Circumference

There are no straight lines here, no sharp angles,
the corners all folded and curved, the ceilings round
as heavy buckets in rooms latched by drawn blinds
and shades. Lace cloths drape across the arch of tables
and old chairs, gray and brown in the dim day
that filters through the billowed curtains, flow
like ribbons and loops across a convex floor.
Outside, along circular stairways and bowed walks,
past cambered walls of round bricks and smooth
stones, stretch gardens and small meadows, coiling
away like bent and luminous shafts from the house
toward the river. I watch as she clicks lightly across
the grass, shoots like a sudden twist of color across
the long sky, rises with the eddies ahead in blue shapes
among the dark rocks. There is a radiance here
of white water as trees reach for rain that comes
in late afternoon deep-mouthed and abstract
as the sound of dogs in the distance.
There is a brilliance here, no longer oblique and
ambiguous among the clouds, that wakens time,
turns blue and green with the abandon of sudden grace.
There is a reflection here of what is past and what is yet
to come, the sibilance of water that translates the present
to currents of steel that stretch before us and after.
It circles where the shadows cower, prefigures its own course.
I flow across these round deceptions, curve across
these intersections of a transitory bloom.
Darkness is light. Only the present matters,
the frail labyrinth of loose ends. I abandon the patterns

of the past for an unillumined future, for the suffering
of the unintended and the not-yet-born, unsure
of what god could save me. And something within
me turns again, turns and whirls and unlocks.

An Unexpected Encounter One Evening
I stood so close to you that day that you
could have reached out and touched me.
You pointed instead like a thread of light
toward the window of what you believed
was a redeemable world, your heart in your throat.
The air beyond was haze and bright yellow,
the sky ragged with the habits of leaves.
There was thin smoke in the distance,
a gap in the insurrection of morning
the color of your eyes. You asked
who was to blame, the pockets all turned out,
the outcomes of our lives up for sale
and the experience of leaving a room the eternal
satisfactions of a safe return more than you could bear.
I picked up the letter and watched day glide across
the far wall. Your skin sighed as I read.
You gave a wounded smile.
A fine shadow suddenly crossed your face.

The Cold Steel of Morning
It rained today, clouds moving down along
the darkened roofs, lights and dust in the distance,
as I watched you walk barefoot in the wet street
with your shoes in your hand, past the glass
strategies and gray facades of closed houses.
You were calm as a stone's throw, daughter and mother
all at once again, the graceful mourners of the heart.
I stood breathless as you passed by, stray headlights
reflecting against the redness of the scaffolding
and chalk marks on the walls, water brooding
in small puddles in the dusk, the remaining augurs
of a season of hope unruled by any measure.
We were separate then, abstracted from the world,
a genealogy of echoes at the edge of the street durable
as keys in dead locks. I tinker here with time,
am a mixture of fiction and fact, imperfect, obsessive,
a disciple of guesses and hints.
Tonight I am white and freshly painted, a pattern
of emergence and descent that clouds your vision.
Morning, they say, when it comes, may be clear as cold steel.

Bone
When I was a young girl, I found the hollow leg bone
of a horse just below the dirt and stones along the fence
that outlined the edges of my neighbor's yard.
It was preserved, hard and cold and white,
like an old star that crusts to mold as summer
deepens and the weight of heavy air is everywhere

within arm's reach. It clattered dry and smooth
when I kicked it with my foot against the fence post,
the last one in line before the bend in the road,
that half-vacant sound the rustling whisper
of the ghost of a clear day above an empty house.
I could not understand where it had come from,
where the rest of the horse was buried, the red wash
of its blood feeding the roots around me, exhausted finally
and burrowing down and out to the servility of nothing.
I brought the bone home, hid it in my skirt,
pushed it on the floor under my bed, pointing
its narrow end away from the window to keep it
from calling and scattering the light.
I have it still, all these years later, wrapped
in ribbons, under my bed, pick it up now and then
and look through it as if through the opaque glass of time
at a sky green with ebbing stars and a changing moon.
When I hold the bone in my hands and open
both my eyes, I can trace the surface of these events,
see the hanging dog wag its tail across the empty heavens.
I labor through the secrets of the determinate earth,
break like a frail shell ignored by the sun, know where
the fault at last lies. I'm cold, love in the heart's ash.
The day is over. My life, my life, my incandescent bone:
a seamless wicker of time that shapes the taunts
of God's lost narrative, the quiet hunt for morning
and the undiscovered beauty of its name.

When the War Began
I pick up the bucket and pour the water out
for the last time, picking it up and pouring it out
in currents and swirls as if for the last time,
picked up the rusted bucket and poured
the green water across the sand where
the thin stone path crossed for the last time.
The sky was a red river, the gray face of the receding
moon a hollow boast in early morning, the shoals
along the shallows below washed to a perfect dead calm.
This is how the day began when the soldiers came,
she told me, when the day began in the small town
on the edge of the country, their menace and resolve
stumbling ahead in slow procession as the day began
and the stream of water crossed in front of them
on the stone path still cool with early morning
as she picked up the bucket and poured.
She remembered only little things, she said, that day,
as the soldiers came: the way stirred wind blew
in her hair as they passed by, the color of the weeds
as the sun rose in the distance, the sounds of the bell
above the outlines of the town. The water overwhelmed us,
she said, the immeasurable black cloth of history and war
covered in the dust of fallen stars draped across the opened
windows. Nearby, she said, a solitary apple dropped
from a thin branch, a fly floated on the surface of the spill.

The Invention of Zero
On the table, wind.
The left hand pressed against the outside wall.
Footsteps across the cobblestones.
The dark rider on a pale bicycle.
Wax that will not melt.
Blood in the corners of the mouth.
The holy fire of night birds healing.
The lost salt of living.
The small chains of the century fallen to silence.
The cold dew on the cross posts of the gate.
Statues of mist as the fog lifts.
The eyes of women hiding in the dark.
The third knock.
The sun today set on the wrong horizon:
black and white, two and simultaneously one,
the double and the contradictory, certainty from
uncertainty, a search for what we have not yet lost.
And I am everywhere, rising like a sudden shout
on the brink of a world in which I play no part.
I turn, a shadow between generation and death,
the final shape and substance of the narrow orbit
of the closing north, the self-intrusion
of the assonant emptiness that betrayed me to dust.
Under this hesitant step, in a world cleanly divided,
I stand triumphant and immortal
at the center, the circumference.

The Hand of God
The blue jay in the spruce tree does a dance for me
and its eye flashes.
The sun reflects off the windows as the sky lightens
and arcs across the floor, the painted wooden shutters
and lace curtains open, the apples in the low white bowl
a splash of red on the oak kitchen table.
Changing shadows play among the cut flowers
in the summer heat, float across the ceiling, glide
into the blue shirt hanging on the back
of a bowed brown chair.
Outside, love slips along the radiant streets
and blood simmers in the petals of roses.
The birdhouse moves back and forth, the whisper
of daylight delicate and yellow in grass greener
than I imagined, trees free as crystal and clear as glass.
This is what I have been waiting for.
This is the bloom of summer when the train stops
ahead in a warp of heady steam and smoke.
This is the crescent of her shoulder as I press myself
transparent against her.
This is the immovable silence of fire.
I want to save myself.
Hold me in this sheltered room, push away the hand
of God as it reaches blindly to touch my face,
call out the kingfisher and the sword.

The Midday Sun
The hill in front was green with the singular deep colors of summer.
On the right, the weather vane at the highest point of the roof the outline of an old man
driving a dark carriage in whatever direction the wind blew, the inflexible edge of
morning an illusion of safety in his hands.
Just beyond, the hard features of the yard, the fence down along the side edge, a
brick walk,
untended flowers thick with the mercy of rain and heaven steaming slowly in the
noon's heat
The strum of cicadas in the distance.
Inside, in the small back room, she slipped past the darkened shades, past the leather
chair that pressed against the bottom of the window, past me, fastening her stockings.
She counted out her steps.
The floor hunched to blue ceilings and dark rugs
The dresser drawers were partly open.
The room spun.
Nothing is an accident.
She passes silent between worlds.
I blend into the colors of the walls, a thin roll of cigarette ashes on the window sill, on
the floor a curl of red string.
I stir like grainy sad dust across the floorboards, try to catch the quick rattle of the lamp
as the door closes, the lull in the sound of clouds passing across the trace.

Folly Beach
It was the first warm day after nearly a week of a cold hard rain.
Daylight, thin and misty, came slowly across the door
of the open cupboard, past the steps and the stretch of wood floor
that floated in a faint glimmer to the open screen on the porch.

Outside, down below, stairs of old planks weathered to the color
of dried leaves, grasses mustered on the pale margin of sand,
a ledge of wind piled up and back against grayed fences.

Just beyond, the water was a wash of eddies and lost surges,
comforting the passing of time across the sea oats and dunes.

A curved line of brown pelicans skimmed the changing waves,
dolphins in the distance broke the crest of the tide, followed
the tracings of old quarantine delays against the far shore,
the discovered remains in the dark sand of later wars.

The past and the future neither forgotten nor anticipated,
faces that undergo slow changes as the morning stills,
the impatient hand that knocks against the wall
with the cold fear of life and death in the unfixed sea.

We are counted with the living here, transfigured
by the light that comes ambling up the walk.

We have visions of water parting, diving deeper and deeper
into the wake, the tide line flooded across the border of being,
the sky unhanded, and the echo of the year's slow wandering
soft and near.

Across West Ashley Street

The events of that day were distant, almost abstract,
as he stood thinking about something at the window.
Wind blew in off the water like an unexpected premonition.
The back door was locked.
Music was playing in a farther room, fragments of sound
that discouraged the glass, turned fragile against
the flat white walls and ceilings of the house.
The sun was setting, casting shadows in the curtain
across a horizon that was growing small and dim.
There were faint images in the distance negotiating
the curve of the invisible.
His white shirt reflected in the wood-framed panes.
He was silent there for a long time,
his high face drawn and sad,
his right hand pressed against the sill to hold himself steady.
He knew where the corner began and where the wall ended,
the texture and smell of summer dust, gray and yellow
in the cool shades of the floor.
In his left hand, he held the woman's glove he found
washed up by the waves on the sand.
Summer, he thought, felt heavier this year.
He touched its frayed lace, outlined its fingers one by one,
listened to the deep sorrow of the passing moon.
Outside, beyond the wooden walk, the steep and downward
climb of sand across the bent dry grasses,
the senseless faint light of stars.
He touched the glove to his face, moved his lips across
its stitches and strings, remembered the color of her hair.
He is lost in black water.
He stands watching her face float in front of him
across the darkened window.
He hears the ignorant voices of the tide.

Stealing Mulberries

It is as painful as the tending of a blistered hand,
the cobwebs of anonymous pages.
The world seen through smudges of soaped glass,
evolving to the dead sound of water against distant rocks
as a hot wind rises and drifts slowly away into smoky trees
like steam hissing loose and quiet at dusk.
That memory of climbing the mulberry tree in the yard
across the street, hands and faces stained purple,
wide-eyed in a mirage of leaves and air, catching a bent
branch to keep my balance as the fireflies fell.
I wake up in the middle of the night sometimes
and remember him falling, falling,
the sound of the train on the other side of the woods
and marsh ground repeating the howl of his name,
falling to a dead run of sky along the far field
as the lights disappeared, falling as if running backwards
in the air, trying to wrench himself forward
and away from the arching of his back.
In the middle of the night sometimes I stumble awake

like a loose screen on the hinges of the back door,
the earth beneath the wide mulberry tree still flat
with no clear answer, knowing the distances
we could not travel, outlined and crossed as the twilight
of the boy who fell, the passing sounds I always hear
in the slow shifting of silence, the places we wait
to be rescued still. In the middle of the night
I drop myself awake sometimes and lean my face
against the window trying to look out at a single aching
moment in a distant landscape that can grow whole
only in sleep. I see myself there, falling.

Navigating the Waters
In the center of all my uncertainties and fears,
among all the old feelings that settle into my chest
like the convulsions of a dry cough that will not stop,
in the fog in my head, the gray confusion,
a single clear thought, cold, unannounced,
like a clap of thunder above the roof,
like a bullet between the eyes:
> The old waters sprawl in death and waking,
> deep as a pillar of light, and the heart takes heed,
> takes heed, as small ghosts haunt the shoreline,
> roaming weightless across the last blue rocks
> of a lost summer.
> The heart is held fast, held fast, quick as a hazel
> wound and the hesitant step of first seeing, the disbelief
> of hands when water turns to dust and grief across
> the crest of a pale moon.
> And there is this ebb and flow, this shudder
> of triumphant air, this eternal margin of a
> desiccated time that salts the sea to flood.
> And nothing in these layers aligns or withdraws,
> nothing unfolds, and the sky hides its wings
> in the ether and clay, and the boatman smiles.

Points of View
The pale wind came through the unopened door
and down the stairs.
The day grew opaque.
The thin young men banked the light on the wall,
bright as blood.
The yellow heart of time rattled against the dark grayed houses.
The long walk of redemption, hands tied behind your back,
ebbed to old incriminations white as the rising moon
as it carves the infirm ground blank in late summer.
The crowd followed after, graceless, rough to the touch,
accustomed to the sounds of the bells in the sunken tower.
The space around him is empty and free as sibilant water.
He shakes his head, the moment of surprise in his eyes,
echoes a truth he does not feel or understand,
roots the insistent phrase.
The night wakes where trees weight the empty air
and shadows brush vulnerable or dead.
The sky is stained thin and red.

I wander from room to room, life curled at my feet,
roused in new colors and motions.
And then the abrupt, incredible flash.

Conjugation in the Square
Even in this we don't yield to despair,
know as sure as a sign of faith
that everything eventually heals.
The sun was burning too bright that midday,
too hot, as the three stood
in the middle of the square,
shoulders bent, blood pulsing in their ears
as children cried aloud
and dogs barked for their meals.
It was not a true measure,
fused here for a moment,
the landscape around them quick
and abrupt, with no color or motion.
It wasn't clear who came to stare
at them that day, from behind fences,
through windows, past ledges and doors,
whose faces they saw, warm in the sun,
as the day bled to this deep
afternoon's commotion.
The present and future between
this life and the next,
the emptiness that makes
a comforting sound that draws
like chalk across the dividing wall.
It catches scattered in our throats,
stirs the humid air,
and then tolerantly flickers away
and fades to a narrow disillusion,
a quarrel lost at the exchange
that makes you small.
Others too will fail like us,
others like us will fail and fall.

Notes from the Last Weekend of Summer
They were convinced they would live forever, the years drifting
        south to an ending that never came.
Fire licks the hand, the wings of birds embroidered on my back a flying night
        too frail to encumber.
The red stain of a truth I did not know, the broken tower an angle of blind lines against
        the stir of the sky.
The bell sounds the hour, the outline of the train on the horizon clear as partitioned glass
        at the top of the stairs, coming back to where we started.
These marks that need more than your breath to give them life.
The transformation like that of the face of a stranger waking early and unremembered
        in your bed.
The innocence of the white leaf wandering, the clutching roots of trees that give no shade.
The sudden emptiness of the sea wall when night comes in full defiance, weaving
        threads of time too fine to name, discouraging the currents of a more universal fear,
        the silence of the yielding voice.

The weightless sun setting just beyond the bend of the road, moving on dangerous wheels.
Summer surprised us then, coming up over the southern lake, skirting the rootless hills.
Two figures in a photograph faster and faster and faster, the world theirs for the taking,
whatever the heart savors and patterns too vague to change, the deliberate disconnection,
        the fragmentary scene.
Witness of flesh as the season turns to call the old widow in the brown house on the corner.
I slept deep and sweet beyond the intensity of light, hear the redeeming whispers of children.

The Middle Voice
Putting down her book, sitting in soft profile
against the shifting light of the window,
she says quietly that the moment is immortal,
that time and space expand and contract
as everything around her dies, but the moment,
only the moment, is immortal.
The slow clouds moved against their will,
hung in solace on the steeples of the churches
above Willow Brook, dying away against
the hewn gray stones that barely cleared the ground.
Memory walks across a landscape it has never seen,
quickened by the brief dignity of onlookers
on a farther hill, the slow afternoon the only epoch
to call its own. It ebbs and vanishes in the long-
empty reassurance that abides in change.
And nothing else moves but the candid light
in the great curve of the circle across an
innocent space, our lives a dream of its silent
circumference, a gathering of infinite points
we cannot reach across the valedictory
of this momentary place.

Corwin's House
I am the last of them and pass by quickly.
The shapes of the town dissolve behind us,
layering to the deep brown of cold stones
that cast low shadows sobering to a locked night
that time cannot erase. The air is heavy with the past,
memory an old country, a symptom of withdrawal
that slides like cold scissors across the nape of the neck.
It was a feckless beginning, a dull familiar grayness
that coats the road when the fading light angles and tilts.
It covers us like an accusation, the slow black
drought that transfigures the year.
They say the haggard ecstasy of that fall
began with a girl who wanted to see her innocent future,
her husband and son, and ended with incantations
of prophecy and curse and the staged command
that those who confessed went free,
not in the shells of their bodies but safe and away
from the angers of a bleaker and eternal season.
Some listened and cried out in water, some,
they say, died well, tied arm to heel, freed at last
from those secret matters as families settled
in the meeting houses and watched the deep-cut
flames of salvation spread wide from the domination

of tended hearths. For some, it was an ending
that came and came once more. Others held a glass
they knew could never break.
The torn page of a book remained like a scar
on the table, the congregation a great crowd
of people pressing together in their own darkness,
generations coiled toward a cold and harsh redemption.
When the time came, the souls gathered in that room
filled with the dry smoke of confession
and in that season of shift and change were equal
once again in the covenant ground at the foot of the hill.
I don't know who had the last word there.

Redemption
In my dream there were cold spots on the floor
and bed, the imperfect silence of the shadows
around the corner, the fire and ice of our hard age.
If morning comes and the day does not follow,
if the day comes and there is no night,
if night comes, if night comes like a warning
or a small burning in the grass, an ache of the wind,
prayers that prevail on their own accord
among the difficult stars   those cold spots
will be a dead whiteness, a hollowness,
the first thing you see on the crossing
of the dark earth against the late sun.
I sleep alone, write freely when I wake up,
feel no need to speak, move endless
and bright and unbroken.

Hope
It was the humming of the water
that caught my attention that morning,
airy things growing small, the persistent
tenderness of tears on her cheek.
I had planned nothing that day and felt
as if my mouth and throat were filled with dust
as I kept repeating over and over again
that the world is the same as it has always been,
gone light then dark as it ages to forgetfulness
and dry seed, the solitude of fire.
Our arms brush against one another as we pass:
hope the square root of doubt,
as if the world would end then and there.
I remember I had the oddest dream:
the face in the mirror, when it smiled,
had transparent teeth and its eyes turned
to avoid the long white blur of the room.

A Long Way Home
We watched the slow contraction of eternity,
twice as high as the inextinguishable stars
and broken by the bundled slow push
of another wind. A cool mist rose in the air

and the man stretched on the hard ground
shivered, turned his head as if listening
to something in the distance, far below
the horizon and snapping away like
a low curve in all directions. The short dark
street alongside came to an end not far
from where he lay, dropping blindly against
snared rocks and a steady line of trees.
The moon was strong, flat and uninvolved.
He was confused about the time that had passed,
felt as if he had fallen into a hole so deep
he couldn't see even the smallest patch of heaven.
He did not understand why he had wanted it
so much and tears came to his eyes.
He would sleep when daylight faded
from the edge of the road. His hands
locked behind him and that vacant gesture,
painful and impossible there on the ground,
eased his mind. He could not cry out or move.
He roused himself with a shiver, felt
a vague impersonal fear, heard the wind move
unbidden past his ears. He believed nothing,
he believed all, steadfast in a weary destiny
that neither surrender nor love would spare.
He saw the sleep of things unfold
in the narrow spaces among the trees,
the bitter moment riddling the indifference of faith.
He pressed the empty paper to its manic collapse.
There, in the distance, he crossed
the boundary of the passing bell.

Double Vision
I had to leave in a hurry.
I saw the woman in the shadows,
stood dumbstruck, prayed
it was a simple mistake,
hoped there was a place for me
as well, somewhere I could go
and they could not follow.
It was an artificial note written
in a thin hand as the picture faded.
I may have been too suspicious,
teeth clenched, skin warm,
and the wind left me behind,
once then twice.
I know what I need as she moves
out of the shadows in a long gray dress,
sunlight glancing off her white arms
and shoulders. I think for a moment
that she has risen up from under a dry sea.
I smile inside, feel something obscurely,
stand up suddenly and then,
just as suddenly, turn and kneel.
I've never seen the sky so beautiful:

140

an oblique and pointed rudimentary dark,
the absolute transparency of the surfaces we seek.

The Mirror
A white marble table stands in front
of a large mirror that someone had polished
early in the morning with a coarse cloth.
A hand moves forward across the table,
patient and calm, in the sudden stillness
of the hallway reflected in the mirror.
There seems to be time for all things, and time
for none, as each morning the knot loops in
upon itself ever tighter and the end of the string
loses itself in the confusion of the mirror.
Pale blue figures move out of sequence
like streaks of clouds that race all day across
the face of the polished mirror.
My movements are filled with neglect and unease
as I walk back and forth in the dangerous places
and treacherous seasons deep in the mirror.
I lie down. The room is bare.
I feel the impetuous rush of the day.
For the ardent necessities,
the low sweet futilities of such a life,
I blame the mirror.

In Effigy
There were no lights in the house and the paleness
of the morning sky oppressed the shuttered windows,
penetrating the corners and bleeding slowly
across the ceiling and floor. The gray coat lay disheveled
against the baseboard in the front room, not far
from the small table on which a solitary candle
slowly burned itself out, casting vague shadows
as daylight yellowed the walls. The door to the street
had glass panes flat as the back of a hand.
A red shoe on the small green carpet
was a reminder of how quiet the day would be,
moving in slow motion, frame by frame,
a wistful resignation of the previous night.
A white blouse fallen and drifting like some
anonymous horizon, ready for a useless chance
or the limits of infinity, and stockings draped
across the back of a chair quivered at every sound.
A brown skirt laced with thin orange lines
yielded to the deliberate air, outlasting
the flaws of the wind and the long frustrations
of entangled flesh. The figure of a woman,
weightless and naked, stood in the doorway,
her hands clenched, head bent down,
as light crawled to a cryptic noon.
It was a frame struck white, the touch
of shadow on a delirious heart. The hidden
choice that stills the blood penetrates

the fallen blossoms with the dullness
of desire and breaks the common silence
of the dream, the slide to being that the season
did not spare and the long calm rising from the dead.
She stands, turns, moves iridescent in a daze
of fate and love. The day declines into night.

The Innocent Air

I slept late again today, woke under a white rising sun
that believes it might catch the ground on fire.
I think for a moment about what would happen
if it all began to burn, like the foretelling body unloosed
and the wandering child quickened everywhere
by the coming of day. I remember how we stood together
in the dark then, and when I look back, when I look back .
That day the trees yellowed with fall to a limitless
horizon and clouds without measure turned gray and blue.
Above our heads, the sky glided to red.
I reached to dip my finger in it, left an infinitely
small break in the darkening flow for the sun today,
half black half white, to rise. The terrible brilliance
of the season gone to ground, the earth peeled
to a mask of light without ceremony or form.
I watched you later at a distance wanting nothing,
a blank self fallen to a flight of birds and dancing
for a moment in a changing sky.

Something Waits Beneath It

The afternoon follows its own course.
The October sky holds fast then suddenly quiets
as you turn away on the stairs leading to the next floor.
You stand weightless and white against the gallery's
dark green wall, the scar on your heart a soundless
thin line you thought could not exist.
You are alone except for the brush on the walkway
of impermanent leaves, the self-accusations of night
passing to nothingness: the taste of the soft curve
of her neck a dark invitation, the smooth horizon
of her body gone from any bed.
These cold dreams tonight that chase an old regret.
My hand curled, ever unable to straighten.
Memory a savage eternity hiding in the autumn grass.

September's Roses

It was the old cemetery near the railroad tracks
that ran through the center of the east end of town,
faintly visible from the street as night turned
to the first cold streaks of daylight and the iron color
of the sky blended with the rails just past the horizon.
To the right of the gravel path, beyond the juniper trees
and maples and the small pond where children fished
in early summer, where I once hooked a tired perch
thrown back too many times, the musty smells
of damp earth from newly-dug graves marked

the grass like the grasp of old fingers. I saw him
under the trees when the light began to rise,
dressed in a coat with pockets he could put his hands in,
and he nodded and looked away as if in danger of losing
his place as the hard packed earth pulled his arms down.
He rocked back and forth slowly like heavy paper
in a low wind looking at the deep red rose some other
hand had put on her grave, rocked back and forth
trying to imagine what she felt, if the dead feel anything,
as that hand moved across the front of the stone,
touching the letters of her name, leaving behind a
faint trace of something indelible as if life itself
had returned for just that moment before the two
of them turned slowly into circles of air,
the deep sweet sleep of shadow and light
in the turmoil of the senses, the cold hope of day
as wind rocks back and forth unexpectedly in the trees.
He recalls the familiar expressions of the distant street
as it turns down and again along the hills to the posts
of the old tracks, the authority of her world carrying
everything off and away. He takes no air as he tries
once more to breathe. I heard steps in back of me,
turned and saw the source of the light.

Doppelganger
The train skims past the outline
of the old brewery, scattering autumn light
across the bare ground of November.
The day ebbs and flows, sputtering like the wick
of an old kerosene lamp.
If you reached for it, you could almost touch it
with your fingertips, a thick mix of white and black
seeping up into a changing sky.
The heater in the car didn't work and a low cold
worked its way up through the metal floor.
He shifted in his seat to stay warm.
He sees his face in the window on the opposite side,
a sudden glance in a square of glass that the darkness
outside has made into a mirror.
I stand by the side of the tracks, watch him
reflected in the far window as he looks away
from me as the train slows. His image becomes
more and more transparent as the lights outside
brighten the car and for a moment he is there,
a single solid man with his back toward me,
and at the same time a ghost of himself
in the opposite window, a vague transparent figure
in a private light that shines through darkened glass.
He is at once both meaning and sign, a concurrent
stillness and motion, one beyond the two
so clearly defined, the face of God in vague relief
sunken to the figure of a moving link that is neither
here nor there. I watch alone as the train pulls away,
fading like a lost hope in an old wind that fuses
in the sudden void. I am reflected in neither place.

The Emperor's Ashes

He refused to come into that room,
passed the darkened doorway without looking in,
heard the two voices without speaking back,
brushed past the transparent walls without moving
abruptly through both.
His face was suddenly quiet, transfixed, seeing truth
traced on a patchwork of air, hearing echoes
resounding in the empty hall.
His hands were fragile as glass when she died
and left no lasting shadow on the curtains,
the moment finally hers like a solitary bird diving
in a distant sea, a brisk and fleeting recognition.
She did not leave much behind in that room,
absence that dissolved to unexpected rectitude,
familiar objects in slatted patterns,
nothing else cataloged or labeled, the pale margin
of the day before reticent and sad.
Time seeps away.
The year is a casualty of innocence lost and forgotten form.
The empty hands of memory locked to the stillness
and sleep of grieving things.
It is what the heart wants in waves of transformation,
the urns and scattered ashes, the burial place
in the surrounding gardens, the voice high and away
of the idiosyncratic gnostic who trembles
like a slow fire from darkness to light.

Penelope's Code

The day buried itself in the backyard, alongside the path
that led from the house to the woods.
He had not come home, coveting a world cooling
against the glare of the sun in the corners of the city,
breaking against the hard lines of fact and dream.
It was the interruption he waited for,
the irresolute walk forgotten in familiar streets,
the curve of a fervent darkness moving overhead
to silence and ice.
He had not come home, shuddering with a folding history
in the moribund passing, the sentiments of gray rain
immeasurable in the curve of space as it falls to iron and night.
It was the necessity he waited for,
the tremulous gravity of a wavering vision,
the anguish of the pitiless fire
of an inevitable heart.
He had not come home, pushing away the edge of the hand
that floats like a knife across the clouds,
claiming the measure of time as night glows green
at the end of the road.
It was the consequence he waited for,
the momentary shallows in the lull of fall,
the incoherent absolute that curls like a fluent wire
across the bow of his ship.
The day buried itself in the backyard, alongside the plunge

of light across this abiding sky.
He has not come home.
The wheel of constancy rattles and shifts.

The Habits of Fall

The day was a bowl of cold water tipped
on its side at the edge of an old field.
A black bird perched in the highest branch
of a tree that reached toward clouds stirring
across the permanent spread of the sky.
The last leaves were still.
The door to the bedroom in the house below
Walnut Hill was open, the room's white walls
absentminded with daylight, deep and watchful
as eyes that fill unexpectedly with tears.
A voice spoke, carrying past the high ceiling,
then a long dry pause trembled across a sky
half full of stars. He leaned toward her
and kissed her, his arm around her waist,
the sweet smell of her skin unsettling and slow.
He thought his heart would stop, breathing hard,
and felt his face flush as her legs moved.
She was quiet for a moment then, touching
the wall, longing for the place that picks our bones
apart and rebels to desire and love.
And the light flickers, the door closes and locks.
The world is divided in two.
Time's dissemblance the sudden echo in the hall
that stumbles back into itself, her name
the quiet agitation of the eye when the last song ends
and the circle breaks.

God's Pardon

When I close and pack up my old books,
when I see the leaves reddening and the webs of spiders
float outside the windows on the north wall of the house,
when the horizon thrusts across the flight of white birds,
when the fire of evening empties to night's proud words
and endless desire rises like a blue dream deep
in the corners of my mouth
the soft heavens open and the noises born at night
shiver across the sky, under white stars that ripen
in a shifting wind that wheels the trees to ground.
Listen to the songs of glass, taste the metal of the moon,
brood through gates of water, lay your head against
the diminution of color that witnesses the grief
and certitude of stone. The gates of November
swing open as if to prove such things and the season
makes its journey forward like a snapped twig underfoot.
No one can remember the arc of the last pendulum of day.
The deep end of time steeps at the edge of the street
and the world slides away. The flickering breath of hope
does not fade on the years' pallid glass.
The blunt hierarchies of windows celebrate

the orphaned hours where the sky has fled.
These are the only truths I know today,
the contours of a life shaped from air and light
that folds to quick patterns overhead.
The sad fall from heaven to the world as it is.
And then the incoherence,
the burning rounds of distant bells.

The Red Cloth of Eternity

Two days ago, before the sun echoed across the city
and the last birds flew by overhead, when all the fires
went out and the sky was like layers of feathers and down,
we tried to make it what we thought it should be,
strangers on the narrow street below, the future
washed away by cold water, the bottomless finality
of this closing season falling hard across our lives
as the world pressed randomly against us.
The light in the window was steady and durable
as stone, your eyes dark and beautiful
when I undressed you and my hands trembled,
touching the small trapped bird fluttering in your breast,
your mouth open and wet against my face.
The long flicker of the moon, the endless web of shadow
and light lost in the timeless tilt of your throat,
the lines of your body, the slow soft parting
of your arms and thighs, your hair falling across your face
in the silence and disorder of the evening sky,
you moving slowly, so slowly, back and forth
among the luminous shapes on the wall, holding me close,
holding me close, as time slides away and wind drowns
smooth and blue in the refuge of the closing trees.
It was a moment of grace, beyond interruption,
that overtook me a lifetime ago. Tonight,
in a different season, when words have no weight
and the day stumbles to its edge, I think of you,
of love, of eternity and the sound it makes
when it rushes in as I move inevitable and free
within you and the clock strikes its hours
against the ashes of the brilliant night.
I move, deep and still, and the red cloth unfolds.

The Sin of Language

It was the sin of language, the trace of words
that lift a heavy body. I drink the secret terror
of the flesh, glow in a sleep that divides the subtle
branches, triumph in the beds of withered roses.
The women are blue and cold this morning
and the future burns its hour across the contours
of a breast traced by uninflected eyes,
the fiery lightning of my lips.
The pomegranates burst with eternal desire
and the trees blush fierce and white.
The soul is empty of words,
mourns the blasphemy of sleep,

succumbs to morning's ineffectual star.
Look! The world is ardent and white.
The ecstasy of another light deep in the flesh
is rising here.

Skimming the Air in November

It was like a darkness at noon, the angle of the sun
veined across the face of the old man dead
in the woods, the dust in the curtains of a vague room
full of old books, the low trace of the invisible
weightless orbit of the changing earth.
The innocence of blood and bone, the fire at hand,
and the strange grace that drives the autumn to night.
All these things.
Do you remember that late November afternoon
when I found a piece of opaque glass under a hollow
of leaves by the side of the road and cut my hand
as I threw it like a skimming rock across the surface
of the air until it disappeared so white and mute
into a distance lost beyond return?
As it slid across that place between the earth and sky
it was like the movement of indistinct form
to ultimate clarity, the infinite from the infinite,
running and standing still all at once, all at once,
from darkness to light and then back again
to the far dominion of dead leaves, the silence
of time before the beginning that hangs like
a blue shadow on a distant wall.
The sky once again drowns to the quality of stone.
The moon, stark orange as it rises against the far horizon,
rocks silently in a noose of clouds and wind.
The bones of my feet are light as feathers,
the white road ahead a graceful stem of faith and fear.
I understand the resurrection possible for the things
of this earth, the driven truth that covers the world
from all sides even as the heart refracts
to quicksilver and change.
And I float like a piece of glass cast across
the heavens, unravel a hidden fate, transcend
the barrier of time and place to eternity's grand mistake.

The Last Root's Call

I could see the city in the distance,
troubled by a hand of wind that drifted
from the coast when winter ledged
the far corner, as I climbed the hill.
The last days of autumn, passing like water
under the ground, staggered to gray
and green shadows in the white birches,
the year's second flowering lighter
at this second turn.
It was the hour of indecision,
a time when old men pray,
a time for secrets and the coming

of a distant chill that turns history to dust.
It lingered in a spindle of moon waiting
for the world to end or begin or load
to the pointless nullity of war, the withering
of the reddest rose or the passing
of the fullest cup.
The last light of summer is in my eyes,
encouraging my deepest self as it glazes
across the fall of time.
This world is not my own, caught
in the whine of a random infinity
as the indifference of death drags it
to radiance and void, the cold
a pitiless witness where the dark
gray sprawls. Evening comes early,
spins the melancholy of hidden things.
The earth shakes and coils.
Anonymous days harden to winter
beyond the last root's call.

The End of History
And then I watched the motions of her hand,
slow and long, in a world that never meant
to be unkind, that never meant to want such changes.
Migrating bones and inquisitive dust that cheer
the shadows and the light. The sound of my desire,
as the skies converged, a late tumbling against
her walls, a braid of storm and wash tied half away.
When I breathe now I hear the mute singing
in my chest, my heart turning as weightless
as thin steel shavings gone to rust.
And I draw back in that absolute hour and the lights
are dim and the loose reins of autumn thrum the sky.
I watch her sitting in the corner of her room,
an old white blouse held tightly in her hand
as if to stuff the hole in the universe.
Little by little the dark rolls in and covers me.
I emerge to my descent. I circle outside,
sink into myself, eyes fixed on the stars,
and time unlatches the outer gate.

Elegy for Winter Light
I watch the slow wind outside.
Snow was falling again, small and white,
across the rooftops in the distance
and the street unraveled like
the ruffled weave of a wilting rose.
I turned as she moved against me,
blind with virtue, made the delicate sound
that a body that does not fit into this world
makes after a night of restless sleep
when it pricks itself with whatever's at hand
to see if it is still alive and finds pinpoints of dismay
under a sky the color of some great imperfection.

I am a straggler cold with yearning for
a different season that's come to itself too late.
I cut an exit for myself in winter's infinite scattering,
search once more for things I cannot hear
or see in this small room, stand transparent
against the panes of the wind.
My fingers climb across the empty floor.
I find my immoveable mark, try to breathe,
unbend the salvage of unsteady light.
The monotony of truth, sturdy in its own design,
lies cut and hollow in this final slide.

Cold Fire

All this talk about aging, absence that stands
fast under the light in the window,
the long cracked tooth of winter.
When I turn away, I feel a slight buzzing in my ear.
It asks me how often I hide behind the stairs,
how the hour slips and the day dissolves.
Thursday, the day was cold but sunny and clear.
This is what I found this morning:
it is all like a film in a dark room with the sound turned off,
as familiar as paper, brusque as the blankness of death
when the solstice falls, the snap of small things in colorful brigade.
The raw earth, black and white, left to dry on the horizon.
The tattered circumstances of old eternity.
Winter, a half-moon setting, disembodied on the blind side.
The vain hard breath of oblivion.
Whatever bends to kiss the ice and stones.
Whatever burns.

The Theology of Snow

Nothing finds its way upward.
You grope through the winter fog
for something to happen, for the crisis of snow.
Walking through the house late at night
I walk on my toes like a small exiled god,
afraid that if I use my entire foot, one step
after another, someone would hear me
or catch me from behind by surprise.
The images swell on the moonlight, disappear.
The stars are moved by the weak breath of early morning.
The incapacity of clouds resists the suspense of defeat.
The heart grips its destiny.
The voice holds.

The Old Hand of the Moon

The snow on the driveway melted and then refroze
to clumps of hard ice, a forest of glass and sharp corners.
I sometimes melt and refreeze when it's late
and there is still so much to do,
when the snow comes, when the snow comes.
The moon tonight is an old man's hand
dragging itself across the dry ice
when the snow comes in sharp corners.

Infinity's blind shore in the ice when the snow comes.
The black window that reflects the dry ice of the moon
framed by the old hand that has no sense that time has passed,
that time has passed and our vision is blocked,
by the snow when it comes.
It is the menace of the moment, a frozen moment,
random as the cycle of the seasons, that traces regret
with the old hand of the moon that drags itself
across the night like the degradation of ice,
that melts and refreezes, back and forth, back and forth,
back and forth into glass
when the snow comes, when the snow comes.

The Third Eye

I have an urge for cold, for the longer strings of clouds,
the salvage of the day as I work my way toward clarity.
In whose blood and hands these further complications?
I too have loved and my eyes flicker and my bones sing,
and when I look back, sometimes, my eyes, as they say,
are blind with seeing, with the winter sun that shines
on the last white houses as it sets, these odd frameworks
of the graveyards of those who failed in the full moon
as it rises, speechless and whistling, as if both it and I
tonight have hit a bouquet of rocks that foreshadow
the same dry footprints ahead as those behind.
I groan like a rope stretched tight in mid-winter,
write this all night in the deep bite of silence,
try to keep from the watching and the cold.

Natural Music

The air has grown warmer in this mid-month
and I was surprised to see a robin in the bush
on the wall above the patio this morning.
I wondered if it had forgotten how to fly,
the gathered cry of morning like a lost feather
in the wind, and I was not sure what the season was.
Tonight, as I stepped outside to see if the bird
was still there, I could see my breath against the dark
and knew that the bird had moved through the spill
of night to the stitch of nothing, the hour of darkness
falling, and that people in the houses around me slept
and never heard how the sky opened so slowly then,
how the horizon thrust itself away from
the quickening of paradise, how I stood with the shadow
of that bird then and sang again and again into the cold.
I don't know yet what's departed on the wind,
what's reflected in the silver light.
I start there.

Glass

Sometimes I think I can complete my accounting,
my history, this memoir, in three days,
especially when a fog of weariness creeps
across the floor of the room and drapes itself

slowly around my shoulders.
Would I be liberated then from all this,
no longer fight so hard, no longer be so afraid
to be hurt or abandoned as a child?
Will you at least leave some token behind,
even your body and blood ever fading?
Tonight, the stars sink without a sound
into seasoned winds, the moon dull as it lingers
in and out among the January clouds.
The year begins with a strange and brittle voice,
the tapping of a weary hand that weights
the day to vigil and faith.
I will wake at dawn, slip out of bed,
breathe slowly, stand witness like a piece
of cut glass to the brightening of the light.

Blue Stars

I see things sometimes with an immeasurable eye,
my hands spurred and raw from touching
the rough places on the moon.
Or sometimes I think it is all a faulty vision
and my eye is made of glass that can turn only inward
to reflect the light of shadows and blue stars.
It is hard, in mid-winter, to keep from descending
to loneliness, to take endless walks as the wind
blows you invisible, to want what you already have
but feel it deeper underground.
I close my eyes and want to touch the naked air
of this cold day, the old red bricks, the wooden stairs,
the hollows of space and time, your face.

The Name on the Window

I glanced across at her.
I glanced across the street.
There was a knock and the color drained from her face.
She said her days pass, one after another, like ghosts
she barely notices and there is no longer anything luminous
in her life at night.
I do not know how to keep the curtains, ethereal as glass
and red as drops of blood, from bruising the window.
The last sound she heard, she said, was like clenched fingers
that could not open.
She gives me a curious look, her eyes thick as old sticks,
and daylight crawls up the wall like unimaginable smoke.
I could not sleep last night she tells me, woke in fits
and starts, idled in the lurch, longed to write
my name on the window.
It's a story she says she did not write and does
not choose to tell: all that we were before we met,
the winter moon dancing in the impossible sky,
a choice of endings too perfect for this life.

Late Clouds

Everything was suddenly over

and we sit staring out the open window.
On days like this, when the clouds pass
and the air is too rich to breathe,
when the count is lost, when the sound outside
can mean anything and the cold birds sink
and dive for the last long sweep of light
and dust that ties your own dark wings,
seamless and widowed, behind your back .
Listen: in my white agony you are the nomadic night,
yesterday's ice and whirling snow, the full moon
singing on a round high wall.

The Shadows of Crows in Midwinter

When I saw him standing in the shadows of the hall
with no light on, only a vague tracing that filtered in
through the high window, I knew that we all will grow
confused when there is less and less time on our hands,
when we let loose the doors that close in just a moment
and lock only from the outside.
Catullus wrote that we are not the sun,
that when our brief light has set, night
is our one long everlasting sleep.
All this, I think today, has been too much
misleading promise, no vulnerable pane,
no courage misplaced.
I see the black silhouettes dive
in arabesque to their fall.
Outside, all around, in hurried reverse,
the shadows of crows.

Winter Gardens

This is what I say to myself as I move
the frozen stones, one by one, across the face
of the garden, in front of the house where
the windows all face west.
Blood hammered in my ears, a cloud passed
across the morning moon, a rankle of words
echoed as if in emptiness in my head.
The whole cloth of winter in a light dry wind
tossed across the closing line of blind circumstance
that yields the point as the hour slips.
The figures in the yard, oblique in the hollows
in the first light, may have fallen from heaven,
incapable of doubt in a sky once full of stars.
On the ground now, among the stones,
my legs grow heavy and cold.
I am past patience. I kiss your hand.
I would tell you I love you if the day thawed
and I could dig in the garden for such words.

Ascension

I pressed close and heard the far cry of a lost bird,
lightning rare in winter reflecting in the white
monotony and whistle of ice.

When the tree fell as the cold rain stopped,
I went outside to count its rings, circle after circle
dragged through the air and round enough,
I said, to enter heaven. I could feel the heat
ebbing from its branches and upturned roots
torn from their cool sleep. I breathed through
my mouth, with each breath tasted the blood-
streams in the air, the long pause between
revelation and night, reached for the lifelines
strung out from nowhere that catch and ebb.

Brooklyn in January
The full moon thaws to shadows
of tree branches on the hoarse snow.
Its thin light claws away the persistent tenderness
and drift of the dark across the sleepless hours.
The river slides under the Brooklyn Bridge
and lacks for nothing in the error of abiding sleep.
The world is what I make of it, here, wherever it passes,
a rope around my arm for safety and the scales
of pleasure in the outer corners of my hands.
Such mad strokes of wings between the tides,
passing warnings that caress the night.
Look down look down: liberty standing sterile
in the distance, the grandeur of the lights and wires,
the river too quick and shallow now to stagger or expose.
I sleep to the sound of your voice, whisper I'll love you
to the end of today. Choose this happiness beyond us,
lean forward: wharf piles draw the river to its end,
the iron arch of the moon patient in the wind,
the water wracked and silent below the invisible ice.

Or
Or: There were two or three of us sitting at the foot of the statue, the lines in our palms the same
deep cut since birth, and we watched the angel, trembling on a loosened rail, move stars across
the paling landscape.
Or: We heard the sound of lost innocence lingering up from underground, floating like the
string of an untied shoe to the comfort of its own extinction.
Or: We asked one another if the days were brighter or the nights, if these were the winds we
each felt and hoped for in these final noises of New York.
Or: We wondered, each as we focused on ourselves, if the faces we watch each day in every
mirror see the hands that brace themselves against the wall or if they all turn suddenly away
when they hear the statues in the streets at long last cheering.
Or: The city as the sun rises blurs in the mineral glass glazed with winter's lust, like me.

The House in the Distance
The light in the window of the house
in the distance, the dry touch of the old door
you scratched your initials on, cold sparks
gathering together again in the blue unraveling
of the year's last January sky, ash to ash
in the slow light of the old room.
Cold and blue, cold and blue
the light of the full moon rises out
of its little box and follows me like a nail

bending under accumulating ice.
I float past on a colorless wind, turn once
and once again, the snow from the light
of the house on the flat of my hand,
the wishbone of unencumbered cold.
This is how we arrive, as glass bleeds
in the windows, as moonlight leans in doorways
and memories stack flat in the clear night
under the cellar stairs. I slip up and out from
the shadows of our last address, whisper and burn.
I fall and fall away. I fall away.

Sleeping Alone
The bed is cold on Wednesday mornings
when I sleep alone and rain implores the windows,
hard as dark holes, to flush and fill with a grainy light.
It seems as if it was a century ago and I have spent
this time hoping to let my soul catch up, hand
itself back from the lugging of the gray-striped
void in the universe. I hope, on this wintry day,
that it is more than just an angel forever approaching
its maturity and come to take its last possession.
This is only half its virtue, left to right,
as it broods in the corners and lives on dirt.
A sick child rocking itself to sleep, a breath
that can hold nothing together, a life preserved in ice.
But I know it has nothing to do with you
or where you go as the day struggles.
I can see it, trapped with you in a slow mirror no one
has ever looked in, and I can't lift my arm high enough
in this small room to stop it from cracking.
It is the impulse of that long obscurity.
It is the gray eye watching the flames on your tongue.
It is that time of year.

Epiphany
The way her face looked in the early morning sunlight
as she turned toward me for a moment without knowing
that I had turned toward her holding the keys to the door.
The way her face looked in the shadows of the house
as wind transformed the shapes of the world.
The way her face looked when she lay down in the light of the moon with the ghosts
        that touched her under a cold glass bell.
The way her face looked in the weather of salvation, the huddle of eternity as the year
        staggered to its feet.
The way her face looked when I saw her later, flying skyward, and through the rustle of her
wings I knew she could not hear me, strapped to her reflection and calling her name out
        down below.
The way her face looked as she watched herself trickle
from the clouds like slow snow reborn against my skin, the short dreams of our hands.
We turned white together. We turned white.
We will what we will when we turn white.

Aubade

The low sound of thunder on the blank screen
of the sky tore a corner of the blanket of snow
last night, a small tin flame, like the hour of death,
in the tops of the trees, the moon sliding beneath
my feet as it clatters and bleeds.
I've waited a lifetime to see this, feel the infallibility
of my eye in the kingdom of ice and coils.
I talk to myself, shake with desire,
watch the constellations drag like coffins
through the clouds, each one a road sign
to a future I alone can name:
the crab, the two dogs, the cup, the lions,
the unicorn, the hunter, the lynx,
and so many others I have forgotten.
The wind wheezes and threads in a worrying drizzle.
Morning, in the distance, scales the small rocks.
The day is woven straw.
Inside, like a dark chain, the fire burns cool and low.
The perfect flight of the pure idea ends in the pallor
of a hollow wooden box.
A new life stands like an apparition in the silence of the window.
I hear glass breaking.

The Revenant

There are days when the windows
and doors of the whole world gradually open,
when daylight whistles in with the thaws
from the wide mouth of the river,
when the margins of the sky shift
with the changes of the season
and we labor together for revival.
I was afraid they would not come back,
sliding somewhere out there
to a more permanent fire,
but today once more black lines
of birds steal home in great circumference
to the treetops and bare yards of the north.
I saw them early this morning flying toward
the horizon, passing overhead like broad
dark leaves blown by a widowed wind.
Though the world lost its legs and ended
weeks ago, though nothing is truly mine
and my heart has broken a thousand times,
I shout out a welcome in my spare corner.
The shadows are quickening
and the day begins seductive and eternal.
I lift my arms in greeting like heavy wings.
I tremble in the gathering light.

The Thin Light of Winter

In the Land of Blue Snow
1.
       after Henrikas Nagys
We trace the child's face in the first snow.
My sister sleeps under wild raspberry branches.
Last night workmen spread light snow
on frozen ground white as my mother's hair.

We trace my brother's face in the first snow.
The guard's epileptic daughter crumbles
dry bread on the echoing ground.
We hear it falling as the wild clouds bleed.

Birds shrug moonlight from their frozen backs.
Beneath the ice rivers flow slowly to the sea.
My sister's doll sleeps under wild raspberry branches.
We trace my brother's cold face in the blue snow.

2.
There are no trees in the land of blue snow:
only the shadows of trees, the forgotten names of trees.

In the hall of cold mirrors dead fingers trace
the breath of silhouettes on dusty glass.

In the land of blue snow only words remain,
lines and letters drawn in cool ash and sand.

Look: above my face old snow is falling:
the sky so white, and the voices of black birds.

3.
A dog was barking outside
and the streets filled
with the slow orphans of wind.

Clouds swallowed the ghost light
of the sky, crumbling to coils
sharp as needles of ice.

The ransomed shadows of evening
framed her face, a black snag
of lightning on the horizon.

We hold our tongues, the earth's
white scar, and the cold breath
of snow recongregates all morning.

4.
We dig roots out from under half-buried rocks,
pull thorns from sorrowful water.
The sky is transformed to porcelain and black crystal,
unfaithful at last.

Weightless air splashed on blue snow, the insignificance
of night and the flash of late stars.

Solitude easy as the red moon outside the window, the promise
of clouds and a light wind from nowhere.

And I shake loose at the margins, unencumbered and free:
whisper, a flicker, a spark.

5.
This is not a trick of light but the cross of wild rails,
ice that sculls the hills in a gaze of slow air.

A membrane of many angles undeveloped
by feeling or time, the sky a dry wound,

the silence before this longing, this terrible sadness,
this slow unlocking of the cadenced night began

in the unanswered clarity of brilliant forms,
in the deepest blue of the coldest snow.

6.
When the time comes they'll bring you to a place like this,
to sleep as you have always slept, invisible and still,
after the long years have split the great meadow
and the city's streets have run away in all directions
and the space in which you wanted to live is filled.
The satisfactions of another year, dust on the sill,
the night like water and the enfolding light.
You have arrived at last and the blue snow scatters.
Tomorrow you will be different again. Try to remember
your name, take your turn at the window.

7.
The month gone, those sad marks,
the clarity of north wind
blue as the snow that rises to meet it
and the fire dances
between darkness and light,
makes a sound so thin
I kneel to find it.

8.
By midnight dreaming of trees and last year's apples flaked with snow.
The stillness in the gathered dark, healed wounds and imperfections,
feeling your absence with my own hands, the emptiness
that hangs like the cold ache of an old thread in the night wind.

The earth here follows you, unties the sorrows of your heart.
Turn your back, fly straight into the sun.
Don't be afraid of the last sounds, your face, small and low,
infinity tapping like blue snow on your closed eyes.

9.
I have considered such things often
in my oldest nights, the full moon shining
how we stood at the window
looking out at the snow,
how her fingers touched my hair.

It had more to do with snow than love,
the thread of something important,
the noises in the street, and if we spoke
it was in whispers and the room
disappeared and she sank to a sigh.

It was a simple thing. And when she left
I was caught between the earth and air.
I was both halves of myself: part water
part glass: the thin light of winter,
the fine dust of the year's last song.

10.
The place is forgotten now. While the snow fell,
slow and immeasurable, the moon mirrored
in the ice and the house so quiet as she slept,
the light and shade where other lovers played.

Taste the patient snow. Stop as the pale wind stirs.
The whole world will happen again, rising
out of itself for the last time as memories
and missed desires swing dark and away.

Forget these words, calm your fears, breathe deeply.
Hold the moment that opens before us:
in the weight of things, in the faint blue light
of the dream's last hour, life sings itself out to the end.

The Woman on the Bridge
1.
It is a long path of laid cinders and stones
curving past the small spaces between white trees.

Up ahead are the ripples and curls of a river
below a dark stone bridge.

Flurries of dust and loose dirt sift
in patterns on the stones of the road.

The horizon hangs low above the bridge
and its brown wooden railings and posts.

I see her from a distance, dressed in a short coat
and skirt the same color as the bridge.

She stands at the near end as I approach,
presses her face close, calls me by another name.

Something falls from the sky.
Time breaks.

The black flowers at the bottom
of the bridge suddenly blossom.

2.
Night has already fallen.
I light a lamp for her in the dark room
but she pushes me away.

I adapt without complaint to this new pattern.
I sleep fitfully
and when I wake my hands are cold.

Morning comes tapping at the window,
moves erratically from point to point
in the empty room.

3.
There seems to be time for all things,
time enough for everything,
even for the silence between us.

I rise and follow her across the yard
to the cinder and stone path that leads to the bridge.
I am aware of the vastness of the sky above me.

She holds out her hand to me
offering something, all feathers and bone,
a soul stirring its wings.

On the bridge I have no fear now.
If I fall into the air I know I will float away,
receding, separated, drifting.

4.
The hours pass in a flat hard place
without shadow or depth
and time is dry as paper.

This morning I do not know
if it began or did not begin
or the possibilities of abstraction.

The body grows silent
among the changing echoes
of what was.

The shifting light
of all that has disappeared
beyond the hope of what will come.

Perhaps in time
I will learn
to howl at the moon

watch birds
settle to roost
as light thickens on the bridge

skip over
whole days and nights
as if they did not happen.

Space decomposes and recomposes itself
before my eyes
as I move down the slope to the river.

5.
It was how the story ended:
sand already in the boy's mouth
settling in, claiming him

carrying him
through the shallows
into the darker depths,

part of his essence
not here but in the future
like a shadow cast before him,

the dark haze of hope
he can never catch
as his trembling at last subsides.

A fly settles on his cheek,
cleans itself,
circles and settles again.

6.
She asks me
why I live
in the green hills

I smile
I do not
answer
I am completely at peace

a blossom
floats past
on the current below

I tell her
there are worlds beyond this one
among the white stars

7.
A day must have passed,
must have intervened here,
something must have changed,

but I am wary
of such suppositions,
impatient with the flow of time.

Sunlight pours through the window
onto an empty bed.
The door is locked.

I help her undress
in the airless silence
of this place, my heart quickens

as her brown skirt falls to the floor,
a suspension, a moment
before the return of time.

Her body is mapped with the signs
that she is beyond her term,
eternal, thrashing about, transparent

struggling for air
in the faint turbulence
of the time that passes.

8.
It is time for what comes
out of the ashes to come.

Time for that which shows
through the flesh.

This is how the trap is laid,
how they are caught.

The dry earth soaks up
the blood of its creatures, never sated.

If this is my fate I'd rather be
a stick in an empty field.

On the far side of the bridge
something pale stands out against the sky.

It will be a difficult day,
a day for waiting.

9.
They have made a room without a window.
I cannot see but I remember how

morning after morning the day passes,
dusk falls, and then darkness comes.

Here, someone switches on the lights
and there are dissatisfied murmurs all around,

discontent at the dissolution of the membrane
between the world and the self inside.

I must have slept. When I opened my eyes
she was kneeling beside me, feeling under the quilt.

For a while I was nowhere, shook my head,
this is my hand, I say, this is the bed, this the floor,

my soul alert, darting, and in the morning
when she reemerged at the edge of my oblivion

swirls of mist floated past her, a dark speck
moving against the stillness of other dark specks,

embraced the bridge and floated away
with the spirits and wraiths,

the great beam of my vision illuminating
the helpless complicity of all who watched,

all they said to one another in this windowless room
in the closest dead of night.

Days and nights wheel past as the lights in the room
brighten to gray-green and then darken to black.

In a week or a month I will
have forgotten everything,

will look around intently and no longer know
who waits for me to step into the shadow.

10.
Heavy rain sheets over the edges
of the roof, swirls of water on the grass
and trees just visible through the window.

The earth returns into itself
and the leaves fall and the stars dip
low in the clouds on the horizon.

I think of you on the bridge, wound together
a thousand times, and feel the stirring
of the air as I call to you in the dark.

This is the grace of things to come,
the one sorrow I walk through in my sleep,
the shine I move toward as the wind shifts.

The rain is the only line drawn between us tonight.
The veil of grayness outside the window grows lighter.
Out ahead, the pale blue of farther skies.

11.
When time drifts like a heavy truth
across the bridge
and the sky comes down
and covers me completely

I am held by nothing and hold on
to nothing, see nothing inside of nothing,
sit bewildered like the man who wondered
all his life and discovered and then forgot

the hidden meaning of things
set loose in the landscapes of sheer earth
in moments of no importance
that spill themselves like dry leaves

and move from one stillness to another,
to the indecipherable taste
and bitter dust
of dry seasons kept from decay.

Revelation, intuition, inspiration:
it would be better to be an empty mind,
the dull and dimly lit, than to live
with the weariness of this uncertainty,

to be neither still nor in motion,
neither force nor will, not dream or guess,
but everything at once, the eternal now,
where nothing returns and nothing repeats,

searching for the metaphysics of the spirit
not the small realities of the body,
the swift-colored thing that passes
in canceled desires and the rising of the dead,

not knowing and not keeping,
dissolved to a drift of smoke
as the moon swings dark and away
and the sky withers and the ash falls.

I have considered such things often,
have fallen with the weight of things
everywhere and unobserved,
have understood how it all begins:

at night when the lights come on
and life changes its face
in every crevice and corner,
I see her in the distance on the bridge

breathing the last breath of dusk,
pointing with unmistakable clarity
to what we had come for as the wind shifts
and darkness invades the day.

12.
There is magic in this world
I'll stand where I'm standing now
here on the dark porch

The spirit moves forward
and the self persists
where the winds and waters meet

I stand outside myself
the finite in the infinite
under the rock at the white shore

I have seen what I have seen
the mind in the air
the swift tide of longing the clean tear

The joy of being
the sigh of the soul pale body
and the naked ease of myself

The word made word and flesh
thick waters dropped seed
the blue expression the whole of light

Where the river lies still
clear night telling who comes and goes
the breath's moment that moved on

Time folds and the sounds I hear
in this vulnerable place
tell of dust leaves ash idea revelation

13.
We let the day take us where it wants
like a slow shifting of the bridge.

Just beyond the gate
everything stays as it is.

The straight trees the curved sky
the slow falling rain.

Day after day
nothing repeats itself.

The window reflects a chair a lamp
a changing moon.

The end of it all weightless the sky the eye sees
the landscapes of the past it cannot find.

The light begins to thin the light we move toward
all dust and colorless moan.

We are the last to leave
after all the others have left.

We stand on the other side
whispering something.

We hear it gathering around us
disappearing calling us back.

14.
I dreamed of being lost and covered with leaves.

I woke up shouting, my throat full.
It was night again and I licked the mirror
into which I was staring clean.
White light reflected in shards of glass
on all sides and in a minute all was done.

I have gone over that moment a thousand times
in my mind, have thought about it for a thousand moments:
it was a sadness, a pillar of smoke dry as the world
around my neck, a disturbance of the soul,
all lightness gone, the desperate silence of a deserted house,
and I understood that I am the last of my kind,
living in the old way, drifting through time:
even if I lay low and breathe quietly
they'll hear my heart beating, clenching
and unclenching like a stranger's fist in my chest.

I no longer know what to do with my face.
The sun had set, the wind began to bite,
a half moon was coming through the clouds.
I took the old road, waving my arms,
and inside my head I heard the green music.

No one is forgotten.
In a moment of astonishment
I tumbled into the cauldron of history
and saw the burned posts of the bridge,
the vast airiness of space between heaven
and the green lines of the river,
the outlines of the words of love
she mouthed to me soundlessly there.
I felt the shame of private knowledge,
the moral dimension of my plight.

I am drowning,
arguing with cold clarity
for all that is unheard,
gripping the bars of the gate.

I listened
and nodded
and dreamed,
shivering with cold,
and my fingers
would not
straighten.
Something has fallen on me.
I crept away, touching the silence
of airless places, was pulled this way
and that by the shrunken tug of the moon,
leaped and groaned at the far edges
of the sky, watched patterns
of chaos manifest themselves
as moments of transfiguration.

I welcomed that dissolution,
pondered its sounds.
Night pushed a stick into my mouth,
left its thin black mark on everything.

Tomorrow will be a new day.
Tomorrow will not be today.
Today I am so tired that I reel on my feet,
sob from the heart like a frightened child.

I am hollow:
unthinking, inarticulate, without imagination:
I come to speak but have nothing to say:
today is the day but today has passed:
how will I know how I lived in this place, in this time:
swept over the brink, a cold wind blowing,
rain falling on barren soil.

An hour must have passed
or the blink of an eye:
events overtook me:
the spark flickered and lost itself at once.
I followed the reflected light,
crystalline and bloodless,
and gripped the earth to steady myself.

The thought began to float away but I clung to it:
there will be another time, and if not, then I don't mind:
I am a blind man dancing, as if in another country,
struggling for a foothold in unfamiliar sand.

All my life I waited for someone to call to in the dark.
I see them I call out here here I am here.

They skulk in the open, stand in a circle around me,
don't know what to say or do.

I am, to some or to many, the beast
that stares out from behind the gate
or from across the bridge,
an unborn laboring creature,
the obscurest of the obscure.
I whisper and tumble free as the odor of smoke.
I stumble and fall, reach out a slow hand,
wince at the sharpness of the light.

The fear of the past day has lost its tense.
I will defend the cause of justice,
the precious safety of the fragile and the liquid-eyed,
will forever shake off the weight
of the resentful gazes that rest on me,
will say my part, will understand how to speak of this.

God's time is not our time.
I dream but I don't think
I dream of God
or that God dreams of me.
I dream that there is water everywhere,
paths that lead nowhere:
holy ground:
resurrection from the earth:
the soul emerging, a creature of air:
truth frozen in its tracks,
the future disguised
in the name of some present abstraction.

The wind dropped, the air was clear.
The silence was so dense, there was nowhere to hide,
and the ground sighed as my body returned
not to the great cycle but to the jagged time
of rise and fall, of start and finish, of beginning and end.
Time stopped and then started again.
I did not want to be drawn away,
struggling and lost, gesturing from horizon to horizon
in joy or lamentation, living between reason and truth
in a secret life I do not see or understand,
a spirit invisible, but the vision faded
and the dust came and the leaves.

15.
Tomorrow
when the war ends
when the moon seeps like dust
through the crack in the door
and draws the fictions of our souls

Tomorrow
when we hang our lives

in the attics of old houses
and fragments of time
are like a knocking on the wall

Tomorrow
when we see dead faces
in the mirror on the pillow
and feel the brevity of our days
in the window and water below

Tomorrow
when we repeat the sounds
of the letters of our names
and touch the thinnest edge
of the voice of God

Tomorrow
when the haze in me lifts
when every hour is mine
and the song of the infinite
is like a silence of the heart

I will empty the drawers
undress bathe breathe go out
sketch the anguish of regret
redeem myself feel the pain of separation
complain softly rise up float across the skin of the earth
feel the scales thicken fan my wings
pause stare out into the distance
render myself into words
let go of myself let go of you
be stunned astounded free of feeling
be turned to stone see the long night ahead
sleep dream wake wait until tomorrow

16.
That year there was no spring.
After winter came winter.

The air grows dry and light
by late December as the heaviness of fall
slips away into the folding corners of the sky.

The day passes uneasily, the simplicity
of the moment passes, and time flows
like a snapped twig on the current under the bridge.

I am whole inside. I speak a language
of distance and perspective, though I have
no words to explain why my bones grow cold.

I can run away, emptied of secrets, utter
my life in words no one else understands,
or sit in the corner with my mouth shut.

I am beyond name and form,
stillness and movement together,
and when I see God I will be very small.

It is a confession I am making here:
I am asleep with no sense of time
and dream that the moment of waking is at hand.

The flow has ceased. Winter is coming again.
A cold wind whistles across the bridge.
A thin sheet of ice covers my face.

17.
The yard filled with smoke and then
the rooms of her house. I go outside.
Time slows, the horizon lifts.
The trees are indistinct black smudges
against the enveloping gray.

I close my eyes, feel my way inside
with the fingers of my hand. Life is
ordinary again. She sits in the corner
weeping but does not see me,
pale as old bones in dry light.

I lay my head on my arms. Night filters
through the window: embers of trees and
burned grass without substance or form.
The future invades my mouth, quivers
like the empty smell of smoke in the room.

There was a long silence. She says she is
a drop of water, a colorless bird, a piece of glass,
a cry in the dark, flesh of my own flesh,
and asks me to give her my fingers, one each day,
and let her stretch her life across to the far shore.

I will never be warm, I think, I will never be warm,
the thought coming and going like a wild piercing
of the smoke, blood and earth, a sudden stirring
of life in the womb. In an instant I am gone
and in another I am back again, facing the wall.

18.
There was a smell of wet ashes in the air.
I cross to the window. It was nearly dark.

The world outside was blackened with burning,
moonlight and briny ice. Today is the day.

I am standing by the river, waiting for someone
to show me the way across. Truth without flesh.

The month is gone and the day. A woman's cycle.
I am standing by the window. It is nearly dark.

There is no one here. I am already across the water and home.
I was bowed under the weight of the day. I am lost.

I kept my vigil for a day and night. It was nearly dark.
I returned to the riverbed. The flames flow from me.

They burned the thought of something of water that stands and runs.
Before this longing the flames in one small fire, the eyes vague.

I have fallen and she catches me. Tense, resistant, hard.
Now there is nothing to hold her. After a while I was still.

The smoke dissolved and the heavens opened and the light
burns down penetrating and sharp. My voice tastes like wet ashes.

I yield to this contagion. The ghosts are gone. It was nearly dark.
They fall and are washed away before they cross. I howled at the moon.

19.
All things are possible at the same time
everything from all sides
and nothing needs to be done.
I have seen all things.
I have witnessed nothing.
I have been around every corner.
I have been inside every wall.
I have failed in everything, in nothing.
I have returned from everywhere.
I have loved everyone, and hated.
I have seen my face in all faces.
I look at life passing by.
I am blind and deaf.
I see and hear everything.
I wait for what I do not know.
I am beginning to know myself.
I divide what I know, everything that exists, exists.
I am now and everything I never will be.
I am living right now.
I walk by, everything's hidden in the night that remains.
I lie down in the grass.
I am the landscape, the sky and air.
I think about nothing.
I speak I stop seeing her I write.
I forget myself.
I am the bridge, I am the sky, the first and final star.
I pick the black blossoms stirring my wings.
I am naked and plunge into the water.
I feel the edges of the world.

20.
Below the root
the water knows my name

its delicate hesitations
drained dry as seasons
drift and go

cold winter
salt and flesh
and the river falls
running down
and standing still
against the panes
of the wind

invisible at night
splashing the lunar sky
its glide breaking
the erratic ice

between the surface
and the slate-colored bottom
the shapes
that cannot be seen
fresh weavings
of earth and air
over the snow at night
and the ghosts of the heart
in the ripening light

Nocturne
1.

    after Nijole Miliauskaite

I know a place where when you
brush your foot across the sand
the sand moans sadly
as if weeping

sometimes
a woman appears there, dressed in black
with eyes emptied of tears

wind carries her across the sand
like the shadow of a cloud

blows through her hair forever

2.
Night and a weightless moon
washed cold and blue-white:
to lie naked in the sand,
hear the silence above the sunken tree,
rise and fall in the long moment,
slip through the slide and ache of your heart
and feel the slow pulse in the hand of God
as it touches your face in the lingering hour.

3.
It was the only way it could be known
the secret when the world began,
the centuries of dust, small things
sleeping forever in the earth,
the dry road, the shattered glass,
the withered white of a single day.

And everything then seemed a single day
the pain she felt, life on all fours,
a wrinkle in the sand, as the old men say,
dark collisions in the clouds, the votive stone
in the ground crying to come up
and out the way her soul might rise.

4.
Silence on your eyelids, clouds on the fragile face of the day.
Old roses in late September, petals falling and falling.
The night's slow song, the moon spread across the cold of morning.
The moment of turning, become another thing, as the ground clears
and the roots climb. Your grief that day was something like this,
your prayer rising to heaven, sand the color of nothing
sifting through your hand as it clenches and unfolds.

5.
I stand by a low wall
indifferent to the stars
and watch all night.
She passes by like a thing
thrown into the air,
a little square
of fading black cloth.
In another world then
as now, the lapse of time
as I look toward morning
and see salvation.
Overhead,
the light of oncoming rain,
the sky fragrant and close.

Two Seasons in the Orchard
1.
So little remains at the center of things as day settles
into a corner of the sky letting go of its colors:
a small enclosing darkness filled with uncertain shapes,
a pale light that unexpectedly brushes the water,
a sudden memory of thin clouds scudding east
in the late summer night and the look
in your eyes when a vein of blue skimmed the pond
and I touched you for the first time, damp
with the cool smells of apples in this sweet orchard grass.
That memory comes and goes with slant of light
the color of dry leaves that holds the afternoon like
a meditative hand before sheeting to dusk. Its shadows

simmer soft as the grayness that clings to the edges of water.
This night, low clouds pass across the pond
with the nesting birds, weaving their grizzled hues
along the horizon, and the cadence of the season
floats blank and troubled on a rising wind.

2.
Time drifts like water on drying glass and leaf
by leaf the trees chip themselves to winter.
Light falls to carved shadows delicate as the air
before sunset, fixing to perfect lines on the water.
Night comes in clouds tangled as soft roots
that loosen above apple trees rubbed to autumn
and late flowers hiss and bloom unexpectedly in the dark.
These are the risks we are born into,
possibilities that flutter to uncertainty in the night air
like birds lifting from the weeds in sudden flight
and spilling to broken circles across the dimming sky.
The moon rises sheer and gray as a shiver
of recognition and the image of your face pressed
in the grass beneath these trees washes through
the brown weeds around me with the sound of wings,
scattering into the distance like brittle leaves
or dust caught in a chill confusion of wind.

This Morning
This morning, the house rests in the mountain's sharp circle.
We are overshadowed by it, its green peak damp and fresh,
one face in the sunlight, one washed in shade.
I set out to find that place, walk across pastures
where leaves from the past settle through clouds
and mist to the kindness and beauty of rain.
This morning, the air sings with winter soon to come,
another November, another year, and life moves suddenly
away on every side. This morning, there is light in the earth
and in the stillness of words I want you to say, in the things we
have lost and the promises we kept. This morning.
Day shifts to afternoon along the edges of the far rocks.
In the quiet fields at the foot of these hills,
in the slow water of the river, the wild geese have arrived.

Salt

mano vaizduote pakele mane nuo zemes,
bet ne dangun lig dievu

Salt
1.
Salt flowers on a cast iron balcony,
the windswept weeks when the clouds
spin a dark fire

Salt flowers among the flashes of war,
the night damp and the beds around us
empty and cold

Salt flowers below bare trees in the half season,
the flood waters rising beneath
their black whisperings

Salt flowers over blue flames and ashes,
the echoes of my heart where it beats
against the hours

Salt flowers

Salt flowers Salt flowers Salt flowers

.   .   .

2.
The voices stopped too soon.
The words I hear are not shouted down
from the sky but come at night
like frost on the grass, like salt
that dries on sea rocks in the air
that remains when the tide goes out.
How hard is it to believe this,
tie up loose ends, understand the laws
of the universe, feel the ecstasy
that radiates from the tips of the fingers
and makes the windows gleam?
Explanations do not interest me,
the tumult of discovered remains,
names that can be crossed off a list.
I hunch my shoulders and wait,
the instant frozen and abstracted.
The stairs creak, there is silence.

3.
The water is married to the stone.
The air is brittle.
Old husks make new designs in the far fields.

My soul is caught in a cage of green wind.
It slides across the blue, falling endlessly as the rain falls.

In the city of salt the eyes look up.
I was gone when she opened the door,
the white light flickering.
We exchange addresses and I answer them
in words they understand.
Something grazes my cheek.
I put my finger on the pain you feel, size up the dark.

You ask me to remember all this, to hunch down,
unencumbered, run bare fingers through these landscapes,

move closer to the cold glow of your flames.
But I remember little as far as names go.
In the round night I run back to myself, duck and hide.

4.
The walls of the house peel away.
The days are numbered.
Dust between the fingers,
darkness between the lines,
a tired voice in the air.

I open the roof, see nothing whole,
watch the door to heaven close.

You can't get rid of the skin you are stuck in,
the body unexpectedly heavy, the smell
of the salt of the earth in your clothes and hair.

At a time like this it's best to keep quiet,
belong to no one, wake alone, fall slowly
through the boards of the floor like old snow.

The current slides: I know it's so.

5.
This is how I spend my days.
Whatever it is I long for
does not come or comes in such a way
that I do not recognize or understand it.

An emptiness, a shell, a thin crust
of ice on still water.

I put my hands on her shoulders,
slip my fingers under the neck of her dress,
touch her soft white skin,
call her name
or the name of some other.
I close my eyes,
probe the sore place
in her mouth
with my tongue,
taste salt and blood.

6.
When the moon is dark
and the night is still
I lie for a moment
looking up into the blackness
and then slide back
into the dream
the wind pours dust on us
I carry her
in my arms across my shoulders

endlessly though there is no hope
of reaching the other side
for either of us
in the hour before dawn
I feel the chill of the earth
enter my bones
I am conscious of my thirst
tell myself to wake up
before we both become skeletons
uncovered years later by the wind
that pours dust on us
she clutches my arms
we do not speak
I smell the salt
of her skin hear the blood
in my veins the sound
the heart makes in its
own darkness when
the dream crawls out
and dwindles
an enigma drained of secrets
an empty soul
carried in the arms
across the shoulders
when there is no hope
of reaching the other side
and the moon is dark
and the night is still

7.
Do you understand? Do you understand now?
How tedious these confessions, these demands.
Something lifts inside me when you ask
a veil of grayness, a curtain, a cloud
then dissolves into the day like salt
stirred into boiling water.
Everything was for nothing then:
there was a sound of breaking glass, then a long
stunned silence, then the sound of her voice
low and breathless as the damp earth,
like a body risen from the dead,
wet, ignorant and blind.
That is the story I choose
or the one that has chosen me,
the place I start or the place I stop,
the place where I join the world
or the place where I leave it.
I look at them and they look back.
There is no time to lose.
Do you understand now? Do you understand?

8.
The white bellies of fish gleam
in the shop windows

I do not wish to be at the center
of the world only a small part of it

passing the days in the midst of a beauty
that protects me from the knowledge that one day we all die

so my art cannot be the art of memory
but seduction, the hunger of the wind

not collected lists of things
but the landscape brought down to zero

the dry light the smell of leaves in an old room
the reliability of darkness the constancy of salt

and afterwards in the frenzy of shadows
in a time heavy as bones

I will be the one who knows
that only the dead can be born again

that the wind continues on its way
beyond the autumn screen

that the future hangs like fog
in the cold street as we pass by

and gleams white as the bellies of fish
in the shop windows

9.
Your body stretched out quietly
in the cold air of the winter room
smells like dust and salt.

You scratch the bed linens
with your fingernail
writing something
on the white sheets
a mark that cannot be deciphered,
a sign impossible to read,
a word that cannot be translated
into any language I know.

You turn your face to me and point
and I understand that at a time like this
we can speak only for ourselves.

10.
A landscape empty on both sides,
heavy rain in the hour before dawn.
Creatures cast up by the sea
stalled on the sands, dusted here
and there with dried salt.

To be turned once again to water,
tears not of sorrow but of sadness,
imagine them passing: here light there dark
against the pale blue of the sky.

In this imaginary country
time is the only durable flesh
and lovers flow together like water.

In this imaginary country

My heart aches to think about it.

11.
A minute and all is done:
grieve if you like, grief is the lost moment,
the salt in the wound.

I sit down to rest, the front door
is open, the broken glass
sharp as a woman's cry in the dark.

I am pushed toward it, following
the faint yellow glow
of all my life has come to.

It's a hard task but I am learning:
breath against breath,
the wedge of light scratched on the wall.

12.
salt is regret, the forgotten, the invisible grief
the abandoned, the long past, the hand
that bleeds on the margin of the page, the holiness
of birth and death, flesh and the word, the rocks that swell
with salvation, seeds and scattering, the moon that hangs
above the earth like a cold heart, invisible and breathless
in a crucible of air, the new dark, gatherings of ice
and dust, night drafts and dirt, desire and ghosts
in the walls, crosswinds and waters, the unspeakable ebb
and surge of our lives, another year another year,
the far edge, the sad tunes, the burn that lights the road home
to the white sky the white sky the white sky

13.
The woods, the pond from the farm
in deep daylight.

The roots of the trees starting to take hold
inside of us.

I wait for the wind, body moving,
feathers dancing on stone.

A moth, white and dry as salt,
settles unexpectedly on the door.

Hold me! Keep my movements close
as I shake loose in the ghostly passage!

14.
We walk hard up from the river across the first gray hush
of dusk

      the fire turns and the salt of the earth

Raising up and setting down in the blue eclipses
of the sky

      in some other life, the great spaces

Clear night, the first stars low fire in the backlit net
of clouds
our love is ghost light, bright water

An easing of the spirit, bare hand and invisible seed
beneath the earth

      fine dust, white faces rising on the hill

And all is self, born of the marrow, the nothingness of light
that cuts to the sea

      there are bodies all around dancing in the wind
      and everything is salt everything fire

15.
In the other world
I have dreams but do not sleep,
press my lips against hers
as she stiffens and endures.

In the other world
they tip me into a hole
and say prayers, bitter as salt,
to white clouds that glower on the road.

In the other world
I flail for the comfort of bodies,
the irreducible pleasure
and crouch of earlier days.

In the other world
I know I am something else.
In the other world
I am something else.

16.
Nothing's wrong

nothing's happening
the shadows freeze
the last tear turns to ice on her cheek
someone's breath moves across my face
the old scars waken
the air bleeds where it touches my skin
and all this time
the needle's eye is a white grain of salt
the hand of the stopped clock
the sound of snow at the gate
the expiration of the light

17.
I am awake I am not awake
it was like this before
I am beginning again
I do not fear the dead
those who do not exist
those who burn before the stars fall listen
listen as they grow fainter
watch them pass like water
into dry ground
remember shut the door at day's end
before the rain begins
before you are caught and held again
in this world remember
you are not the name but the hour
not the hour but the hunger
not the hunger but the night
the edges of things
the lightness of being it is me
and always was it is me
and always I move among them
a shadow a bird's cry a light
I recognize their hunger
their voices in my mouth
they have forgotten who they are
they remember who is forgotten
they answer without moving
they touch the faces in the sky
they taste the climb of silence
the cold salt of their lives

18.
I lift the four dead birds
their feet a tangle of claws
a drop of blood like a pearl of red salt
at the tip of the beak of one of the sparrows.

The funnel of the sky turns a darker blue
and the stars emerge for a moment
before the clouds wash across and cover them
and the place I sit once again becomes hard and dark.

Of all the places in the world
only I know where I am.

If I cut my hand the blood would seep dry
the skin would stiffen and contract.

I would become small as a dead bird
shrivel in the wind in a day
be preserved unexpected and whole.

I do not want white but black
not wet but dry
not light but dark
not water but salt.

19.
I ask a question of salt
I get a white answer

I renounce myself
for the deepest secrets of love

avoid the falling of dust
the night the solitude the cold

the overwhelming voices
the fading letters
the figures of speech
theories of language
ideas that freeze water
the minutes of the day
gaunt and pale
bones brittle in rainy weather

I consider the darkness
the light
that wakes in fear

I think about the angels
that fly with my lover
about a god made of salt

who comes like blue flame
in the nights that follow days
in the days that follow nights

20.
The water is asleep when I wake.
The circle beneath the earth,
black ribbons and the dust
that never settles, the shine
the water moves to in its dreams,
the streams of air that seep
through my heart and pool

in the black leaves, the hollow
through which the blood flows,
the slow rise through
the trick of light
that sculls across the surface
of sleeping water.
It was a blindness,
the cold source of stump and bone,
clear night in the black fields,
birds jumping at the stars.
Here on the white plain
under the white sky,
far from the silent water of the
one sea, salt washes from the mouths
of weary gods, their old shadows
everywhere, lowered and fixed
in the clay like a message
locked in frozen breath,
wakening for a moment
ahead of us and then
vanishing because of something
I remember, the lost son,
while my body hangs above
the water of nothingness,
the dry threads of desire
knit no hope of change,
and the river of heaven
watches the night.

Through the Window: Dark Figures and A Solitary Red Bird in the Center of the City in Winter
An empty square.

The whole city white.

I wake, cold.

The woman alongside sleeps
curled into a ball.

I can't shake off this feeling.

I open the curtains.

Outside, dark figures.

I call to them.

A sheet of ice covers my mouth.

I call to them.

They dissolve into the air.

These are brittle days.

Around the corner, unfamiliar people.

Hollow voices echo.

Night burns in the distance.

I spend the time that remains
touching her thighs
and when she wakes, she mine.

Snow falls.

Above the city, a solitary red bird
with dissolved dark figures in the air.

The End of the Day
At the window, I make it out the best I can:
the red flare of shadows as the day drains,
the slow wakening of night among the roots

in darkness and rain, the moon,
orange and blank, scouring the slow drift south
of clouds the shape of dark birds.

The month is nearly gone and the world out of focus.
I think of you and do not know which ending
is right: darkness and light darkness and light.

It happened, I remember, it must have happened,
it is like a fog, everywhere and nowhere, a suspension,
a vision or dream, a private space in the heart,

some deeper grief I could not bear,
an impending form and then gone again,
great wings rising and falling in white water.

I give myself back to the ordinary, the light diffuse,
my own ghosts turning in the wind,
and listen to the dust falling inside the walls.

The Fifth Wind
1.
The second week of June. Green leaves in a blue wind,
the grass warm, bees and blossoming plum trees, dogwood.
I open the door. Last fall's apples on the table,
the bed made, candles the color of new bone alongside,
all the poor furniture, dry flowers in an old pot,
a tattered dishcloth draped on a chair,
the unwavering mirror, shadow everywhere and shade,
memories strewn across the rooms like old clothes.
All these lives, the world brought back to innocence,
the form and grain of the morning light.
Now I understand: the wind blows, the door shuts twice.

2.
Whose face comes and goes at the window?
The ghosts in the attic pooled like black leaves
against the walls by the wind,
here to watch me, and lights and lights:
unburdened and borne away
something out there on the other side of the glass
caught in the shadow of its own sorrow,
the husk of its own death and all that followed
wrapped around the darkening blues of the air,
the great distances it must cross, one absence at a time,
rise gradually on the long long waters, the lost road home.

3.
The news arrives from nowhere
full of the east wind and anxious for nothing
on its way out to the far edge of the sky
a wind with many doors
a wind that digs deep across the red earth
a wind that makes me nothing,
green music, the moon down,
the grass whistling with the dogs,
all the beauty there is, dust and the last sound.
Now there is no one here, only you.
 I will come back as another name.

4.
God's transparent hand bears me up,
rises and falls back
on my shoulder: draped in white at the window.
Perhaps night has not yet begun to fall
under the great eye of heaven,
the moon cinder and howl at the border of the world.
Perhaps there is salvation to be found
in the core of this silence before morning rises.
At the window I am naked as a blossom
in a cold wind, not knowing what gestures to make,
a bundle of grief, wet wings, secret and light.

5.
They are all here already, cast up at our feet,
the taste of salt and rain, the odor of stone,
the touch of steel and blood taken deep by the wind.
Already there is the road ahead, signs nailed
to the columns of the dark porch, and voices calling me home.
She is here too, unfaithful and cold, brought back
piece by piece, a last sigh, the seed planted
just deep enough, the color of nothing, circles
and scratches on the floor. I am the last to know.
The nights press down and sing and set like dust
in the grass as black moths gather at the door.

The White City
1.
We have sold our shadows in the grim

game's short flutters and whirls.
The winter's black and blue tints
written in indelible ink.
All those who screamed there
holding the inconsolable mirror.
Dullness of sight and shortness of breath
in the hour of judgment.
Bodies pressed together hands
on faces in unfamiliar laps.
The bullet and drum
inarticulate instructions for survivors.
Patterns of skirts and blouses the laws
of genetics infinite and bitter.
She sleeps entwined with her children
helpless enthusiastic.
White claws coal and the days
falling out of borrowed pockets.
Disorder addresses smoke signals
signs of speech and umbrellas.
Whiskey. The slow uncertain song
in the hollows of veins.
I cover the windows protect figures of stone
from the wounds of wind and rain.
The expectations of first love
flame in cold ash.
A single summer day
landslides and volcanic eruptions.
Water cold in the dry river beds
no wisdom no green.
A white banner of dust
delegates of war a gray insoluble slide.
Old doors the children's hour
in the unfathomable room.
Tell me something
I'll count out the hours for you.
The ghost of blind elation
breathless in the great Nothing.
Like God but he won't allow it
listen someone's coming.
Bread moments of comfort
the sighs of branches in random places.
Barbed wire in the new landscapes
the sudden silence of prisoners.
The spirit declines, remembering the dead woman,
terrible and stunned as the blind.
The firm contagion of these things
the white image the light of the white city.

2.
I cried out spindled in lung and bone
deep as the night sky.
Your white face marked
by a line of sudden blood.
The white dust sheet gauze

in the darkness and marrow of light.
These lives that unfold
behind glass windows.
Hooked tight wild-eyed
the blood in the wheel.
The precise dryness
of the hand that feels the pain.
Sight drained in the dry corners
and stumps of memory.
Transparent figures old roads lights out
the zero of a stranger's death.
The scenes dissolve into explanations
collusions with no place no name.
The echoes of passion shining
new mouths new fingers.
Bodies that fit badly
lasting flesh the soul vivid and dense.
Love stiff as new clothes
chance meetings the changing pulse.
Going out and coming back
sentiments arranged inch by inch.
Lines under the eyes the body
suddenly heavy the lie in the throat.
The taste of the world
the hand pointing the empty space between.
No one leaves no one speaks
the bones of the wind rattle against the house.
A woman in white at the window
doors open to heaven.
I touch her shoulders
a strange map on the bed air to float on.
The same questions the white of the eye
the night thick and deep.
White steps these sad marks
on the water tongues in the wind.
The edge of the white city
midnight the full moon the red grain of night.
No sound the color of nothing the gray
of what keeps passing.
The worm in the belt of stars the old address
above the rooftops.
Ash and cloud in the sky rising and falling
drained to flesh made word.

Rain in Late November
1.
When I shiver with cold or fear
or tremble suddenly in the gray
of early morning, perhaps I am being called
out of my body, in a rain of light,
to huddle in an empty field
as the horizon lifts, a brittle creature,
all dust and air, dry wings sighing,

while the skies open, and the cloud arcs,
and the great white glares down.

2.
The one note that strikes the ear:
the soul ready for further flight,
some deeper and unchanging form
shaking loose its ascent into
the final reaches, the cold trails
of space, where the ghosts of love
loom and fear of my own death pulls me
back from the edge. Something broke
inside me when you left, a silence fell.

3.
It was something I no longer remember.
I am falling, I say out loud,
I am falling, floating without end
on the dark shine of water,
drifting through time, eyes closed,
the skin transparent, bones imprecise,
passing through the curtain of light.
And in the afternoon the sky turned
above the empty sea, the rains came.

My Uncle's Watch
1.
he arrived after the war with his parents brothers sister
leaving behind the youngest in the Virbalis cemetery
dragging from camp to harbor to converted military ship
a half-empty wooden box nailed together from barracks boards
tied with an old stolen German rope
and everywhere they turned all around unseen unfamiliar people

2.
there was he knew there was people said there was gold in the streets here

3.
they led like melting steel
to the foundry where he found the only job offered
and worked and worked

4.
he wore a raincoat tied
with a cloth belt at the waist
on Sundays
the future an eternal crease
across his shoulders

5.
it was all his own fault
his mother told him
again and again
everything stays as it is

6.
as it should be for him she said
all that he deserved
part of the family of dust

7.
or not at all or not at all

8.
some evenings
he would sit by the window
watching the neighbor's dog
licking the moon in a puddle
left by an unexpected rain

9.
sit silently by the window
tense as a rope stretched in the cold air
and dream he'd go back someday
dispel the constant darkness
of all that had disappeared

10.
but work in the foundry bought him
things he'd never had or imagined having
a used car a gold-plated watch
a well-made suit polished leather shoes

11.
and perhaps someday
he'd wake up
and have enough
a family of his own

12.
a woman he could sing to in the evenings
sitting quietly by the window
    doesn't anyone hear it but me?

13.
he would bring his mother shopping
to the old Lithuanian store in the center of town
and on the way home bring me a bar of chocolate
and I came out from hiding
among the pots a strange lonely child
some would say five years old my uncle's son

14.
out from behind all this groping in the dust
out of the darkness I know
I made and from which he called me
whenever he came
to a place where everything was real
and bright where everything rises

15.
these shadows don't fade

16.
he died late one Saturday night in April
when the car he was riding in skidded
in unexpected puddles of rain
the first in our family in this new land free now
withdrawing quietly from those moments of welcome and grace

17.
my father told me he heard
their mother wailing from the street
standing outside her door
hands clasped for the last time
when they came to tell her the sad news

18.
all this day I recall something

19.
I was not at his grave
rain tapping on his coffin
but have begun to wear his watch

20.
more than twice his age now
nephew become uncle
how will this passage
of our lives be told now
rising and falling and rising again

21.
we can't get back to what was
walk again among the veiled furniture
reorganize memories
the color of nothing
like old photographs
no one wants to see any more

22.
it's quiet in the room
quiet outside
the watch ticks quickly
through the night
the sound of things to come
the place we dream in
all night long and half the next day

23.
there's something I still want to say
something in words he'll understand
late in the afternoon
the lights just coming on

24.
I let the wind speak
it tells us
what we will know
when the time comes

Epiphany
All the lives that inhabit me come suddenly
flying out to a single sound.

The sea cannot hold me,
the earth or the sky.

I rise out of myself and lie down with you,
the moon a wafer of light on my tongue.

And everything here comes all at once.
And everything here is desire.

Midwinter's Roses
The snow falls, white as the cold,
and we kiss as the slow high walls waken.

*

Outside the window, a hush in the air
still and old as fading paint.

*

The clock keeps striking one in the center
of the city, the shadows deepening.

*

The streets are empty as far as the eye
can see, baring their layers and veins.

*

Your touch is like icicles under my skin,
the whine of wires in the chill of the winter moon.

*

Half my life ago:

*

I say my first word, my first confession:
now all I want are a few minutes to finish what I am saying.

*

The flowers are colored and numbered,
the black ice under my feet the end of the past.

*

I touch your hand, press hard, leave no mark
or scar on the cold slide of your skin.

*

A white self helps me up and I begin again.
I look up and see my face, the light of myself.

*

What I love is near at hand when the wind sighs
and I think of roses roses roses.

Reflections in God's Mirror

1.
These are the edges erased by night,
the fragile face of the day,
the shifting view of what was.

The things that happen outside,
among the distant trees,
wind in a cage the long bite of the air.

This is the absence the fingers feel,
the place that keeps slipping away
across railroad crossings, the chairs rearranged.

Each error, each turn in the road,
comforting flesh, the space you once filled
among the reflections in God's mirror.

This is an empty bed an old kettle whistling
whose meaning I saw too late
in the white of the eye behind red leaves.

Laughter and the last hard breath
words lost in the dark burning year after year
and nothing happens white numbers.

And you've arrived at last blood in the moon
scratching away uninterrupted
no one noticing the noise of the glass.

Give yourself time wait for everything here
the earth is a wound the windows wet
the roots a flicker of light burrowing down.

I am not one of a kind
I appeal to no one to all
I point my finger at what I was at what I still am

2.
Go and steal it
Take the house and close the doors
Cover the windows leave us
Night settles down
There's nothing to hear
Eat and drink in silence
Hollow your heart in the dark room
Open your wings
Come in at last out of the rain

3.
What I don't know let me say
What I can't see let me do
Let me fly on my own breath
Let me shed my skin
Let me hide in the whirlpool of stars
Let me lift the light of the sun
Let the waves of the bright sea wash over me
Let the moon grind its bones against me
Let the sky draw up
Let the passing song of eternity pass

4.
When I stop I am alone

I am in the old room

I am where the candle flames
in the dark hours
before the stars fall and the void wakes
where the cold voice in its sad code
asks for breath and the face remains
in the sorrow of broken glass

where the dry thread unrolls from the stalks
of my fingers and old mothers knit
the last crosshairs of my dreams

where half-parsed prayers rise up to heaven
stepping down from the reprieve of sky
to the raw chill of mud and stone

. . . half-bridge cracked light
unclarified breath unencumbered night. . .
the loss of form the slip of smoke
waist deep in the silt of memory
the odds and ends of past lives . . .

leave me retrace your steps leave me
here alone between what I am
and what you have made me

open the windows turn off the lights

listen to how dust moans
in a wedge of the wind
how night flowers blossom
as time's fevers fall and fall

5.
So many names,
the night like snow,
the eyes at zero.

My mouth cut
by imperfect truths,
the hollow echo
of the absolute body,
the hunger of cold rain.

No way home,
from this moment on,
a vision of higher things.
Shaken loose,
an endless scattering,
the name of silence
darkening the roof,
the light at the end of light.

6.
The dry throats of strangers
some days long after
their arms rivers that dig in
beneath the cold blossoms

Faces under old streetlamps
spaced far apart
the white hand of the wind
touching the world's sad marks

The cracks of the past day
under a stone sky
the soul, dark migrant,
moving out from the cold:

I knew I was late arriving
in the half-forgotten room
the moment hastening to its own absence
in the clockwise spin of April light

to this shining to the soft movements
of all that time and place
the smoke and smolder of stars
as dawn shifts between the lines

and blood becomes the root of water
and the dead grass whispers
our names, and the white shadow
gains on heaven, and the ice moans

7.
they are gone at last
shuffling through the empty rooms

carrying away the secrets
they did not bring

climbing the stairs as dust
keeps falling on our heads

at the end of the day
in our glass sleep

and I heard them long after
hurrying down a side street

as the wind shook
in the empty doorway

in the breath of things
you do not see

by an old brown wall
under a dim light

keep your distance
don't make a sound

8.
Some things repeat themselves,
fill our pockets like an old landscape
we drove through all our lives,
as the light rises, and the darkness prays,
and the fear inside me says old friend old friend.

9.
It was a moment in a dry corner
standing in dry air
no moon in the sky

the wind shifted south
sharper than a sword

time was horizontal
an overturned glass on the table
outside the sky fell
vast and hollow as green fire

I have come to a still center
I rise and try to walk

this is how all beginnings come
as the saw of night keeps cutting
as the needle of morning threads

10.
I pace the room back and forth
unsettling the dried flowers,
climb the stairs, come to the wide wall,
look for the empty doorway,
watch the darkness let itself down.

It is an old feeling and this is how
it always begins, sorrow burning
like a dim lamp in the hallway,

my shadow hiding among
the shadows on the floor.

I know it will wait there until
someone comes to lead it away.
It won't be me. I add my footsteps up,
count out the floorboards, breathe like
a tiny star fixed in the long night.

And no one will come to call me
though I stir in the dark as the moon
drags its light across the floor,
though the sky goes on living
and I hear the endless falling of its seeds.

In time I will learn what to say,
will whisper into a different ear,
will reach the door that opens on both sides.
The name for it, everywhere and here,
is the same the same the same.

Where Rivers Have No Names
A slow spray of water moves over
the low white rocks where the shadows
change, where darkness is forgotten
and the light is open and wide
and shifts toward me softly
on the river's tight banks.
There is no sound in the trees,
no sound among the birds, no sound
in the lapping of water as the wind
slackens across the shinings
of the water weeds and fields.
There are no names for rivers,
no names for rain or clouds
or the white paths on which
the seasons move here.
The light is not yet divided,
the deep chorus of this place
turns to a single sound,
a radiant stillness deep at the root,
and my soul is nearly my own,
the wind at its back.
And I live with the grasses and stones
in the water, with the currents
and winds, and the light speaks
to me as I move among them,
as I rise and fall and feel the slow
touch of fish I cannot see passing,
the echo and pulse of myself,
and the day flows past,
and I belong to no one,
and I breathe with the birds,
and my body glows.

White

Spring Perspective
The water of melting snow
and winter rain in footprints
alongside the house

Helpless birds in the yellow March grass

Windows cannot hold back
the wind the glass shatters you suffocate
while leaning against it
in the dark room

The walls creak
the white response
the crack in the door answering
—say
powdered earth
crumbled dust
black ash

Where does the illusion begin

All around are black flowers
red and green spores of life

How thin the moon

Bones
1.
The day hangs like an old white shirt
on a rope beneath the winter trees.
In a room filled with women I move slowly,

whisper past without making a sound.
Their faces hang on a rope of light
in front of me beneath the trees.

You dream of names wet with blood
and when you wake you write *my brother*
with a sliver of bone on the walls of your room.

Thing becomes memory:
love discovered in the tiny lines around her eyes,
the corners of her mouth, the yellowness of her hair.

The thin brittle line,
winter's letters, words of ice,
the cold that binds my tongue.

2.
My heart begins to pound more quickly,
I cower as if from cold wind, and consider once again:
when I die, all that will remain will be clean white bones,

a dried skull, empty eye sockets near the fence where
spiders weave their webs, catching everything
that flies or crawls past. That will be the penance for
my sins, fitting punishment or lost redemption because
I wanted a magical emancipation, an unconquered heart,
one chance at last to touch the timbers of the moon.

3.
When I touch you, stars fall,
gather together dry and dead in your hair.

When you touch me, clouds
lift and tremble, burst into seed and flame.

Yesterday is a scattering of broken twigs
near the fence of an old house.

Today is a ragged sigh of a soul
measuring its losses in a burling wind.

Tomorrow is desire, heavy with sorrow,
a bone with wings brittle at both ends.

4.
Your shoes leave no marks on the hard ground.
You turn your back to the waking of the world.
Each day you struggle with the wind.
Each day your blood thins to water and rust.
The bones in your feet are light as feathers.
The white road ahead long as the echoing air.

5.
I hear their whispers, their moans,
their steps on the floor of the adjacent room.
They lay together all night, waking, drifting to sleep,
and this morning their smells seep charred
through the walls and door:
the metallic smell of her first blood,
the bitter scent of her repeating excitation,
the milky sweetness of his nightly response.
His voice, when he says something to her,
is hoarse, full of derision and shame.
She answers sometimes, quietly, carefully,
understands his unspoken thoughts,
reluctantly enters his soul's black fissures,
the deep cuts in the cells of his bones.
Each day it's clearer to me:
they create emptiness, no matter where they go,
leave behind emptiness, their own emptiness,
meant for them alone, above all else—cold, dark,
the martyr's wounds, the blinded heart.

6.
He lives in a house made of yellow bones.

He says his body is the name of the north wind,
the grave of the sea, the shade of the heart.

The tattooed girl sleeps in a pile of dry grass.
He lifts her, shaken by the east wind,
and warms her green body with his hands.

I cobble a blue bed on the floor, hammer its tangles and whirls.
They talk together all day and night, as the west wind blows,
about the forgotten, the lost, the living and the dead.

A dark light circles around them like a broken clock.
I mourn their vain parable of the lengthening night.
A black bird burns dumb as a candle on the smoldering roof.

7.
A woman I've seen somewhere before stands outside the house
gathering gray bones of dragonflies from the window screens.
She tells me to believe only what the fingers can feel,
the ghostly sun's heat in the white chaos of the clouds.
A dark hole appears suddenly, a wound in the body of space.
She stretches out her hands, eyes closed, offering the thin bones
she's gathered to the gods she recognizes with her skin and hair.
Time gathers its own course, transfigures the substance of things.
A broken corner of the moon falls against the window screen
and her hands shake as she reaches for its delicate bones.

The Door
Light in an empty room filled with old furniture.
Careful angles and dark corners everywhere.
Each thing in its place.
The sound of distant trains, the ruts of the road.
People talking about the cold days and nights they have endured.
The transparent weeks, one after the other.
An unexpected noise in the hallway.
The clocks outside striking all at once.
Everything that was once here and important.
In the evening I don't recognize familiar colors.
The sound of love at night so close I can touch it.
I catch my breath, shift relentlessly, one pulse at a time.
The door will open. Nothing will happen, everything will change.
Quietly carefully I make my way toward it.

Light
Whom can you believe, what can you trust?
Forgetting is a form of loss, memory a loss of form.
Names erased so easily from a dusty black board.
For a moment time stands still.
For a moment I remember.
The house in which I live is growing cold.
Dust on my fingers. Pain in my hands.
The white line ahead. The black line below.
The touch of the face and belly
of the one I want to sleep with all my life.

I see her, from a distance, we talk sometimes.
Lives not shared, one body passing by another.
This is how things happen, one moment at a time.
This is the time it took to get here.
I meet myself standing quietly in the dark.
I stand alongside myself, try to take my sight away.
Look. Around the corner the ineluctable light.

A Poem in Honor of Li Po
                  after Li Po and Tu Fu

I have forgotten my friends
my old friends
my lost friends
my dead friends
          turned to earth beneath the pines

sometimes I meet
an old man in the forest
we talk and laugh
and I forget
          to return home

let's drink more wine
I'll dance and sing
out loud
while the clear moon
          rises
*
I sing
and the moon rocks
back and forth

I dance
and my shadow
shakes and falls with me

I know
we will meet again someday
in the white river of stars above our heads

Confession
the rifle
                              emptied
lies
          on the floor   near the window

he sits   leaning against the wall
             pressing into the curtain
             covering himself with a dusty cloth
in his side
                              an open
wound

199

I draw near

             kneel   alongside

he doesn't turn his head

                             I don't know

          if he hears me

he stares at the empty wall in front

     seeing something   in the distance

infinity

         perhaps

               or

                    the redeemer's face

           forgive me

                      he whispers

               deep in the earth

underground rivers flow
in dark caverns

                in caves

he floats
on the current

               a white

flower

      in the darkness

dreaming of rain

he drinks cool
drops

        trying
        not to give

himself away

        not to reveal
        his infinite

terrible

                         thirst

I understand

          there's nothing

to be done
I get up

quietly

         like dust

falling

           on the curtains

    someone

           whispers

       I forgive you

Northern Solstice: The Feast of St. John, The Dance of the Dew
A table and chair near a window shuttered with old boards.
Above my head, bowed rafters, gray frayed shingles.
On the floor, under my feet, a thick layer of dust.
Wind blows through the cracked clapboards.
The dust stirs, and in the far corner of the room something moans.
Roots tremble in the margins, an empty mimicry of being.
A muffled voice by the window asks how to enlighten the world.
I am the only witness, sitting alone by the door
covering my eyes with my fingers, embracing my knees.
A muffled voice answers that this is the time of fire,
the time of water, the time for that which will grow
at last out of the ashes and dew: the heart's chord,
the radiance outside, the day of resurrection an unbreaking
note before the great cold comes and the gray sky grinds out.
Death comes quietly here, admitting to nothing, rattling its stick.
In the great reckoning of this room, coiled tight against the future,
I am the white self on a black road, the shuffle of whispers
through a broken window, the whine of wings rising and falling
as darkness deepens around its mouth and the mud slides
and the rain sleeps and the lights drift down.

The Dry Season
There was no rain this summer
and the days have carried over,
one by one,
into a vast white airiness
hanging thick
between the earth and sky.

I am awake once again long before dawn,
staring up at the thin strips of the window.
There is almost nothing to see outside
from this angle, only a few dim lights
in the distance reflecting in the glass
and the high rim of trees as it traces
itself against the clouds and air.
A few last stars twinkle in a clear black sky.
A thin coating of dust gathers
in a corner of the far wall.
A small brown beetle scurries past.

I doze, then wake unexpectedly,
confused and thick-headed,
listen to her fluttering about the room,
recognize the sounds of her quick movements
as she stops here and there
the way she does every morning.

I flatten myself as far as I can,
push my face hard against the floor,
shift slightly to ease the stiff weight
of the bed's wooden slats
as they press down onto my shoulders.

The bed creaks as she sits
to pull her stockings on
and breathes a small sigh of effort
as she lifts and lowers her legs.
I lie still, breathing softly through my mouth,
stiffen in response as the slats
press harder against me.
I know they will lighten when she gets up.

I wonder with an inkling
of pleasure and satisfaction
if she knows that I am here.
Even if she does, I have
no plan of escape and she
will not chase me if I run.
The years here have been
acceptable to me, the unseen
participant in her routines
and exceptional events, though lately
it all seems all the more commonplace
and dull and not what I had imagined
when I first crawled that night
into this rectangular space.

Or perhaps it's because
I have not eaten or drunk in a day
and the heat in this small room
grows thick and more stifling
with each passing summer.
No. She is relaxed and oblivious,
accustomed to the sounds
of the house, lost among them
my occasional twitchings and stirrings
each morning and small groans in the night.

Some days I hear the birds sing
if she opens the window
and from time to time long to feel
the air in which they live on my skin,
or want to lay myself down
in the sweet fragrance of flowers,
eyes fixed on the clouds like an old man
gazing upward consulting the spirits.

But I cannot see from here what stretches out
into a blue distance I barely remember,
try to compose myself among the dust
and lost pins, know it is only as matter of time
before I am discovered with a shriek
of fear or surprise or finally give myself
away at some sudden hour.

It is the day I wait for:
to arise, powerful and transfigured,
and walk into the world, all light,

with the confidence of a blind man
who has never developed a fear
of darkness or the night.

But it is not today.
And after all, what is there to see
when you do step out
and open your eyes wide?

This morning, again, after she has left
for the secrets of life outside
that hangs in my memory
like a shapeless gray dress,
I pull my knees up to my chin,
biding my time, the white walls
around and empty bed above me
reminders of where I am,
my slow and practiced movements
on the floor in the shifting light
reassurances that I am all spirit
and from here can fly when I want,
inexhaustible and free,
away into the ether.

The Solstice, Early Morning by the Window
when she left
the fingers of my right hand
webbed together - - - -

      then I could feel
      the worm's storm of lamentation
      the dreadful ocean of compassion
      the clear needle of sorrow
      the absurdly crumbling ice of love

and the snow
that misted
over everything
evenly
blindingly
in which
are born
the pains
of death's
new kingdom
the deepest
final white
point into which
the whole world
this morning descends

Lullaby
night

                            the light melts

among the trees' roots

                             where are you running
                             child
                             through pools of fading light

those who died
there
are long dead

                                   disappear
in the darkness

swollen with sun

                                 dried by the wind

                                                 frozen with cold

                             where are you running
                             child
                             through pools of fading light

my fingers

                                 stiff and dull

                                           reach forward
seek
the
place
these
words
will
never
touch

                             where are you running
                             child
                             through pools of fading light

November Song
Knives of light scrape away the blue of the sky
the music of the earth begins
and in my ears drums the hour of fear

the years will pass
years without us
we will sleep a hard sleep

a pleiad of wild geese shines in the heavens
listen
is it my name they're singing as they pass by

Immortality
Serious contemplation
of the moments
that have
just passed by

the face in the mirror

                                      is my face

                                                   and will be   my face

even if I burn it

                                    in fire

                                    or

throw myself

                       into the deepest hole

don't expect   miracles

          from the body
even I will die

                                                     no

I don't think so

my heart

                                                        begins to pound

                                      when I think

        that I won't pass on

                                    or that I can come back

               a second time

I
am probably

                                                         the only

                        one

                                      I'm prepared

I know

                                  that others

                    won't like
                      my good fortune

      I laugh softly to myself
         humbly bow my head

The Last White Blinding Radiance
when you live
with prophecy
for so long
the very
moment
of revelation
is terrifying

the clothes

                    of old age

                                        fall

      from

             our   bodies

                      like

                              dried

leaves

she rises
                        lightly and easily
                                              into the sky
her face
                        not a face

but
                the very expression
                                        of
ecstasy
she reaches
                        the layer
of clouds
        penetrates it
                                in reverse
                evolution
through
                the heart
                                              of primordial
light
time
                                but not
eternity
        rising
                before
                and
                after
                                    time
        near
                the sudden
                                        horizon
        where an unfamiliar
door
        unexpectedly
                                              opens
we
                                        stand
naked
                redeemed
first she
and behind her
                            I

before that last
white blinding
radiance

Returning Home
there is an empty kitchen
and a cold stove
lattice walls

in the room beneath the roof
        like interlaced evidence of the past
        a worn man's suit
        a baptismal gown
        daguerreotypes
        documents and testaments

I take off my shoes
        touch
                the cold ashes
                        between the grates
            in the fireplace
    feel
                how
                warmth
                releases
                the bones
                of my
                hands
                and
                feet

Discovered Foundations: A Novel
sleep   among the roses   in an eternal furrow   he shoots metals

sun   power   radiance   a
white winter day

                    love   darkness
                    the blue milk of night
        covers the stars

a thousand insane tongues

song   cry   the lost woman's heat
the debt paid by the unclean son

a waxen gift
                a dead glance   foaming
                    bitterness

mourn   inundate   for a moment
                                of beauty
                                        blow
out   the burning cities
                    don't let me leave
                                        I am
beat only sweet
green humanity
                    abomination
                            fly
        the way you wanted to fly
                    and my
                            life

207

heated to the point of redness soldiers

                        with ball gowns

under their tuxedos

a woman
who cut the music beneath the machine

                            go   have it

look

the quick-tongued apparatuses ring

                        pray for the pains

of hands and feet
stop   bloody reins   a blind place
she begged me not to rob her   the lake

                            still

she drags herself along   awkwardly   like all the rest

the weakened finger will deify you

use it with   whispers   if not theirs   then
knife   apex   moon   lie   all inclusions
          above   higher   one
you will have
villain

                  reprobate   war

show or   contemplate   do   say   want   did
emptiness   the fullness of the fields   the
graceful
stem of fear
and a woman knows

friendships always   are about
a man remembers this   here

                no one gave
then

                and together
had
pick our delicate   fruits were
    then
                  that
one
who   will
later
he felt himself   falling   she will do
someone some
day
               she
        sees   all
little one
let his desires
beat
hard and rabid

sleekness   rust   hymns   they could

be

I am a delicate violin
in the forest
splendid

never   wash yourself

in the ocean
of rain

eternity

light
mother I love you   uncommonly

goddess   vision

beat   depress   hit

I am skin

shake   slander   force to kneel

a real diamond
you slaver madly
longing for her

locked to the water
you adulterate like honey
the refreshing mist of sorrow

I sit on a rock
shadows pursue

me in the wind

the symphony

of heaven

my wife

spring   aurora   casting about
a nauseating enfeebled
autumnal harvest
moans like black death

a woman's

plague

two said   no   do you think
it was so easy to leave

ask them later

how
the bitter wreath
essential to summer
propagated in annihilation

through him

with her

they are

she

was

then

Revelations of a New Existence
bone gives birth to rock
and the soul's filled fissures congeal

the mind of grass disseminates
in the manifest presence of dawn

the flaring merger of body and blood
obliterates the past

the primitive and magical culture
invests the shudders of civilization

the covetous action endows thought
with divine and immediate form

powerswallowspowerswallowspowerswallowspower

the productive totem and metastasizing incantation
give birth to the hierarchies of law

the metabolic rites of fire and water
drown in the forests of ghosts

the renunciation of faith hangs among the shadows
and fear of love among the swollen shapes of being

the pleasures of desire play expressive mystical melodies
at the ragged edge of desiccated dreams

somewhere far away the wafting fragrance
of the future echoes past

After Rain
1.
you are so cold so quiet
after rain
where the hill once stood
in the afternoon darkness
in a distant light
three people hang in the trees
where the future begins
where the dark rainbow ends

2.
a hand rises and falls
hits the stones in the road
leaves sad marks
in the dirt
signs preordained
in the needle's eye
as the wind changes
as the strangers pass

3.
God turns
in the night wind
a lost old man
unable to recognize us
sleeping in rags
at the edge of the world
look: stars splinter the sky
the door opens on a wire stem

Evolution
All your life you wanted to be like water:
        I carry you in a small transparent glass

All your life you knew it was too late:
        each day you grow in the opposite direction

All your life you heard water calling your name:
        all your life you heard water calling your:
            all your life you heard water calling:
                all your life you heard water:
                    all your life you heard:
                        all your life you:
                            all your life:
                                all your:
                                    all:

                                            :

Excerpts from the Autobiography of a Man Who Casts No Shadow
Before getting out of bed in the morning early while it is still dark
I gather up and hang my bones together
attach my hands and feet
finding them wherever I left them the evening before
pull on my skin
inside out sometimes
to frighten the neighborhood's children
sew up my body's wounds with strong invisible thread
pull on the face I plan to wear that day
selecting it from all the others arrayed in the dresser drawer
with difficulty push into it my forehead cheekbones and chin
fix my nose ears eyes eyebrows lips moustache
smooth the wrinkles on my cheeks
find and combing slip on my hair
choose the appropriate shoes gloves hat shirt pants socks
so I would nicely cover the entire form

while outside the window
above this day's head
the sun is rising:
mote of dust
flake of snow
barely living thing

*

it doesn't matter to me why I am
how
or
from where

I don't care about the stories of the human voice
destiny
or the daily works of God's hand
the consequences of original sin
the hypotheses of brave imagination
the security zone populated by ghosts
or you

what does it matter anyway .
I care only

that my head hurts today

I look into the mirror and see nothing

I walk in the sun and cast no shadow

I stand in the doorway breathing heavily

*

after I was born
another raised me

for two years

my parents worked
in factories
otherwise there wouldn't be enough money
to get by
 each time they came home
they found me
injured
a broken arm
a fractured bone in my leg
a swollen lip
bruises on my forehead or cheeks
fingers dislocated
thin red scars on my back
like the lines on a map to my peculiar future

in my dreams now I see her face
painfully touching me
hear her voice

people say I called her name
at night
and she hearing that
thought it was out of longing and love

she reminded me of that
when years later grown up
I would pick her up to visit my parents
and sitting next to her in the car
would remember
the strange odor of her hair
smeared with
the same grease
she used to heal my childhood's wounds

perhaps that's why today
I am afraid to live with others
I am afraid what people will find
when they come home
and look for me in every room

I am afraid whose name I'll call out
at night in my dreams

*

I found myself a wife
because I am no longer young
because I did not want my blood to die out in this world forever
because the bed creaks frozen on winter mornings
because I crawl up the stairs with empty hands
because I have begun to fear the twilights
because dusty holes gape open in the corners
because the rooms have no windows
because the doors are open

- - - - - - - - - - - - - - - -

I wander through the house closing the doors
the front door
the living room door
the dining room door
the bedroom door
the bedroom door
the bathroom door
the bedroom door
the kitchen door
the back door
the cellar door
the bathroom door
my room's door
her room's door

some were already closed

*

I am
a quick shadow on the wall

I am

                              an indistinct contour
a barely noticeable smell

I close my eyes
listen to her breathing
on the other side
of the bed

sometimes I dream
that
I am
                              an indistinct contour
a barely noticeable smell

a quick shadow
on the wall
on the other side of the bed

*

every day
in my arms or over my shoulder
at the end of an old stick
I carry
a bag

in the bag is a
box
in the box is a
bundle
in the bundle are a
woman's ashes
mornings
I sit in the kitchen
waiting for
the coffee to boil
holding the bag

afternoons
I walk barefoot in the yard
chattering and whispering
quietly to myself
touching the box

evenings
when the lights go out
and dogs bark somewhere far off around the corner
I stretch out on the bench
caressing the bundle

she who was turned into ash
is here
between my fingers
but she is also
a spirit

let loose with the smoke
into the skies
reconciled
with the clouds
that's why every day
in my arms or over my shoulder
at the end of an old stick
I carry a bag

I know that
in this way eventually
I will arrange things
will create
our only
almost familial
life together

it is pleasant to imagine

at midnight
kneeling in the corner
scattering ashes around the room
consecrating
the walls and floor
I begin to laugh

*

a son was born
a daughter-in-law was born
                              two grandsons were born
the older one
was sickly since childhood
early one spring
just a few days before Easter
he became deathly ill suffered
unearthly pains died and was buried
the younger one
opened a small kiosk on the corner
near the city's central square
sold his dead brother's
photographs clothing
toys books pencils
tufts of hair fingerprints
bits of his body pieces of his bones
the relics of his life and living
after a time
he opened a shop
in the center city not far from the church and government offices
sold
his brother's remains
and leavings
and became rich
built himself a house somewhere outside the city
associates with priests politicians academics

travels to foreign lands
conducting the affairs of his strange business
doesn't write doesn't call

a daughter was born
a son-in-law was born
                          three granddaughters were born
the first
weak-minded raises cats somewhere
weeds gardens
at night kneeling
in the middle of the yard
catches flies
her hands are red
washed in the blood of vegetables
in the life juices of flies
among the clods of earth
she searches for happiness luck her parents' inherited fortune
the second
always sits
near an open bedroom window
longing to escape into the night
and never come back
but is afraid
to die in life's wilderness
so much hardship
so many misfortunes
so much loneliness
so many troubles
there
outside the window
she finds her accustomed place
presses herself between the window and wall braces her back
knows that always somewhere in the world
it is snowing
the third
consecrating herself
entered a convent
prays for her cousin
dressed in black
sitting
in a room washed in light
eyes closed
his relics in her hands
taking deep breaths murmurs quietly
holy holy holy
prays
for us sinners
now and at the imagined hour of our
deaths

a daughter was born
died
                   giving birth to a granddaughter

sixteen years old
                          without a son-in-law
in her high school best friend's
dark attic room

a sinner
calling out that boy's name
the innocent child
the granddaughter
died
hopelessly thirsting for air mama's milk a future
her cousin prayed
for her
not knowing
then the hour
of her birth
or death

a son was born
a daughter-in-law was not born
                          no grandchildren were born

was born

was born

was born

was not born

died

so many children

so many grandchildren

as many
as people say
as were necessary
I had enough of everything and everyone
joy
mixes
today
with signals
of danger

*
they taught me
for many years
and I learned
this and that
earning
all sorts of degrees:
every thought

has a sound
every sound
has an image
every image
has a form
every form
has an idea
every idea
has a thought
every thought
has a sound
every sound
has an image
every image
has a...

and so on

or perhaps
it was different

e.g.
every person has a thought
not all thoughts are sound
my desires are not acceptably exemplary
if in the world there are forms
then my ideas rule your thoughts
that's how nations arose
or something similar

I don't recall now
maybe I didn't hear it right
in my ears there were too many loud sounds
in my eyes there were too many images and forms
in my mouth there were too many ideas and thoughts

and after all
I was never interested in
history philosophy politics religion literature
or other weak inconsequential branches of learning

and to tell the truth
how can they know
that that's how it is
that that's how it was then

*

I had a very good and important job
my principal responsibility was quite simple
I'm educated enough and prepared
well-trained and experienced protected by the right union:
to discover something new necessary fundamental
beautiful essential and dangerous
I discovered god

I didn't tell anybody where I found her
most people but not everyone
liked my discovery in the abstract found it useful
and terrifying nothing to argue about
or everything to discuss
something to make love to or fight wars over
challenge other deities with salvation or demise
rake the sidebars of the universe kill everything you want to
with no remorse
piss wine
I made a killing receive royalties
been guaranteed a pension
I'm photographed with celebrities and politicians
have my choice of women and wine (!)
now they ask me to discover something else
I thought I didn't have it in me a one trick pony as they say
but now now hold on now
I have in mind wind sun clouds stars rain oceans time
peace love tranquility the morality of existence
the virtues of being acts of consecration
forgiveness love redemption
the opposites of turpitude the elevation of the flesh
but it's too early to present those people there
with such valuable and progressive things
politically correct and all that bullshit
they won't understand will begin to misuse them
will stumble down stairs paddle in circles
walk on ceilings slide across floors
feel the earth undulate beneath them
as they seek to rise and fall
like sirens wailing in the night
shatter their golden calves
I'll write down the instructions
in several languages
(half of which only I can understand)
on how to create them
will write secret testaments and dead sea scrolls
will require easements considerations
proper payments to my estate
more than those who find them will be able to pay aha!
they might be able to decipher my letters and words
or else will have to give me a call for directions and pay aha!
and they'll have to find the right pictures of me drinking
making faces scribbling in my diary at the dining room table
not flinch as I become invisible and white

*

I want to eat
I am so terribly
hungry
I want to be fat
so my chin would glisten with grease
so my hair would shine
smeared in oil butter whey

219

so I couldn't walk
so I'd crawl on all fours
so children would make fun of me
mimic me
stomachs stuck out cheeks puffed
I get up in the morning
my intestines sing
I go to my neighbors'
from door to door
like a man fallen on hard times
though only pretending to be so
begging for bread milk butter cheese
meat bacon livers kidneys hearts stomachs
tongues ears snouts eyes pig fat
cows' newly-peeled skins sheep's swollen hides
they can be uncooked even raw I say
just give them to me
I say
just give them to me
and I swallow everything I swallow
walking down the road to the next house
to ask the same there
all day
all day
while at night I am afraid of falling down stairs
getting lost in unfamiliar yards
falling down near the fence

I go home
lie down but do not sleep
impatiently wait for morning
know that when I get up
I will want to eat
I will be so terribly
hungry

*

god
my god
my dear god
the clothes
aren't laundered
and the dishes
haven't been washed

if I squeeze hard enough
the glass will shatter
blood will drip
and will mix with the water
that washes everything clean

*

so many governments
so many leaders

so many national heroes
so many of those
whose voices
I have been
trying to forget
for a long time
Truman
Eisenhower
Kennedy
Johnson
Nixon
Ford
Carter
Reagan
Bush
Clinton
Bush the younger
they promised everything
we got
Korea
Cyprus
Viet Nam
Dominican Republic
Grenada
Lebanon
Panama
Persian Gulf
Iraq
Somalia
Haiti
Rwanda
Yugoslavia
Bosnia
Kosovo
Newyorkafghanistan
Iraq revisited
and etc. and etc.
my classmates and friends
fought and policed there killed and died
I miss them

on the other side of the great puddle
as far as I've heard
things are the same

*

I had a friend
a good friend
of all the friends
in the world
the very best

all his life
he was so afraid
to die

221

that one day he died
of fright

now
I no longer look
for such friends

I don't want
to be such a friend
myself

I'm afraid
to be afraid

*

writing my autobiography
I decided to call it
Hope, rediscovered while stretched out
on a freshly made bed in the stable

the first page began like this

we carry the bed outside
through the door into the stable
all three of us together
and lift its corners onto the rafters
tie them with a rope firmly
protecting it from the wind
which perches hard spread-legged
on the roof howling together
with the evening glow
dust rises from the sheets and pillows
and settles in the corners
on the straw and spider webs
when I lie down
it's my room the last room a special room
the only room left untouched by people and winds
not only a room but a dark passageway
to the other side where I can wander at night
blindly tapping my fingers on the walls
a room without windows
where closing my eyes I hear
the creaking of the wood of the house
the scratching of mice beneath the floor
the whistling of bird skeletons
in the ridges of the roof above my head
requests for sympathy and mercy
when dawn breaks
their songs come from nowhere and go to nowhere
have no past and no future
hang quietly in yards
in the neglected unhappy present
not feeding anything not seeing anything
not understanding anything

awaiting only their own true final resurrection
listening to them I thought to myself
do I really need this today
I turned over onto my other side
and for good measure slid down deeper under the warm sheets
I'll write the second page when I get up tomorrow

*

I don't sleep
I can't fall asleep when I lie down
if I fall asleep I can't stay asleep
if I'm sleeping I wake up
or I dream that I wake up
or I dream that I dream that I wake up
occasionally I manage to catch a few winks
an hour or two
tossing and turning I dream about many things good and bad
I remember some of them e.g.
my canonized friends in black robes in churchyard cemeteries
childhood's disguises masquerades masks
old age's apprehensions doubts pains lies
city plans the maps of rising and ebbing tides
the trails of night birds in the clouds
bronze soldiers and the swollen injured flesh of bodies
the splashing of oars on the open sea the fluttering of sails
hands holding plucked feathers black wings
flowers watered washed drowned in blood remains of leaves
lovers and angels with cups filled with stars
the shells of locusts and rosary beads around necks
two foreign men in the shadows behind
the dying wind's wheeze on earth the earth's moan in the wind
uncountable seeds and new grasses sprouting on sides on backs
white leaves dry stones brittle bones shards of broken windows
a wooden chair in a cold room
dark sweet smelling roses wilting in the distance below
the pleasures of fingers and mouths the softness of her belly
the cold sleeves of my lover's discarded dress
all those I've loved and love all their faces their names
the yellowness of solitude the redness of longing the gray road
home sycamores oaks mountain ashes distant empty fields
recently dead widows knitting my unlived days
your mother floating in the air with hair in flames
wreathes of bone scales of blood the enclosures of existence
light filling the empty room painting the black walls with splinters
something enormous too great to comprehend forget
the dust we are the color of nothing the lost moment
hope's rot love's mold daily sins
which give my life its holy movements resulting form hard shape
so many truths
so many realized perceptions
so much consciousness
that I can't doze fall asleep sleep
I wake again and again I wake
in the whole world others sleep so sweetly so sweetly

while quietly in whispers in a hoarse voice each day each night
I talk to the sun to the moon

*

I am
the grass
beneath a running child's feet
a flower
that opens unseen for one day in spring
and slowly eternally closes in the evening
a drop of water
hanging on the spider's web in the night air
a single glass tear
on a young girl's cheek
dust of the earth
pressed between primordial roots
the smell of ice and snow
the touch of moon and wind
the color of the sun's song
a golden fish
in blue water among black rocks
a shark an octopus a baleen whale
that feeds together with the hermit crab
a widow's mourning dress
an unmarried woman's dozing as the day ends
a dry river filled with roosting birds
dawn's first aura evening's last flat sleep
the fog of error the mist of love
all children all parents brothers and sisters
friends relatives acquaintances lovers
the last fallen angel unable to find its nest
searching the edges of the universe for its lost voice
a white train to the stars
the first human tree
philosophy dialectics music physics poetry
magic and spells war poverty misfortune hardship
applied science conscious knowledge
God's kingdom and the soul's resistance in the land of heroes
fibers of the body and veins of wood
a drawing of the essence
that explains the world
everything that can be seen or touched
matter and form
shadow and light
and all around
everywhere I see
everywhere my hand reaches
everything is
white
white
so white

Lithuanian Crossing

ir tu pati kada nors
tebusi tiktai vaiduoklis
senam name

Lithuanian Crossing

My mother's mother's first lover could not have her
and lay down late one summer night on the railroad
tracks that ran through the fields near her father's house.
They found him there the next morning, the earth gray
and brown beneath him, the neighborhood's dogs trotting
uneasily up and down the dirt road, the wind whistling
without a trace of an echo in the branches overhead.

It was a story I heard from time to time from
my grandfather before he drank himself to death.
He would mumble, too drained of strength to rise,
in front of his wife or anyone who would listen,
about how quickly his life had passed, having poured
out, like the blood of that man on the tracks,
in a ceaseless and unending stream.
And my grandmother, with both malice and remorse,
would call her husband by her lost and long-dead lover's name.

The death he chose was full of misery and shame,
the indelible trace he left on my grandparents' lives
as they wasted away to pain and regret, beckoned by
a memory that would not fade to join him in the world beyond.

I remembered all three of them when I stood on those tracks
in the middle of those fields near the remains of my great-
grandfather's house, understanding how even those who perish
in obscurity, half a world away, leave their marks on the faces
of those at night who close their eyes and listen to the silence
after the trains in the distance have passed by.

The Angels of Wine

He died before my children were born and I tell them
about him sometimes, when I tell our family's stories
uncle and godfather, raw-boned and visionary,
alcoholic son and failed father, in the end a weak reed
no one leaned upon, who struggled with his gloom
and self-loathing and was caught in a trap
he laid for himself in the teeth of the wind.

He would listen to me in moments of clarity, drawing
a breath as if wanting to speak and then letting it out
in a sigh and waiting for me to talk myself out.
He would nod when I said that life is not something
that was waiting for us around the corner but was here
and now, and then would ask me for money for a bottle
of sweet wine, too tired and shaky to invent another lie.
It was not for his thirst, he would say, but because
with it everything grew remote and the stars in the sky
began to swim and the horizon expanded again.

Once he said he thought we gave birth to our death,
like something lifting inside us, like the tunnel where
he thrashed and choked and could not breathe
because there was no light. That's how they found him
early one morning as the sun touched the edges
of his room: the artery in his liver spilling his life out
into something scarlet and black, his nose burrowed
between the thighs of the woman he lived with
like a small lost dog looking for the place
he'd come from and where he wanted to return.

I think of him like that but do not tell my children
the details of his final story: lying in the dark in a pool
of his own blood, not knowing what was rolling over him
as a veil of grayness covered his eyes, perhaps dreaming
one last time of the daughter he had abandoned
or the grandchildren he would never see or the angels
that would come to him with the wine in the dead of night.

His Father's Son

It was not until years later, until we remembered
the things he had said, that we could begin
to understand the reach and measure of his death.

He said he had stood on ground where no sun
had ever shined, behind a door that opened onto a night
that was impenetrably black.

He said that shadows sprouted around him like dark flowers
watered by the rain that fell only on barren soil.

He said that something inside him had gone
or was letting go, like a curl of smoke dissolving
in the sky or a whirlwind roaring in the utter silence
that shaped the deepest truths that were the blight
on the heart of his family and his life.

He said he had groped forlornly inside his head,
searching for the tunnel that would lead him out
and away while the whole world spun around him
like the chamber of his father's gun.

The sound of his death was the flat concussion
of a bullet exploding in the spinning chamber
of his father's gun, the link to the past and future
he held clenched when they found him in his stiffening hand.

His bones are turning white in a place where his father
has never been but knows how to find.

Rhapsody

We sit on wooden chairs in front of a small raised stage
on which a man sits on a wooden chair in front of us.

He is dressed in a white shirt and dark pants illuminated
by a harsh flat light that casts no shadow.

We watch him, with no sense of concern or alarm,
as he begins to burn.
We have been here before and know it is a question of who can endure this the longest:
we who sit in front of him or he who sits in front of us,
he who burns or we who watch him burn.

We know it is a question of how long we would be content to watch.
        Until all that he is peels from his bones?
        Until the blood no longer beats as hard in our ears with each new wooden chair arranged
and illuminated on each small stage?
        Until the last such spectacle ends in truth and resurrection?

He would not move when the flames began, saying the moment was his triumph and destiny,
and later could not.

The first dry moan finds its way from his throat,
the sound of what was once a man now broken and lost.

Some around me clap and stomp their feet,
some whistle and laugh.

A Physical Phenomenon
Somehow I find myself tangled in white sheets
lying at the feet of a man with sores on his arms.
The echo of a thin moan circles the frayed edges
of his body and gathers in the wisps of his hair.
His hand reaches for me and I roll my arm up
in a corner of the sheet and stretch it forward,
afraid to touch his skin. The bones of his hand
rub through the cloth and grate against me
and I am wracked in dry revulsion.

I stand in the tub washing myself, scrubbing away
the touch of that skin and bone, chafing my flesh
until blood begins to appear in pinpricks on my legs
and arms. I tremble in long ripples.

He lies in bed and seems to be sleeping, a long white
bundle with one eye rolled back.
I feel my heart grow heavy.
Clean and washed free of the touch I recall
half in memory and half in imagination,
I wait for the tremors in the bed on the other
side of the room to subside.
I eat and sleep and am at last content.

I breathe fast and shallow, my belly and arms
pocked by sores and small scabs.
Somehow I am dressed in his clothes
and lie tangled in white sheets and moan softly

as someone I do not know stares up at me
from the foot of the bed.

I stretch my hand out to touch him.

The River

The sky is pure white and the air is still.
The dogs drag back and forth across
the grass, whining with eagerness, kicking up
tufts of earth clinging to old roots.

The bodies of the rabbits are lined up neatly
in rows on a flat slab of thin metal, marks
made by dirt and the work of the dogs
distinguishing one from the other.

I dig a hole on the banks of the river,
shaping a shallow pit in which to bury the rabbits,
forming small neat piles of earth in a circle around it.

When the hole is made, I pick up the slab
on which the rabbits lie and walk slowly
back to the hole, kicking up the dust
and tasting the smell of the soil.

One of the rabbits falls off the metal slab
and kicks its hind leg straight out unexpectedly.
It lies crumpled and abandoned on the ground,
moving in fits and starts.

My heart quickens as I watch it.
I find myself in a pocket of air in which time
stands still. I bend down and lift the rabbit up
by the loose skin of its back and press it close
to my chest as I grasp its head in my right hand
and snap its neck. Its spine will not flex and breaks
just above the shoulders.
The pocket of air and time in which I stand
fills with the dense smell of the rabbit
as I carry it back to the metal tray.

The flies are there before me, rising in a cloud
from the rows of furred bodies and buzzing
impatiently as I wave my arms above them.

They will not follow these creatures into the hole
I've dug along the riverbed.
When they are buried, I will live alone again,
awaiting a similar extinction.

In the years to come, when the river rises and roars up
in flood, perhaps it will wash over all of us buried on
these banks and mix our bones together.

Entering the Tiny Kingdom

The cricket under the table in the kitchen tells a story
in a language I have never heard, with a voice muffled
as the cry of someone in the desert drowned in sand
and loud as the tumbling of dust.

It is a story about odd creatures who slide away
into the night, who hiss and rattle in vengeance
and threat under rocks and dead holes, who form
the core of a universe of predators in the world's
hidden corners and great flat plains.

The cricket tells the story with a conviction so intense
that its voice is thick with admiration and wonder
for the things it cannot understand and yet describes.

It is like a ceremonial of cleansing, a numbering of visions
and signs, a chanting of the beliefs of generations forged
anew each night in this retelling beneath the dull dark sky.

I find it here in the early hours of the morning, a comfort
when I am unable to sleep, the story it repeats continuously
as much a part of this room as my breathing.

I know that all stories end, that the hours pass in this land
and that one and in all the rest of the world.
I face that fact more frequently now and it is no longer
a moment of astonishment or pain.

When the time comes, I want to die in my bed, in a familiar
place, and be mourned by my children and old friends.

The cricket understands this, accepts me into the weaving
it makes of its answers and truths, and I am borne up
like a scrap of paper on the wind and then sink back
calm and free into the dark river of its words.

The Word

The word she hurled at me
in the kitchen was a nail
driven through my hand into
the polished wood of the table.
I can no longer leave this small room.
I accept the limitations of my destiny,
express no regrets, voice no complaints.
I fix my gaze on the glass of the window,
watch the whole scene repeat itself
as the light outside changes
to the color of gray rags.
She tries to pull it out each night
as I sleep bent across the table,
but the nail holds, it holds.

Metaphor

It is a house I have never been before,
filled with rooms I have never seen.
I walk through, talking to a woman
who looks like my mother.
The staircase on the left side of the house
is solid wood with a painted railing.
I begin to climb it and quickly discover
that the stairs are not connected
to the second floor. I climb down,
looking for another way up.
There is a ladder hanging from
an opening cut into the high ceiling
on the right side, or possibly in the center,
of the house, in a room lined with books.
To the ladder is attached another ladder,
made of rope with wooden rungs,
to be used in the event the first one fails.
I start to climb the ladder toward the opening
in the ceiling. It is square and very small.
I can barely fit my shoulders through,
but above it I can see rooms painted white
and doors and windows of light oak.
The woman who may be my mother stands
beside me and then, as I climb, below me,
urging me on. I want to let the other ladder
loose, to have her climb up as well,
but do not do so. I know that if I did
she would not come. The staircase
on the other side of the house breaks
loose and drifts back and forth across
the floor of its room and then out through
the rest of the house. It glows with
a steady light that brightens suddenly
to green and just as quickly darkens to black.
Something begins to lift inside me as it moves,
like a stirring of the air in the curtains
of those rooms. I look but cannot
make out her face. In dreams we are
always children of indistinct mothers,
and I have been told by that woman
that this is a vision of my birth
or my death and that she too has had it.

The Deer

The deer stand in the shadows
of early morning on the road
that leads away from the house,
where the trees are silhouettes
against a sky that stretches out
to a light mist on the grass
and the air is filled with the songs
of birds that drift through time
announcing the change of the seasons.

I see them here each morning as the sun
rises, and each morning I hold out
my hands, palms upward, unable
to speak, stretched out in a gesture
of rapture and welcome, longing
for the touch that would at last unite us all.
The silence between us as we
watch each other is as heavy
as sleep in the eyes of a child.
As the deer move across the yard,
pausing here and there among the trees,
I feel the weight of the silence in the house,
the silence of time before the beginning,
the sound that settles deep in my chest
when I lie down at night or wake
disturbed in the early hours.
I think of myself then as a child
in a long white dress in my mother's
house waving good-bye to my father
 as he left for the last time, letting go
of myself, letting go of this house
and its trappings. Some mornings,
as they pass by, I understand the
resurrection possible for the things
of the earth, the white light that covers
the world from all sides, how to renew
the touch that has been broken.
And I know then where I have to go
as the deer come again and the birds
at dawn whistle me down,
whistle me down and away.

Undeveloped Photographs
Our son would have been photographed
in a garden, among the fruits and
blossoming flowers, light streaming

evenly across the sky, his face luminous
with curiosity, his dark eyes a reflection
of the deepest desire I am capable of.

Our son would have been photographed in a garden,
running to you as a soft breeze stirred the leaves
and caught and lifted the hem of your summer dress.
Our son would have been photographed
in a garden, and the pictures we would
have kept in albums and desk drawers

would surprise us when we found them
and we would say then that this
is how life should be.

Year after year the garden pours forth
its seeds, resurrecting itself, and the things
that grow here are tended with love.

As I make my way among them, I am comforted
and at last content to know that our son would
have been photographed with you in a garden.

Navigating the Waters

In the center of all my uncertainties
and fears, among the old feelings that settle
into my chest like the convulsions of a dry
hammering cough that will not stop, in the fog
in my head, the gray confusion, a single clear
thought, cold, unannounced, like a clap
of thunder, like a bullet between the eyes:
I stand on one side you on the other,
one on one bank one on the other,
facing away from each other
without looking back.
If we had a boat we might cross
the black weak waters
of the most neglected sea.

An Act of Creation

A white marble table
stands in front of a large mirror
polished with a coarse cloth.
A hand moves forward across
the sheet of paper on the table,
hangs in the air above the blank page.
The paper absorbs long, luminous
threads reflected from the hand
by the mirror, then broken threads,
then the black spaces in between
the first words on the first page
of the first book than can only
be read in the dark.

The Lace Maker

These pictures of solitary women
in light-filled rooms, allegories of faith
and innocent desire, soft brooding
moments filtered through leaded glass,
the dissolved contours in variegated
perspective and composed balance
all purity and harmony, the blurred strands
of red and white thread that fall
onto the lace maker's table, her face
consecrated with the sanctity of simple
pleasures as if life itself was gathering up
to embrace her, the significance of ordinary
things, simple actions treasured as divine gifts,
and the light enters her and she draws
breath again, the breath of truth, obligation,
and piety, and in Vermeer's hands
when she is gone this is her life,
waiting for the passage that grows no darker

as the days pass, never moving from that fixed
scene to mystery or transcendence, her soul
showing through the flesh, beyond the farthest void,
the distillation and fate of her love, the deep down
stirring of the knowledge a woman alone has.
I think of her when I lie in bed at night and stare
into the dark hole into which I am falling.
I wonder if she is an angel come to show me
the way out. She goes before and I follow,
my eyes shut in order to see.

October Garden
Like all gardeners, I am bound to the patch
of dirt I cultivate and to the seeds I plant,
each a universe of labor and each
a point in the tally of the passing days.

In the cleared ground are the remains
of neatly tended vegetables and flowers.
The last few tomatoes on the vines
in the small plot of garden alongside
are very small and deeply red.
Their leaves are already furling and
drooping and the creepers that shoot
out across the ground wind toward
the grass beyond the fence and wither
slowly in the cold dry air.

I come here without fail every day,
even in the fading late afternoon light
of this closing season, to clear and turn
the soil, to make sure the earth does not
grow too hard to tend as the nights grow colder,
as the wind reminds us that work here
for the year is nearly done.

Time bears everything onward and forward
in its flow and there is in fact now
little left to do, only to gather stray leaves
from time to time and turn them over
into the earth, listen to the silence
that drops across the garden when the wind
in the trees unexpectedly stops,
record the changes of the moon.
It is possible in this way to be both
body and spirit, to know that there will be
another summer in which to try again,
another time to be sure the seed does not die out.

Vermont Morning
A pale light, cool and dry, seeps
through the walls and door.
Rain washes the mist that feeds
on stones, prunes trees to cudgels
of brown and green. Clusters of stars

233

dissolve to shadows thin as paper
at the wood's edge and unfold
from ridge to ridge like the slow
pulsations of silence and time.

I remember the shape of the sky along
the curved bank of trees above the drifting
of foxglove and bluet, the wooded crests
of the hills trembling with clouds, muddy boards
by the barn, a thrush singing, the smell of the soil
after that April rain, the frail sun huddled
above the surface of the pond lighting
the delicate bend in the wall of piled stones,
the curtained windows, the gentle swell
of her breasts.

As I wake from sleep in the spring
in the darkened room layered by light
that seeps in crescents through the walls
and door, the rain downwind, skimming
the moss on the cedar roof of the barn
near the maze of pastures, speckling the wild
rose that flowers pale each summer against
the morning sky, smoky as the distant hills,
as I wake from sleep without her,
I suddenly remember.

A Moment at Sunrise in a Country Rain
The unexpected long high note
of bird song brushes the boxwood
at the far end of the field
like an old memory as the north sky
unfolds along the curved bank of trees
that tapers the wall of piled stones,
cracks loose, stirring the empty gray
meadows laced by the cobwebbed
glitter of light as it threads through
the brief clarity of morning air cusped
in the changing patterns in the east
above the locust trees, simple leaves
traced by water crisp as glass,
that unravel with the slow cadence
of the season to rings of thistle greening
against a white drift of sky while downwind
rain simmers in dissolving shadows
quick with the whistles of red birds,
hollows out a pale arbor
that holds the cold blue fading
of this night we longed for at bay.

The Things of the Eye
My eye is a flower shut tight
at the center of a closed circle.
I sit on the bus by the window

beside a woman who smells
like falling rain. She talks quietly.
I hear the landscape of rain,
the hiss of lamps on street corners
dimmed by rain, the chiming of bells
and dreams of glory, the melody
of expectation and promise
full of movements and pauses
enlivened and animated by rain.
My eye is an insect on her lithe,
white thigh. As it moves,
I know that I know women,
and how women are like rain.

Of Stones

Sometimes I wake up in the middle
of the night and walk through the house
without turning on the lights, quietly
so I do not disturb my children,
listening to the breathing of the stones
beneath the porch.
Sometimes, when the air is right
and the pods of dawn rattle quietly
in the distance, the stones speak.
Their words proclaim
the independence of their lives,
cloister in solitary gesture,
console one another softly as they
move apart, away from the foundations
of the house, having buried their
dead here upright.
On such nights, I turn my back
to the wall and wait for the wind
to repeat the only word possible.
Sometimes I stand there until
the sun rises, aware of a unity
of which I am part but cannot
control or possess.
And I know then how to keep
my distance and my place,
how to listen to the murmuring
of the stones as they pass by,
how to be still and silent.

First Light

It was the things they sang about that caught my attention as I opened my eyes that day for the
first time:
    a face full of earth, deep, impenetrable, restless, in a room encrusted with beetles and dirt;
    toads croaking unexpectedly in the enormous silence of solitude and cold;
    a dog howling as winter startles the dry leaves and uproots the delicate heads of flowers
from the hard rock of the ground in tiny gray bits and pieces;
    the roll of muffled drums trembling in the silence of the frozen battlefields, the night
banging against its own stars;
    a bird, flying low across the line of the horizon, suddenly erased by snow and wind.

All these things, after a sleepless night broken by the fall of dawn as it emerges
from obscure corners, and the same voices this morning that persist in my ear.

The Sound

The sound that rounds the corner
is dry and brittle as old wood.
The dead who lived here are long dead,
having passed through the gates
of their bones like vapor, having lifted away
from the flesh that love transfigures
to mystery and sorrow with empty hands.
The sound rounding the corner
is the abstract clothing that memories
and fears are made of, elusive as a wisp
of smoke, ineffectual as the flicker
of hope in the hearts of prisoner
perched on the brink of the ditch
into which their bodies will fall.
The sound is the embrace of longing
and regret, the descent into the sleep
of wingless creatures that toss through
the night with one eye open and rise
listless and haggard at the coming of dawn.
It is a message that never changes,
and as I listen I don't know who else can hear.

Epiphany

I once believed there is nothing
worse than what we can imagine:
the body stiff with solitude,
the face blank and featureless
and little more than a varied
bulge under the skin,
the soul an old parcel of eggs
hidden in a deep dark corner
of an abandoned barn.
The protection of imagining
the worst has not protected us.
There is a time and place for everything,
and today, quite unexpectedly,
the worst is here.

West of San Juan

All these passing moments,
all the ephemeral things of the world,
and now, suddenly, something
I can embrace and keep as if forever:
the tiny white-bellied bird
on the red flower swaying in the wind
near the green and silver waters
of the sea in Mayaguez!

Advice to the Adept

Marcus Aurelius wrote that living requires
the art of the wrestler, not the dancer.

Thirty years later, I finally understand.
Staying on your feet is all that is important.
No matter what they told me then,
I know now there is little need for
graceful movements or fancy steps.

The End of Mythology
She could not use the gift of prophecy she was born with
and closed her eyes for hours on end, waking up suddenly
from one formless dream or another stiff and cold,
a human spirit beyond classification, the last of her kind.

It was wasted, she said, on someone like her, who lived
in a place where words could not enter, having coiled away
in inconsistent directions, and from which the visions
she monitored could not emerge.

It was there, she said, that she defended the world against
the beasts that stared from under dead roots and out of holes,
forming their bizarre shapes into answers to the questions
she deciphered among the gestures of expiation
and the genuflections made by those around her as darkness fell.

> She hears them, turning in the direction of a sudden noise,
> a steady building roar in which no single sound can be
> distinguished, the stuttered revelations of ecstatic souls.

> She keeps her eye fixed on the gates, hearing nothing
> but what goes on inside her, wrapped up in the pulsing
> of her blood, watching for the figures that come through
> unexpectedly from the farthest void.

> She lives a life unmediated by words, apart from the
> quarreling of voices, outside the dominion of ideas,
> omniscient as dry bones held together by dust and
> cobwebs in the urgent present of the eternal moment.

> She understands that the truths we know lie in inessential acts,
> in the silences between us, yet she fails to see the moment
> at which together they wax and wane.

At the Water's Edge
I wrote your name in the sand
and watched the waves
wash it away as gulls
on the wharf piles and piers,
open-eyed, dived for bluefish.
Now the night above my head
is frozen to stars. The wave
that took your name beckons
the solitary bird that each night,

far out at sea, crosses
the track of the moon.

Sometime after I gave her those simple lines
she asked me how and why I had come to write them.
It was a cool day that August in Maine.
The sun was setting and I sat in the sand letting it
pour over and over again through my fingers.
The wind was still and on the air came only faint
and distant sounds: the rustle of grass, the call
of a bird, the splash of water. I was part of a vast
airiness, the space between the heavens and the earth,
and traced the letters of her name there, touching
each one gently, as if touching her, as darkness fell
across the sea and moved slowly along the land.
Everything was calm and still then, all was receding,
separated and drifting, and I knew as I watched
the water and her name as it disappeared beneath
its surface that what is left of that world,
what is still mine, I am trying somehow,
in these letters and words, to possess.
Today, as winter sweeps over the brink and memories
of that day rustle past me like old leaves, I write
something new for her, to keep myself from giving
myself back to the expected and the ordinary:

Night after night I return
to that small place between
the rocks, curl up in the cool sand,
and turn my face away
from the water. The shore is awash
in a dark blue light whose pull
is as strong as the tide's. Beneath
the waves that wash across
this stretch of rock and sand
is a tug as constant as the moon's,
drawing you to me and me to you.

The Ghost in the Kitchen
I have not seen the ghosts in this house
but have felt them touch me from time to time,
emerging from between the walls in various
rooms and brushing my back lightly with the tips
of their fingers, like a stirring of air on my skin
moved by the flicker of brittle wings.
The first time, I turned with a start,
a cornered, uncertain look in my eyes,
thinking there was someone else
unexpectedly with me in the house,
feeling suddenly cold; the second not
remembering what I had planned to say
if it happened again, the thought eluding me
like a wisp of smoke in the wind;
and each time after feeling the first stirrings
of welcome for whatever would come
to put an end to thought and dream,
for the moment when the door clicks

softly shut and the ghosts move slowly
through the house to put together
the pieces this life has disarranged.
I often write in the kitchen, alone late
at night, hunched over the table
with a single hanging lamp above my head
shining down on the paper and glinting,
as it moves almost imperceptibly back
and forth, on the ink as it dries.
I lay out the pieces of those pieces,
emerging translucent and blind
from the recesses of the page
like the ghost who stands behind me
whispering in my ear.
I write because the absent are present
when we think of them, groping in memory
for a grief past weeping, for a bridge
however makeshift or temporary across
the silence that has fallen between us
in the passing years. Sometimes
when the words don't come and something
still presses, nudges inside me,
I look up from the page and down the hall
at the chair standing alone in the dimly-lighted
room at the opposite end, and see myself there,
sitting quietly at first and then suddenly
dodging from shadow to shadow,
ready to climb up and into the darkest
corner of the farthest wall.
Something happens then, though it is
different every time, slow, mysterious, and
dense, and I stare fascinated and afraid,
reaching out from inside the wall to touch
the next one in the house who passes by.
But the hour is late and no one comes
and once again I struggle to climb down
on my own out of the corner of this wall,
find my way along the hall back
to the table in the kitchen. Time is short
and the question here is always the same:
who are the ghosts and who are the presences
in our lives; who is inside the wall bursting
to get out and who leans against it, bending it in?

Water Light

Priam's Daughter
I. Touching the Moon
A slice of light, half-curled above
the tree line, settled to smoky threads
along the horizon as night dimpled
snow in the dark fields and the creek's

cold edges thickened to a polished spill
the color of old birches. After dark,
the wind right and pines hovering
close to the ground, clouds rubbed
against a cut of stars that slipped
in a darkening slide to a clearing
half-lost in the mountains. It was a place
where dark flowers grow and cicadas grate
in solitude and vacancy, the sound
of their strumming suspended
like dust in the faint light that draped
the faded edges of the sky. She found
that place alone, listening to the wind,
as we quivered among the noises
of that starlit night and watched her
climbing over shadows that lay
like dark bruises on the season-plowed soil.
She climbed to touch the moon,
to break the trance of the nightfall
that surrounded her, push through
the cold clouds that curled north on the wind
where the hill ascends and reclaim
the emptiness she said was ours.
We were all divining life in those
dark corners then, skirting
its dangerous edges, each stirred
by a different pulse of the wind.
Caught there like a sift of leaves
against the tree line, we did not want
to understand when she said that nothing
lay beyond the things she feared
and lived by, that morning
always came to her in a heaving
under clear sheets of water,
that hollow trunks of trees
are warm as blood and their dark wood
opens to seed beds where the year's dead
are transfigured by the moon
and skim the earth like feeder roots
pulled loose from the lost ground below.
We watched her, in a dream
without sleep, waiting for a signal,
a wisp of smoke or quiet tapping of stone
to pierce the shadows. Her face was
as disconsolate as the moon she reached for
and all around gaped open burrows
where small animals slept, their soft skins
hardening white in the unaccustomed thudding
and jostling of the night air. Its odd light
seeped to our marrow and we moved
toward that place with arms extended,
drifting past each other like dark footfalls
in empty passageways before stumbling
into silence. The patterns in the sky

unexpectedly changed and she was
suddenly gone, a rustling of birds
in the veerings of the wind.
Although we had come to sink with her
into a nuzzling of thorns
in the gray scrub bushes, there
was nothing else we could see
in that place, only clouds and trees
awash in a dark green light
that dissolved to an abstract of angles
and lines on the water. The chill
in the wind smoldered in the darkness
and the hours before dawn opened slowly,
like the shell of a dying newborn bird.
In that light, traced like panic against
the paling sky, we knew she was gone,
a scuttle of mist thickening to the cool dark
of the earth, a quick return to dust,
and we were left alone with the moon
hanging black against the stars,
silent and forbidding, and the sound of the wind
whistling endlessly across the hills.

II. The Nightingale's Song
The air tasted of metal and the sky
was passionless as glass. In that slow
realization of light, as clouds
unraveled the fine dust and swept lines
of the moon above my head, I stretched out
my hands and the frozen flowers
in the meadows blossomed, rainbows
in the trees' hanging branches
glowed with the bodies of fragile butterflies,
time drifted like moonrise across wet ice
in a spark and warp of heady smoke.
Wait! I can hear them. But I don't think
they pity us. We blend to sorrow and strife
in the wounds and leavings of new birth,
and hunger advances in the wild hour,
and I wait here for my breath to settle,
for the fear to go away as the nagging surge
of needled hearts startled in every direction
probes like braided wire for the parch and peel
of blood. I lay for a long time near the stumps
of the yellowing pines, a patch of fallen white
against the fading green, bristling in flutters
and shivers, and heard their voices
pulling my bones this way and that,
whistling in the caverns behind my eyes
like the climax of some unspeakable hour.
They could not hear me when I cried
that this dream was not enough,
the work of the spirit falling to elegy and ruin,
the way back a lost moment hammered

in secrecy hard as steel in the forge of night.
I am blocked whatever way I turn, in cough
and blind panic. And I know there is nothing
beyond the things I've feared and lived by,
nothing they could find or name, only the darting hiss
and click of the moon's pale blood, slow hunger
stinging eyes fixed on the grass, stamens
veined and coiling. They don't believe me,
bloodless and apologetic, though all my life
I've named that weariness of the heart
that scatters quickly into the night like dry leaves,
building patterns that long for extinction,
a hundred gray shapes that pass among the trees
like a tide of blind mouths flying off to oblivion.
Root clenching root, blending to hard earth,
the hypothesis of dark desires,
and the life that moved within me
silent now and thick-fingered as roots
sprouting from clods and dead holes
stretched and laboring forward, sinews oiled,
tasting stone. I know they didn't pity me
even as the years passed across
the dry-veined sky and clotted hard
among the oaks and pines and lines
of cedar angled thin in the snow.
They don't remember that now
or understand why I need the moon's
pure light above me, high in the hills,
a vacuum into which everything collapses,
stripped to the numbness of bone.
I cannot reach it. I cannot reach it.
Listen! Do you understand I am not
this empty space that splinters to light,
the womb of earth, infinity's blind shore?
I climb only to touch the moon, to reclaim
the thing that once was mine, afraid
that my story has already had its end. Deeper
than the eye can follow, its pale light stiffens
in the mist, plain, placid and clear, and trails off
forever in a welter of silver that glowers
and pierces every shadow. I've heard them say it,
and in my deepest heart I know it's true.
My life is sprung bone, dull with reluctance,
longing to be filled in a world in which nothing fills.
And so it begins. I can hear them behind me,
voices borne on the wind at night
in a rustling of birds. The moon is up,
a halo of clarity that thins and thickens
and is sucked out again into the dark
like the ghosts that vanish as I touch them.

The Metaphysics of Wolves
1.
The old woman rides the wolf

through the grained scarlets
of the sinking sky.
Wind licks her face,
thrust to a clouded howl,
and her blind eyes rest
on nothing, tongue stretched
in a scratching lurch
to the dark and shearing
blood of night.

2.
No protection, nothing
to keep the blur of wind
from tearing at our bones.
We cross packs of ice
hard and dark as a clot
of blood, backs arched
to knives of fear: ahead
a ragged line of skittered
shadows hunches fanged
in the cut of the field.

3.
Slices of shadow stalk
the sun, withering
in the fraying light
that pulps the weeds to dust.
We leap with the wolves
through the driven grass,
tethered jaws stretched
tight as wire, and string
them up like hunted birds
on the crisp and shredded air.

4.
Bones, wolf bones, shafts
of fire sparking
in the soil, steaming
in the hard beaten rain,
the long sift of ash
coiled in the darkening rain,
the swift bones sawing
through the soil, burned
to white stone in the quaver
and pump of silting rain.

5.
Morning chars the green
and pitted sky,
crumbling to white spines
that crackle like broken glass
under the skin of the red moon.
These things are fibered
vapor: the wolves still stir

in the bone yard, cusped between
their frozen dead and wailing
low in the wind and flame.

6.
There is nothing left to fear,
only thin bands in the sky that strobe
toward a foam of clouds leeching
the new moon, stars sprawled and brittle
as old bones, broken shadows sputtering
like flocks of wolves across the dark grass.
Do you hear them? Those howls,
hurled from nowhere to nowhere,
are the despair of another season
ground to powder under our heels.

7.
Those were the signs
we watched for, in that time
of pity and addled hope, things
that can be named like blood
in the cheeks or marks on bare wood
clawed to a lacework of exhaustion
and sorrow that smothers
the air. The rapture of self
in the shells of these creatures,
the sound of wind in an empty place.

8.
Nothing is plain, stirred
by the gesture of an unseen hand,
discouraged and cold as the dead
no one comes to remember
when the wolf moon rises, sheer
and gray as a shiver of recognition,
beyond the fullness of care and neglect
and the lost reasons of our lives.
Its light tonight is all
that makes the world persist.

9.
The sky clears to a dead bolt
of gray and the promise
of snow cracks like a dry branch
in the wind. The first stars
are out, streaks and pulses
and whorls of light that bite
into the earth. Ah God!
The turmoil of marrow, the singing
of nerves, the bellow of terror
from the depths of our lungs.

10.
The silence of the day falls away

to the low sound of God's name
in the hiss of memory
and old confusions, harnessed
to the shudder of the changing air,
stutter in the redemption of wind
and inwardness of stone.
Listen! The wolves whisper
of life to come quickened
in the depths of profoundest night.

This Hard Light: Fragments
This hard light awakens the chill
and dwindling of the world's edge
to the endless darkening currents of things
we believe in the face of silence

echoes with the pulse of blood
in the slow hand of God
as it reaches to touch your face
in the hour before dawn

reveals the embrace of the contours
of absence in the tumult of desire
that grows like a thin black flower
in the last cold stab of the moon

groans with the lure of empty gray doorways
in the darkest chambers of night
that forever lead to the frozen moment
before the first scream

burns with the transfiguration of flesh
and skin to the sloughed textures of dust
encasing the fragile bones of creatures
that endure and endure

St. Francis at Alverna
1.
The bells swing back and forth in the gray towers
and the town's deaf mutes collapse in the streets.
They are burning the last remnants of this plague.
The eyes of the bodies in the market place
are the color of ochre and melted wax
and take their nourishment from the passing air.
Blackened bandages flutter like banners in the wind.
I spin my trail from door to door roaming blank
across their field of vision, patient and bloodless,
crying out for forgiveness and redemption.
No one answers. It is the same everywhere,
the seeds of the thorn bush that sprouts in the graveyard.
My voice hangs still and vacant as an echo
above the smoldering flames and the dust rising
for the day of resurrection that will never come.

2.

The man with no hands weaves
the day from motes of dust and shadow.
Hovers on wings carved from tree roots.
Speaks but does not answer.
Stands wedded to the impotent stars.
Works quickly, without assistance,
pierced by perfidy and forgetfulness.
Knows which things conceal
the contours of being.
Does not know who I am.
Does not know himself
or the name of God
in the uneasy rasping
of this final hour.

3.

The perfected lie the word that drones
and drones inside my head the clever
madness in this time of confusion and faith
common signs in the limp of night
fixed to allegories of balked desires
uneasy consciousness of absences and gaps
in the pale smoke of each other's signals
the empty shell of language rattling
with the dried peas of forgotten words
the pronouns of intimacy
from the first letter to the last
the mystical contemplation
of the incarnate word
the maze that defines
the monologue of the self
as it swells with envy
in the babble of its cell
all this

I haunt the streets like distant whistling
I cannot stretch my hand out to stop

4.

The announcement was distorted
by an incidental emotion.
No one listens to the explanation.
I call near the window:
Pay attention!
Remember these signs and blood!
The voice caught in the wind answers:
the scar has whitened,
the stigmatic mark.
Amid the grate of bone
and sift of skin to dust
the blind spot hurtles
into the maw of the future.

Maine Aubade

1.

The simple lyrics of waves
and sea flowers stutter
like feathery tufts of light
through darkness brittle
as charred paper. Loose shapes
of birds clip the water,
trolling the banks
of the Kennebunk, and slip
without sound through reeds
pared by the stitch of night.
On this narrow furrow
of shore wedged between
the river and sea, you touch
your fingers to my wrist,
in one cupped hand holding
the pale shells you gathered
to catch the light. The grasses
creak and the moon casts
small circles on the river,
spiking white slivers of water
that hum with the cold
flat voice of the wind.

2.

The tuned gathering of mist
and clouds above water
that cannot hold the tympanic moon
shrouds the horizon like gray gauze.
Waves in the distance break
in a noiseless slide, lines
smoothed to sheets of dark green
oiled by dapples of light
from shore that flash
off the contours of watery foam
ruffled by a wind far out at sea.
Quickened tangles of birches
and scrub pines press forward
in half-relief toward sand
leached to blue shadows
by the curl of the coming tide.
Head down, you stare into the fire
as it reddens the stacked
driftwood and lights your hair,
flames fingering the leaves
of the trees that frame you and moving
like brittle chimes in the wind.

3.

The landscape is suddenly still
as the cramped angle and thin
crack of sky shift blue
along the bend in the river

and flatten to a wedge of yellow
that threads with the current
among the knobbed rocks,
sliding back upon itself
and retreating into shadows
bent as sticks in clear water.
In this place preserved from the sea,
under the worn fingers of trees
thinning to clouds and fog
above the river, you trace
the outline of the dead bird
lit by the moon in the sand,
wing feathers gray as stone,
hissing like the wind hollowed
at dead center, like sagging leaves
fluttering against the scrape of water,
like unmoored things drifting
aimless and shimmering to silence.

4.
The veiled flanks of the river
are flecked with primrose and laurel,
flowers gone to the hard mercy
of wind that skims shoals
thick and black with mussels. The bristle
of water in eddies and pools
thickens an octave to a soft lament
trembling among rocks sour
with the sea's smell curling
in the measured breeze from the east
that brings the first taste of dawn
to birds unwound on the shifting waves.
You stretch strands of eelgrass
across the rocks, arrange pieces
of driftwood softened by water
like a cradle or trap around the tide
pool at your feet, foraging in water
streaked by first light for signs
of life, face pressed against knees
that muffle a voice rising slowly
from your hollows like a small cry
lost between the sea and wind.

5.
Water spreads luminous and thin
across the pale blue bruise
of morning as it shifts to white
in the pulse of reeds ringed
by the crouch of night. The play
of light bursts among the twisted vines
where the sea and river turn to land
and the sting of water hardens
to circles of dark birds strumming
the trees, the shape of something

fragile and small scattered to flight,
trickling through crevices of fog
in the clustered shallows
that mark the end of the season.
Forgotten like a seed cast
on dry sand, your face softens
to a weightless blur mitered
in the scrim of morning by bird song
that floats like mist across the inlet
where water brushes the sky
and touches us, transfigured by light
to counterpoints of silence and wind.

Christopher's Dream
In a midwinter night of air
muffled hard as wire
and shadows spined across
the bowed back of the moon,
he dreamed of a woman
rising from the dark water,
half-snake slither uncurling
below her delicate head,
mouth whispering his name,
open and feeding. He dreamed
of what she had become, daughter
and wife, in the green crest
of water as it looped around him
in coils like midwinter light
hunching chill over flesh
and bone, of skin and the dry
rubbing coddle of scales bristled
stiff in the wind, the face
nuzzling in darkness, the knowing
tongue and teeth at his throat.

Sleep together in a cleft of rock,
faces touching, hands wound
in darkness where the dream
unfolds its last uncertain hour
in vein, nerve and bone
and shadows surge deeper
into night, savoring the pale
spinning and slow shame
of light that sinks
into darkening water,
the hushed coiling
of bellies and mouths
into rings of cold stone.
Nothing else remains
to be carried away.
No rasp of skin or husk
of blood, no shaft of light
to crop the wind, no sound
or breath to scatter the silence
writhing by the sea.

Chiaroscuro
A fine snow falls
across the harbor,
eats like white mold
into the darkness
that straddles the water
at Black Point.

Flaked with tiny pieces
of moon and knit
with dull mist,
the dark iced docks
wink in the distance
with the eyes of hooked gulls.

Wind churns the stiff reeds
and dry sea grasses
like a glistening
black hand laminated
with crusts
of chilled water.

Cold whittles
the raw wood of night,
huddles in the brittle
scraps of things
skinned black red
by the winter sea.

A sketch of white
curves past us back to shore
in predictable rhythms,
tilts to shade
across snow building
in the pale north.

And despite
this memory of loss,
your face is as hard
as rock chiseled
by the dim mottle of light
that pits the sea.

The Shadow of Death on the Open Water
Rows of starfish stiffened
in the sun unfold
from ridge to ridge
with the slow pulsations
of silence and time.

Circles of wind
carry the cold weight
of clouds that thud
across the sky
like dark horses.

Black mouths locked open,
gaunt cormorants the color
of dust and burned weeds
dart through
the ocean's hollow eye.

The finned thing, hiding
its face in the sea's
scored rocks, casts
its silent and odorless
shadow on the open water.

Easter Morning
The boats rock clustered offshore,
cuffed by a cold spray of light
that begins nowhere and sluices
toward piers stiff as old veins
of grass in the hard chirr
of green water. The fishermen
have left on a rising wind,
from low tide and harbor flats
rankled by birds scything crabs
among the gray rocks, clearing
the tide line from the sand
as the sea retreats to Nantucket.

The wind is up and waves
flake the open tangle of kelp
and eelgrass beneath our feet.
We find our way across
the damp sags on this point of rock,
cutting low past the seawall
gaffed by winter on the edge
of this April morning, in silence
inexhaustible as water slipping
across the sand like shadows
of birds cast by a moon tacked
hard and white on the horizon.

The boats hover like gulls
half out to sea, tacking against
a sky shaken loose of clouds
and mottling with the wind
as it lifts to nets of light
that seine the water.
Under the surface, in the small
gray recesses of the birdless wall,
the dim grid of the season unlocks
in a voice that echoes like
a breaking wave swept to a sudden
formless blend of sky and sea.

Circles spread on the sand
as spring jabs the coast, foaming

with the tide through weeds
along the crest of the wall,
leaching salts that wrinkle
the damp places under the shoreline
stones and burrowing outward
in a familiar mix to tidal pools
hardening to sun. We huddle
in the wet sand below, traced
by a wicker of light and washed
by the cold absolution of water.

The boats fade with a shiver of wind
into the streaks of the eastern sky.
On shore this Easter morning,
above the line of thin-stemmed grasses
weaving slowly to the flicker of buds
on frail stalks, a knot of clawed tracks
of something born in the tidal marsh
leads to the darkened edge of the wall,
pausing here and there then spreading
unstoppable in all directions
like the hard snap of shadow
to sudden light that comes by water.

Waiting Birds in the Dead of Night
Wild birds roost in the trees
along the dry river,
the sound of their thin whistling
caught like contempt on the chill wind
that eddies in the wire-drawn shadows
of the dead of night;

like things sightless and uncertain
pummeled by the darkness and ignorance
of the wind awaiting their resurrection
from the dust to black clouds
that pound against the sky like blood
in the ears in the dead of night;

waiting for something, listening
for something far away, the first scrape
of the sun on the banks
of the river, the wind hissing away
its absence to dispel the silence
and misery of the dead of night.

The White Bend of the River
I.
Dead wood whitens
to connecting lines
that snap
with a brittle sting
as the season
dries to autumn.

Water the color
of charred sticks
stiff in the rain
beaks the clustered rocks,
thickening to knots of grass
that barb the horizon.

Drawn by the cradling wind
to the remains of summer,
you sleep in fitful starts,
weeping softly against me
long after the pain has gone,
dreaming

of a forgotten place
swept to silence by the river,
of children covered
in feathers
nuzzling the damp
smells of your body,

yourself, a whispered
shadow unspooling
in fields black
with birds, dragged
unraveling to the dull
white humming of water

where it flattens
to a thin cut around the bend,
its hoarse refrain
whiskering the sallow moon
as weeds spire and click
in the wind.

II.
Your hands are cold.
In this loose moment
of certainty between
dusk and the chill
anticipations of night
that rattle loose

like buried things
unearthed from the hollows
and old holes
lining the hard edges
of the river,
you tell me in whispers

about the thing
you are most afraid
to hear—the congested
flutter of birds

blinded by your
children struggling

in the shallows
among reeds and dredged
rocks, whipping murky
patches of water
to a swollen foam
of feathers and blood.

You are shadow
without light,
you say, the pale
deception of death
in this place
of resurrection,

a shred of darkness
that curls like
a shiver of fog above
the river whistling
anonymously into the gray
backwaters of night.

III.
Light appears suddenly
on the water,
brittle as glass
and the color
of dried feathers,
glances off old roots

straining against
the sear of wind
that jabs the grass
the way heat lightning
scuttles the stiff air
of late summer.

You finger sand
leeched to pallid streaks,
paring thin weeds
strung along the banks
like trapped birds
hobbled in effigy.

And I don't believe
you, even though
clouds wither
around us to
a residue that
stains the land

and the sky opens
in a penance of stars
spilling mutely
across the valley's
dim floor
and spinning outward

under the slow pulse
of your hand
as it trembles,
pure as a child's,
above the cold white
bend of the river.

IV.
It was the thing
you finally hoped for,
this congregation
of birds inching
through the grim
refractions of sky

on wings sharp
as the spines
of locust trees.
The air prickled
and shuddered
in their wake,

moving slowly at first,
then faster, lifting
branches of trees
bent with age
and chipped by
the scrape of winter.

You watched them
settle on the pulsing
surface of water,
clenched figures
floating into
changeable shapes, laced

to the river's twined
banks and dissolving
into radiant strands
of white feathers
that shimmer like silhouettes
on the blackening tide.

And you float gently
into the water, calling
out to the children,
bending your shadow

into the gathered corners
of this floundering night.

V.
The wind blows everywhere,
white and black, a hard
beaten wind that hisses
through the trees
along the river
in scorn and doubt.

The birds tumble
around you on wings
fragile as burned grass,
twisting above
the flat groan
and thud of water

toward some distant
invincible dead-center
without substance
or form, a whirlwind
of indifference
and desire

that whistles as it fills
the small cold darkness
where the ache
sets in and rattles
through the ruts and burrows
with the low sound

of your name in the vaulted
silence of this hour.
Time's blindness
broken by degree,
the marrow of light
spinning across the water

like things that do not move
then rise suddenly
in the endless symmetry
of birth and death giving
shape to the precipice
of river and air.

VI.
Time drifts past.
Only stones desire nothing.
The air is filled
with the sound of birds
murmuring of love
and despair.

The moon shines
on gray folds of mist
that thin and thicken
with a wind that blows
through the wallow
and ignorance

of the infinite stars,
through you, chilled
to the heart, through the endless
drift of transfigured shapes
that creak toward dawn
along the drab flats ahead.

The names of all we are,
all we have been
and know unravel
to simple bones
picked clean by birds
shaking with hope and pinned

among the flickers
of the day's last light.
The resolutions
of this shadowed hour.
The dry noise
of life to come.

The stars dissolve to dust
and the banks are awash
in a pale blue light
vacant as a sudden streak
of white against
the void of space.

VII.
the press and breath of silence
cool and dry as the dust
the flesh peels down to

the spindled slide of stillness into stillness
as midnight settles in against its hollow core
and the long night wanes to element and seed

salted in the natter and dream of birds
as the spirit comes to judgment turning
on itself at the iridescent edge of things

the field of being the white shore
where the end comes as a whisper on the wind
and light is transfigured to earth and air

the press and breath of silence
cool and dry as the dust
the flesh peels down to

the old confusion of water as the river skins
itself free of land where the moon
is hung and the wind whistles overhead

coalesced by sympathy and fire
to the ecstasy of hope in that deepest place
of undeciphered secret and stillborn sound

death and rising caged in the hull of time
of darkness gone and still to come
widening the chaos of the night sky

the press and breath of silence
cool and dry as the dust
the flesh peels down to

the shiver of wings stirring in message
or prayer untangled to writhing sinew
and luminous bone at the edge of the river

where the journey out of the self begins
with a distant chill and threads away
to echoes of wind and fluttering water

look   wings break with light
as birds stream out around you
in innocence in a cloud of white

Seeing Wyeth's "McVey's Barn" Seventeen Years Later
In this place of memory
beneath a sky full of branches
ringed by the far-off hum
of cicadas, light powders
the quiet weave and dust
of straw. Shadows sprinkled
across the coarse boards
crumble like braids of dirt
tapped from dry roots.
A touch of pale color,
like shadings of brush stroke
or line, trembles above
the sleigh burrowed high
on the brown rafters, spreads
in the still afternoon air
like gray smoke, rising and
fading in the loose darkness
of this New England barn.

Small birds gather in the grass
and the blue jay's song lifts
across the narrow yard.
Your footsteps still echo
on these floorboards where we
danced naked that summer

thinking no one would see,
our bodies dusted with light
that filtered through the thin
barn walls with the sweet
smell of late roses. And though
half our lives have passed,
that afternoon has not left
this place, locked in the warm
smells of barn straw and flowers
and dappling the walls like
bird song or pale dust washed
by a haze of fragile light.

Beneath the White Balcony

1.
This is urgent for both of us: a transfusion of dreams.

2.
I kiss you: you disappear in the embrace of pure music.

3.
I want what I do not have: not the body I embrace but your desire. I desire your desire, not the body I embrace.

4.
I do not know, when I am alone, which of us is not here. When I stretch out my arms, I do not know if I reach for you or for me.

5.
Hands, words: they tell us of only one affair of body and thought. What I feel for you is impossible to translate into either one of these two languages.

6.
We love each other without a point of support, in an eternity of anticipation, in the soft corners of a white night without shadows, in the place where death dies.

7.
I say this to you in whispers beneath your white balcony: there is nothing older or newer than this love, and I will never finish beginning to love you.

Inheritance

In his last days, my grandfather
would tell me to search the sky
for omens in the waning hours
of night, for clouds the shape
of crosses portending war, dispersions
of stars swept like white dust
behind the darkest corner of the moon
auguring illness and death, streaks
of light, oranges and bloody reds,
divining the smoldering contours
of famine in the hours before dawn.

Now, whenever the wind trembles
the house and the clouds
are odd angles black against
the paling sky, I stumble
suddenly from sleep and reach
to open the window, watching
the horizon for signaled changes,
pushing back in absence to the dark
of the room to wait for the whistling
of the wind to stop, the dry echo
of my grandfather's voice in my ear.

Freight Trains
for my brothers

There is something reassuring even now
in the sound of a passing train
lifting in the night wind and settling
with the rain against the corners
of the house. It fills the room,
and I remember how still we would lie
late into night in the old green house
on Millard's hill listening for trains
as rain tapped soft and gray across
the latticed shadows of the porch roof.

The freight cars would roll with the clouds
in the distance by Schultz's field, sliding
through the late summer air and whistling sweetly
in towns they passed to up the road.
We found comfort in that, without knowing
where they were going or where they had been,
as if we had found a place screened
from the wind in the dark trees or shaped
by the colors of night as they soften
the edges of things outside the open window.

On those nights now when my children
whisper tenderly in their sleep and I lie
in bed as the wind rises and wanes
listening to freight trains in the distance
roll north up from the yards in New Haven,
I remember you there, so quiet and close,
watching the stars in the trees drift
toward dawn like the lights of summer
that passed the bottom of the hill, their names
the first and last sounds on our journey.

February Snow
It is snowing again tonight
and the sounds of the bells
from the church on the Green
whisper low around
the corners of New Haven.

Light from the street lamps
ruffles through the windows,
silver blue in the snow
that sifts endlessly
in the cool green pines
that border the yard.
Here inside this small white house
where my daughters sleep,
I walk in the dark
with a familiar creak
of floorboards, checking the doors,
drifting slowly past the windows,
each step framed
by that thin-veined light
that comes from the north
with the snow
on silent February nights.
There are memories in it,
of other snowfalls and other houses,
the odd comforts of darker days
now as silent as the stars
that slip away to clouds bearing snow,
a certain melancholy knowledge
of beginnings and endings,
old friends gone, the years
passing as unexpectedly
as the storm's frail sounds
suddenly whisked away
from the house by the wind
toward the harbor.
But there is still this night
and this snow and the quiet
breathing of my children.
Downstairs, the wood stove
is filled with embers
and purling, the fire settling
to ashes on the cold grate.

Spring Blessing
Each year, when the thorn bushes
between our yards tangle
with new leaves and the grass
beneath the willow is threaded
with a twist of soft green more delicate
than any memory of it, Mrs. Berg and I
work our gardens across the dry threshold
of early spring, measuring seeds ready
to burst to hummingbirds and flowers.
There is a simple music in that work,
hands playing roots and mud, the steady
rhythm of scraping soil echoing
for a moment in the grasses and trees
before lifting away on the soft pulse
of the wind with the voices of young birds.

This morning, the light calls us out
to our separate gardens to turn clumps
of earth for the first time this year,
burrowing deep to touch the old roots
of plants whose names we know by heart.
Mrs. Berg stops for a moment and stands
in the spare shadows of the greening willow,
squinting against the sun. Her face,
which has longed for many such springs,
is as wrinkled as the braided bark
of the trunk. Although she's deaf
and cannot hear my greeting, she knows
that I am here again and turns to wave hello,
the gentle lift and fall of her arm
a benediction for our shared season.

Simple Gestures
Tonight, as the air changes
and the light around
the dogwood fades
like the folding of old leaves,
I watch you press your face
against the window
and touch the cool glass
while evening bends
the deepening shadows
of the yard.

The years repeat themselves
in the perfect silence
of that simple gesture,
gentle as the soft scrape
of wild iris across the grass
in early summer,
and in the knowing lines
of your face, the clarity
of coming night
in a frame of pale hands.

Raking
In late July, as evening wreathes
the red maple and clouds pass
east thick with orange light,
we rake tiny apples from the grass
that still lies flat with the afternoon's heat,
gathering the hard green fruit
the trees have dropped and rolled
to the small far corners of the yard.
The weight of their branches brings
them close, smelling of summer,
sweet with the rich tastes
of the season that petal the air.

My daughters help with the raking,
playing with the apples piled

in the wooden basket in a weave
of grasses and twigs tangled
as a bird's nest, their faces,
turning every few minutes to watch me,
bright and warm in circles of light
filtering through the midsummer leaves.

And as they played, I raked up
the body of a young bird,
neck folded awkwardly back
against its stiff wings, from beneath
the white pine I planted
in the spring. It was hard
and the color of the ground
and I took it over to the basket,
calling my children away, to lay it
like a spotted apple among
all the other living things
the trees had dropped this year.

And as I placed it in the basket
among the twigs and grasses,
I remembered an earlier season
and another bird, my parents readying
the garden for spring, rakes clicking
against fallen branches, and my sister
catching a robin with a broken
wing under a wooden basket

and how the bird fluttered and died
without a sound late that afternoon
when I brought it pieces of apples
and bread to eat and pushed the edge
of the lifted basket down against
its back, trying to keep it safe
from the things of night when it tried
to hop away, and how birds since then
sing in my sleep, their midnight cries
thick with a sense of death
that awakens to whistles of forgiveness
in the pausings of the wind.

My daughters don't understand
why I tell them to keep away
but will not come closer, as if they know
with some hidden childhood sense
that there are secrets none of us
should know revealed by the things
that lay tangled together in the basket
they have made their plaything.

And though I sometimes find it hard
to say, I know I want to keep them

from the muffled cries and flutterings
of creatures that die in innocence,
the quick turn toward that other light,
the singing in sleep that shapes
the shadows of things gone long before
we would give them up. So in this
raked garden, thirty years later,
I widen the circle, in my children's play
among the dropped apples trying to find
and preserve whatever it is I lost.

The Silent Life

We sit together again
among the hills,
in these familiar woods,
brushing soft branches
from our faces.
I brush the sun
and thistles
and meadow flowers
from your hair
and the grasses
that climb around us
toward the endless dark.
The wind shivers
and renews our spirits
as the hours
and waters pass,
and we sit silent
and ever faithful, our voices
shining in our throats,
untouched by the shadow
the rocks and sky,
the hollow trees,
the flowering wind,
all shining.

My Father's Wine
after Vytautas Bloze

My father made wine
and buried it in large bottles
the orchard soil
and year after year
the wine fermented
among the roots of apple
trees and cherries.
And then he was gone,
taken by them that spring
with a knock on the door
in the dead of night,
buried far away
by an unnamed road
at the forest's edge.

He could not find his wine
beneath the ground
where they put him.
They would not let us
look for it among
the orchard's roots
and I never felt
its sweetness on my tongue.
But I know
that when we are all together
in the ground
and the light of memory
has changed to something
deep and clear,
we will gather around him
to drink that homemade wine.
My father will lift
the first glass
to all our living and dead,
and the absence
that was ours will touch
and shape that moment
with its sweet last sound,
and our deep thirst
will quicken our resolve
and our desires.
And I know that mine
will be the first head
to spin and that I
will be the first to cry,
to cry that while alive
I never had the chance
to taste my father's wine.

The Last Song of Fall
the sky is whiter
than the bones
of birds
the remains of summer
eternally returning home
to die and live
one for another
as October's colors
thin in the featureless air
when night falls
but I abide
and sing the wind
and watch the river
and know how
we are renewed
by these changes
in the deep center
of things
the other side of light

the place that brings
first snow
to ridges of stone
the holes of old wood
the skim of water
slowing to ice
above half-sunken trees
and in them all
is a dream of journeys
conjunctions
that affirm the world
below the root
and above the leaf
and everything
turns inward upon itself
keeping the secret
silencing the birds
and I know
how we are gathered
how all these things
are enough
for the seed and marrow
of this season
and that other

Winter Geese
The changes of evening
come steadfast as birds
scraping the lake
in the darkness downwind.
A dim chill of light
tilts from the curve of water,
traces a black wave
of geese that lifts past
branches beyond our reach.
Winter comes this way
each year with the birds,
settling across the trees
and hard grass of the late
November hills as the season
turns toward the year's
darkness and softens
the sky to the colors
of weathered wood swollen
with the textures of wind.
Behind the dark windows
of this house,
tuned to the slide
of weather and not sure
of what it is we wait for
in all these long nights
of wind that whistles
through the cracks
of the chimney and repeats

the names of things
that we once were
softly, like some secret
hidden from itself,
I watched as night rippled
toward land in slow circles,
unraveling across the dark
fields to strings of cold rain,
and cried myself to sleep,
remembering in this music
of weather and wind
the empty places and
the dead silence of things
that pass like the circles
made by rain on still water
to the edges of shadows and dreams.
Now, as a thin layer
of frost coats rocks
stung with cold and stains
the roof and walls stitched
with the faint spume
of first light, I listen
in this ebb of time
between sleep and waking
to the whispers
of bitterness and sweet grief
in the folds of the wind,
shaking off again
the deep solitude of night
and the wearying press
of the painful emptiness
of this changing season
that even my remorse
at death could never fill.
Outside, incandescent as ice
in the first blue touch
of sunlight, the wild birds
trill the clear water
to a muffled, familiar sound.
One rises effortlessly
on white wings through
the misting lake grass
and hangs like slow smoke
on the horizon, circling home
to the white hills
in this half-light
like an unexpected sign
of hope plain against
the promised clearing
of this winter's dawn.

Winter's Roses
It is the place
the hands
can never reach,

the stone
that cannot
be lifted

as the hard earth
heaves forlornly
with wind

and emptiness
gathers around
the old trees

that bend
above the beds
of roses

where I touched you
for the first time
that winter long ago

and I am not ashamed
to tell you
that my hand trembled

with the fierce
and inconsolable
brevity of things,

the ringing of bells
that lead us
home,

the elegy of wind
and star rising sweet
as the sound

of falling snow
on these
forgotten roads.

The hush
of the season
on the garden beds

gathers the year
and holds it still
and I know now

how little remains
at the center of things
as day settles

into a corner
of the sky letting go
of its colors,

how the flowers stiffen
as death
leaves us

alone among the empty gardens
and we move
through them like wind

not sure of what
we came here to say
or of who we were then

or how we grieved
without knowing
our lives from theirs.

O my love!

The way back is this moment,
the light of winter's roses
lifted and made clear.

A Point of Departure
The deep end of time
opens itself in the white ledge
and hush of branches
locked to the fragile
meditation of seeds.

This is the redemption
of hard weather
and reluctant light,
of hope discovered
in lengthening shadows,

in the pale bloom
of dust at dawn
that perfects
the landscape
as the journey begins,

in the music
of the spirit
returning in expectation
and wonder
on the determinate air.

Go now.
The sky
is washed in white
and night
yields the way.

Voice on an Anthill

Still Lifes

1.
A blade of morning,
a fighting of light,
a web of voice,
a song of the hills
spilled sweetness
and the dark trees
salty with silence,
incredulous.

2.
Brittle-beaked and shadowed,
seabirds lick salt
from the ocean's stones,
luminous tongues like vines
tracing the rim of rock
beneath the snake-grass stalks,
a crux of rays
trembling, feeding.

3.
Pin feathers lining
a gangrenous foot,
the tree's leaves
stunned like swatted glass,
the unearthly stones
clawed by the notes
of the littered, raw,
incandescent stars.

4.
The hooded glare of apples,
rooted leaves, the painful
stiff grace of birds,
winged feathers,
rain-rotted wood,
the healing light rising
from the mud of the
autumn sky.

5.
Its mouth upstream,
the stitched fish
glows with the blindness
of its skin, the deafness
of its fins, the taste
of its shiver as it leaps
belly-up to the
falcon's throat.

6.
The black terror
of sunset, the blank
fullness and roost
of the branching sky,
the crowded horizon
lumped out of light
at the dipping edge
of the bullocked woods.

7.
The oak of tooled-billed bird,
the grass of mouse,
the glimpse of knuckled tail
and ear, the crest
of moon, the song of dark,
the bruise of flight,
the lick of death,
the owl's stare.

8.
The obsidian stars
pulsing in the night sky,
rootless light
swallowing joggled limbs
and oozing through the
bloodless veins
and wind-flushed void
of the birded heart.

9.
The wolf's cornered cry
on the fallen roads,
delicate as steel,
pumping organs nerved,
a howl of bagged pain
and rawness, spattering
the snow belted by
the slither of spring.

10.
Abandoned to space,
eyes flickering
and wind-shaken,
breath bristling
and cold, a creature
circumscribed by fate,
a masked soul, mouth fixed
on the heart of heaven.

11.
Thorns the shape
of a bloodless face,
the opening womb and
crack of light swaddling

the water, the black
wind hooked to the sun,
the viper rain
crusted and blinding.

12.
The jawbone of the river,
the shore's fingered grip
on the core of night,
the glazed blotched terror
of the moon's bitten flesh
and blind blood,
the bird-hooked cloud tearing
the shell of the puddled sea.

13.
Wrenched and riveted
silence, the rain spinsterish
brown   the numbness
of fall flits bat-like
to the leeched blood
of the open-bellied
honeysuckle, fangs
stuck in the dark.

14.
The claws of the retracting
ice burst the tunneled
roots, split rocks,
vibrate the smoldering fumes
of the lake waters
cracking like dry twigs
in the mouth
of the winter sun.

15.
A single note
of sun in the skull
of the cranberry,
peaks of light
creaking like old
foundations in the
skylines under
the crevassed sea.

16.
A blur of throbbings,
wrestled daylight
filtering the wet bush
and prongs of stars
blackened by morning,
heavy green rain tangling
the hills like the entrailed
strands of hiving vines.

17.
The frost bites deep
into the sly eyes of morning,
the balled coolness
of the air blocking the light
knotted and stuffed
into the raw broken ends
of the fossil moon's
wind-cracked halo.

18.
The eye of the flame
gunmetals the feathers,
flays the hooked feet,
rips the craned talons,
ratchets the burying bones
below the licked skull
and disentangled fluff-belly
of the hedge sparrow.

19.
Rubbled dust in the crystal
of silence, the dance
of tangled flesh,
convulsions of wings
and furred feet,
uncoilings in the shadows,
the underbelly's torn
and gushed relief.

20.
The struck spectrum
of frenzied hunger,
the ecstasy of teeth
hardening the agony
of the stifled groan
beyond hearing, eyes
rubble among the beetles,
spines gulped and coiling.

21.
Dry bleached weeds
and sticks over dry stones,
the oiled centerpin of
lightning, glared
and cut like a cry of flesh
inverted, swallowed, and
larval in the darkness
and stealth of blood.

22.
Trees ravaged with feathers,
spilled light and eiderdown
dissolved in leaves, the green

underbrush displaced and spattered,
the disemboweled bird
singing the song of uncurling,
the joy of deforming, the rooting
of tongue and earth.

23.
The smell of divided
feathers numbing
the reeds and staking
the sands, jabbering
the nakedness of death
disheveled by the birth
of the hot undersoftness
of the tendrilled sun.

North Light
1.
The wind changes, stirring the gray of early morning.
In the old November garden lie blackthorn, seed, and spore,
shadows and bird bones in the brittle north light.

The flecked glow of ice on dry grass, the fingers of cloud
against the sky, the salt veins of stones, the deepest roots
in dry weather, in the bursting and cudgeling light.

2.
There is something beyond and perishing, crackling
in the bark of the oak and poplar. A cry lost on the wind.
An old dream of beginnings and endings in the deepening light.

Things hard and alive. The silence of beating wings.
The rocks dark and singing. The sigh and shiver
of wind where the water meets the north light.

3.
The silence of forgotten things knocks like the wind
against the moon in November. Branches in the garden
washed white by the rain glint in the fading light.

Hours of wind, dusk in the hollows
where the deep roots crack in dryness like dead bones
in the sleep and shadow of the cold north light.

October Wind in the Wine Country
The chattering static of wind
and rain in hills wallowing
with leaves, colors wet against
the gray dissolution of the north sky.
A farm brimmed with grass
and scrubby wood, beaten
to the bones and shine of mud,
the hay luminous tatters.
October. The wild rose

has withered and a new wind
drifts from the north. The lake grass
lies claimed by water, reeds brushed
flat by wind and rain that washes
the stones and the roots that hold
the hills, the burrowing vines.
The earth's smells think and warm
as the smoke of nightwood burning.
Something stays here long after
the wind and rain have passed
beyond the hills and the sun dips
across trees and vines soaked
with autumn's brown coolness,
in the evening's red clouds
and the stirred pond the wild birds
have traveled on. Something
in the rocks, in the shimmer of silver
at the breaking of morning
on the hillside, train water tracing
the edges of leaves and old wood.
Something. And in your eyes
wings, a beauty beyond words
marked by rain, a quickness of wind.

Spider Skins
Night darkens the waters
as shadows sprout
like gray weeds
along the banks
and windswept clouds,
like black fungus,

inch across the sky,
past the pale moon
that lights the spider webs
wedged among the stalks
of sawgrass and sedge
near the tide-water flat.

There is no love here
in the half light
that seeps through
the pores of the basswood trees
and nuzzles the horsetail
and burdock;

only spider skins,
stiff and shivered
with dew,
that cling to the worm grass
and float in the wind that
winds through the bent.

We walk the pale shadows
of the river,

through the blue hollow
of trees and past
the owl's yellow stare
as he scans for insects,

night birds, and mice
that dart through
the bindweed and nettle,
in their jolt for life
stirring the fine dust
where the spiders die.

Green Water

Green water
the smell of wind
in the mist,
ditches shrouded
in sedge and
the silence flickering
in the green water.

Green water
the bitter moon
in branches,
the rhythm
of vine tendrils
stripped and burning
in the green water.

Green water
the sky clear
against the
thick parched land
dark among the membraned
roots floating
in the green water.

Green water
the air
crystal smoke,
the clouds
dead fire against
the trees sinking
in the green water.

Block Island Blues

Sunset: jaundiced, the sun
splashed into the sea
ebbing green and gray,
a tide of bilge and backwash
swelling tidal pools
with sewage, silt, and slush.

Dusk: adamant still, we kiss.
In this last night, sitting
on the mudflat beach,
we talk of love. Now night:
high above, circling seagulls
wail for water, for light.

Churchill Pond

1.
Woodstained water
weeds and rushes
by the drainpipe

remember?
sitting at the pond's edge
whispers tangling

in trees
and undergrowth
desire hardening to wood

2.
The sky
mute and white
strikes us dumb

cold and afraid
your body
wrapped in grass

smells of dead leaves
memories, other girls
laid in this sand

3.
Ducks, ducks squawking
feet spanking water
wings splashing before flight

your voice behind me
tilted day
chill before winter

ducks, ducks squawking
the sound of grass
cracking with cold

Rock

1.
Something bleak and old
waxes and wanes here
in the truth
of the sky and sea
in winter, in the groan
of the water weeds,

in the moon's cold light
on this clump of rock.

2.
Light, sweeps of light,
clear light, gray
on darker gray.
The indifferent, reckless
waves of sky and sea.
The glint and glance
of washed rock.

3.
The salt water stirs
the sea's stone bed
and the wind brushes wet
across the driftwood.
The clouds break
against the night
like pale waves.
We squat, cross-legged
and thin, blue-wooled,
on this rock. It is
sad to meet again
like this, to watch
the salt tides
in the black
crevices of rock,
to hear the dark birds
clamoring for rock,
to shrink, half-afraid,
backs bent, from the sea
toward rock.

Narragansett
Clocks stopped ticking
as we watched
a dying horseshoe crab
in torment
crawl on the beach
pushing sand before it
like a broken plow
toward water
it could not reach. Now

high tide, waves
cover the crab,
its shell cracked,
lichened, a drab
sandbrown; wash up
a wake of refuse,
offerings for the dead.
Mottled seagulls, open-beaked,
pick at the crab's sandcovered head.

Behind a wall of seagrass
we lay hallowed, unstrung,
circled by footprints of dogs
on the run,
our heads resting
on driftwood logs,
seasoaked and rotted,
naked, faces touching,
legs and fingers knotted.

Shells
Empty, light and dry
shells hum the ocean

waves cradling the shore
washing silt and sand

powdered coral, bits of shell
eelgrass and driftwood

echo the wind bending
the grass by the sea's edge

the rattle of torn crabs
gutted in the sand

Hollow Tree
It was a hollow tree like any other.
At night, when the chill of wind
brushed through the quackgrass
and cane and nudged against the stars;
when nighthawks flickered above the river
and ripped through the sodden weeds;
when the clouds hung stiff and dark
and dead above the freezing sea
its branches sang of life in the hollow,
in the beak-carved hollow, where birds
lay sleeping beneath pale feathers,
beneath the weight and warmth
of pale feathers.

Water
This is a still life caught
in a picture without a frame.
Through the holes
in the underwater rocks
the sea brings in foam
and seaweed flags,
brown and green,
and stretches them out to dry
in the dark sand.
All around lie pieces of wood,
bare sticks carved by
the saltwater and the winds.

Starfish cling like children
to their sea rock mothers,
forget the time of bitterness
when they slept in the clefts
of the sea-bottom stones.
Gulls tame the tides,
tall thin grasses whisper
their names to the silent shells.
The water rushes in, then out.
It does not need the sympathy
of human eyes.

August Rain

After a late August rain and a brush
of fog that swept in with the wind through
the trees by the river, evening thickens
the shadows of the earth and sky.
In the yard a cat's eyes shine hollow
in the lamplight as it stalks a toad
that crawls up a grassy bank rippled
by rain waters. Overhead, the stars gnaw
through the blackness of the night sky,
and the moon, stark orange and longing
for the dawn, rocks silently in a noose
of clouds and wind.

Love

after Miroslav Holub

Two thousand cigarettes.
A hundred miles
from wall to wall.
Our lives a vigil
for something whiter
than snow.

Now, words are dry,
like seagull footprints
in the sand,
sweepings, dust.

Bitter, you say,
the world's beginning.
You laugh when I say
how beautiful it was.

Incident

Thigh to thigh
we lay on the rock
where the paths converge

smells of cedar branches
and ferns, droppings
of birds on their way south

in the yellow leaves
and briar undergrowth
thrashing hip to hip

we embraced and kissed
like birds in the bushes
and tangled wild grass

speckled with sunlight
in your hair
leaves cracking

as I touched you
that October
when trees are pruned

of dead branches
bonewhite against the sky
the autumn sun

casting shadows
on your face
reminding me of her

Anniversary
Awake all night
clutching a pillow
in a tight old man's embrace

wrapped in a frayed sheet
you cried for help
dreaming of next year perhaps

or ten years after
in this woman-heated room
slack flesh and a haggard heart

your touch turning in sleep
the outline of your body
in the dark, the silence

Summer Dream
The hour has tensed itself.
Last night I dreamed
of a woman
cutting off my fingers
with a carving knife,
sucking the warm flesh.
Tonight I clamp my jaw,
try to forget the face
I tried not to see,
choking back the deeper sleep.

Night Music
When all else fails,
the mud in the sack

that fills the void
and thumps the skull
of silence.

Tenth Avenue
1.
Streetlamps and shadows
the sky descending
redstreaked black and gray

faces blurred in windows
bus noise, bars
drunks in hallways

a black woman
hair slicked back
whistling at the cold

2.
Night shields him
a shadow beneath the streetlamp
bag in his hand

it is possible
to remain unnoticed
slowly limping forward

walk the streets
a solitary figure
turning a corner

3.
A city of accustomed dread
chainlocks on the door

the drunken Spanish nightshift
stalking down blind alleys

old men, absence in the eyes
listing to a broken wall

Poem: Old Age
The black window,
that vacant eye,
still stares

and winter nights
enlarge the number
of our hours.

We thought
these days
would last forever.

But tonight,
in broken moonlight,
your eyes

without warning
are an old man's,
rigid and immense.

Voice on an Anthill
The sky is the color of death.
The afternoon
has brought the curling light
that sucks away the breath
before it rusts
the day into night.

The sun no longer lingers.
I dig through the mud
of this rocky mound
with bleeding fingers,
grope, and tear
the calloused ground.

I look for life in this hole.
The earth is dark and hollow
where I stand
wrapped in shadows, cold,
a colony of ants
clutched in my hand.

Poem
1.
The atmosphere was frog-like and croaking.
The stars woke the plaintive night,
twittering and sniffing, glossy and raw,
as we edged toward dawn.

2.
There is no transfiguration, no finitude of sky.
No division of land and sea.
All is bliss, downy and undifferentiated.
A world turned inside out, all flesh peeled off.

3.
Vague tracings.
Black rubbed-raw footprints of dreams.
The night creeping in unafraid
and watching, watching.

Books by Jonas Zdanys

Poems in English

Notebook Sketches, 2019; *Three White Horses*, 2017; *St. Brigid's Well*, 2017; *Red Stones*, 2016; *Cormorants*, 2013; *The Kingfisher's Reign*, 2012; *The Thin Light of Winter*, 2009; *Salt*, 2007; *The Woman on the Bridge*, 2005; *The White City*, 2004; *White*, 2004; *Lithuanian Crossing*, 1999; *Water Light*, 1997; *The White Bend of the River*, 1994; *The Metaphysics of Wolves*, 1994; *Maine Aubade*, 1990; *Voice on an Anthill*, 1982.

Poems in English and Lithuanian

Two Voices/Du balsai, 2017; *Preludes After Rain/Preliudai po lietaus*, 2017.

Poems in Lithuanian

Ikaro prisikelimas, 2014; *Tarpdury*, 2008; *Dumu stulpai*, 2002; *Dotnuvos stoty*, 1999; *Ausros Daina*, 1993.

Translations

Solitary Architectures: Selected Poems of Kornelijus Platelis, 2014; *Agne Zagrakalyte: Artistic Cloning*, 2010; *Kornelijus Platelis: Haiku*, 2007; *Icchokas Meras: Stalemate.* Revised 2005, Original edition, 1980; *Emptiness: Poems by Vytautas P. Bloze*, 2005; *Zones: Poems by Kornelijus Platelis*, 2004; *Five Lithuanian Women Poets*, 2002; *Inclusions in Time: Selected Poems by Antanas A. Jonynas*, 2002; *Silk: Poems by Nijole Miliauskaite*, 2002; *@ and Other Poems by Kornelijus Platelis*, 2002; *Snare for the Wind: Poems of Kornelijus Platelis*, 1999; *The Theology of Rain: Poems of Alfonsas Nyka-Niliunas*, 1999; *Smoke From Nothing: Poems by Vytautas P. Bloze*, 1998; *Four Poets of Lithuania*, 1995; *Chimeras in the Tower: Poems of Henrikas Radauskas*, 1986; *Leonardas Andriekus: Eternal Dream*, 1980; *Sigitas Geda: Songs of Autumn*, 1979; *Selected Post-war Lithuanian Poetry*, 1979; *Brone Martin: Reality and Dream & Brone Martin: The Wandering Seagull*, 1979; *Jurgis Gliauda: Agony*, 1977

Edited Editions

Unlocking the Word: An Anthology of Found Poetry, 2018; *Pushing the Envelope: Epistolary Poems*, 2015; *Yale 1972: Twenty-five Years*, Volumes I and II, 1997; *True Fellowship in All Its Glory: Remembrances of C.S.P.*, 1992.

CPSIA information can be obtained
at www.ICGtesting.com
Printed in the USA
FSHW020010020420
68726FS